International Development and Global Politics

This textbook provides a historical survey of economic and political development theory and practice from the 'sovereign' order of the post-1945 period to the 'liberal' order that emerged during the 1980s. Against the background of changes in global politics, it explores how changes in development theory and development institutions have been shaped in a series of wider contexts.

This textbook:

- illustrates how these changes impacted upon developing countries generally and features three detailed case studies on Ghana, the Philippines and Argentina;
- examines a number of bilateral development agencies in the UK, the US, France, Japan and Sweden;
- focuses on specific development projects and programmes, to explore some of the success and failures of the project of international development;
- evaluates how international development is changing in response to changes in international politics including the 'rise' of China and the global financial crisis.

Making an important contribution to contemporary debates on foreign aid and international development, this book will be of strong interest to students and scholars of politics, development studies, international relations and international organizations.

David Williams is a Senior Lecturer in International Politics in the Department of International Politics, City University, London, UK. His previous book was *The World Bank and Social Transformation in International Politics: Liberalism, Governance and Sovereignty*, published by Routledge.

International Development and Global Politics

History, theory and practice

David Williams

LONDON AND NEW YORK

First published 2012
by Routledge
2 Park Square, Milton Park, Abingdon, Oxon OX14 4RN

Simultaneously published in the USA and Canada
by Routledge
711 Third Avenue, New York, NY 10017 (8th Floor)

Routledge is an imprint of the Taylor & Francis Group, an informa business

British Library Cataloguing in Publication Data
A catalogue record for this book is available from the British Library

Library of Congress Cataloging-in-Publication Data
Williams, David, 1969-
International development and global politics: history, theory and practice/
David Williams.
p. cm.
Includes bibliographical references and index.
1. International cooperation--Textbooks. 2. International relations--
Economic aspects--Textbooks. 3. International economic relations--
Textbooks. 4. Economic development--Political aspects--Developing
countries--Textbooks. 5. Political development--Case studies. 6. Ghana--
Politics and government. 7. Argentina--Politics and government. 8. South
Korea--Politics and government. I. Title.
JZ1318.W5475 2011
327.1'11--dc22
2011009516

ISBN: 978-0-415-48936-2 (hbk)
ISBN: 978-0-415-48937-9 (pbk)
ISBN: 978-0-203-80441-4 (ebk)

Typeset in Times New Roman
by Prepress Projects, Perth, UK

For Tanya

Thank you

Contents

Figures

Tables

Acknowledgements

This book is more autobiographical than most. In terms of subject matter its origins lay in my time a student at the University of Swansea. My interest in development was first sparked as an undergraduate in the now sadly defunct Centre for Development Studies. Anyone familiar with the 'Development of Development Thinking' course taught there in the late 1980s will see echoes of it in what follows. At the same time my interest in the international politics of developing countries lies in several courses I took in the Department of Politics, notably on India and Southern Africa. That some of what I was taught there is still with me today, sometimes literally in the form of books and papers, is a testament to the power of undergraduate education. From Swansea I went to the Department of Political Studies at the School of Oriental and African Studies (SOAS). It is hard to imagine a more intellectually stimulating and challenging environment in which to think about 'development' than SOAS, bringing together as it did (and still does) social scientists and area studies specialists. I want to thank Tom Young in particular for his support during that time. We continue to work on issues we started working on then and I feel very lucky to have his continued friendship and encouragement. From SOAS I went to Oxford University, first as a research fellow at Lady Margaret Hall, then as a Lecturer in the Department of Politics and International Relations. It was there that I was really schooled in International Relations and the staff and students provided a rigorous atmosphere in which to learn the possibilities and limits of that discipline. In 2006 I moved to the nascent Department of International Politics at City University. The project of building a department almost from scratch was a very rewarding (if at times difficult) one. I owe a large debt of thanks to those who supported this project, particularly Tony Woodiwiss, Howard Tumber, John Solomos and Christie Slade. I also owe a large debt to my colleagues in the Department: Amnon Aran, Gemma Collantes, Tom Davies, Jean-Francois Drolet, Sophie Harman, Chris McDowell, Anastasia Nesvetailova and Sara Silvestri, and Peter Willetts. Particular thanks must go to Sophie Harman, who read and commented on the first draft of the manuscript. Thanks also to the students who took my course on the international politics of development for helping me refine the arguments that follow. Eleanora Poli did sterling work as my research assistant, particularly on the data used in the book. Finally I would like to thank City University for granting me a sabbatical in order to finish the manuscript, and my colleagues for taking on the additional responsibilities associated with my leave. I would also like to thank Carl Zarecky, Toby Dodge, George Lawson, Richard Higgott, David Goldthorpe, Gregor Irwin and Charles Kenny for their support and friendship over the years.

There is an even longer personal history I would like to acknowledge. My father taught me the value of history, and in particular the power of history to make the present seem strange, and that attitude permeates what follows. My mother taught me the importance of teaching and this book has been written out of the experience of teaching but also with the intent of contributing to the teaching of others who might be interested in the subject.

My largest debts are to my family. My children, Seth and Nina, have both grown up considerably while I was writing this book. One day they may understand why I was busy writing a book without pictures. In the mean time I want to thank them for simply being themselves. Words cannot do justice to the extent of my debt to my wife, Tanya. This book is dedicated to her with love and thanks.

Note on data and sources

For all data on foreign aid, this book has used the International Development Statistics database of the Organisation for Economic Co-operation and Development (OECD). In the text this is referenced as (OECD). The data can be accessed online at http://stats.oecd.org/qwids/. For the macroeconomic and developmental indicators for the case study countries and for regional growth rates, the World Bank's data have been used. In the text these are referenced as (World Bank). The data can be accessed at http://data.worldbank.org/. It should be noted that other data sets do sometimes give slightly different figures, but for the sake of consistency the same data sets are used throughout the book.

All of the individual projects examined are World Bank-designed projects. The Bank's repository of documents on its projects is unrivalled and it is really the only major development agency which makes easily available the documentation necessary to come to any form of conclusion about the impact of individual development projects and programmes. This repository can be accessed through the World Bank's website: http://www.worldbank.org/. It is a fascinating archive and I would encourage anyone with an interest in international development to explore it.

The graph in Chapter 5 on books published in English with the word 'globalization'/'globalisation' in the title is drawn from data derived from the British Library catalogue.

Introduction

Development and international order

In 1961 the World Bank, and the American and British governments, funded a project to build a dam and power station in Ghana. The Askombo Dam created the largest man-made lake in the world, Lake Volta, and was argued to be important because it would make available to Ghana an abundant supply of power, which was thought necessary for economic development. Large infrastructure projects like this were typical of the kinds of development projects funded by international development agencies during the 1950s and 1960s – be they dams, roads, power stations or ports. By 1987, the World Bank was supporting an entirely different kind of development programme in Ghana: a structural adjustment programme. The programme aimed to establish a policy framework that stimulated growth, encouraged savings and investment, and strengthened the balance of payments. This was to be accomplished by a series of reforms, including liberalization of trade, reducing the role of the state in the economy, and improving the 'incentives' for the private sector. In 2001, Western states and development agencies were stressing new concerns such as the importance of 'good governance', 'civil society', the consolidation of democracy, and explicit poverty reduction measures as the way towards development in Ghana. This sequence of changes is not confined to Ghana, of course, and in one way or another is typical of the kinds of projects and programmes funded by development agencies in almost all developing countries over the last 50 or so years.

The changes here are not just in the way that development agencies saw the problem of development, although there certainly was a dramatic shift in what we might call 'development theory' from seeing infrastructure as crucial, through seeing policy reform (structural adjustment) as crucial, to seeing political issues such as good governance and democracy as crucial. There were also important shifts in the way development agencies related to developing countries and to each other. The shift from infrastructure to structural adjustment and good governance represents a significant increase in the intrusiveness of western development agencies as they have become concerned with a wide area of economic, political and social life with significant implications for the sovereignty of many developing states. This is in sharp contrast to the narrow concern with infrastructure. In addition, the earlier period is characterized by a certain level of competition between aid donors and a limited form of pluralism among them. The Askombo

Dam was funded by the World Bank, and the American and British governments, not just because they thought electricity supply was important for Ghana's development, but because they were worried that the Soviet Union and/or China would fund it if they did not. They were right to be worried about this because Ghana received aid from both the Soviet Union and China at various times during the 1960s. This gave countries such as Ghana a limited form of bargaining power in their relations with western aid donors. By the 1990s all this had changed. The Soviet Union had collapsed and China had not yet embarked on the rapid expansion of its foreign aid programme that we have seen in recent years. The limited form of pluralism and competition that had characterized aid donors disappeared, again with significant implications for developing countries.

This book has three main aims. The first is to explain these changes in what will be called here the 'project of international development'. The term 'project of international development' is used deliberately to mean attempts on the part of western states, development agencies and other organizations to assist, direct or otherwise help in the process of 'development' in less-developed states. Part of the answer is that development agencies 'learned' that certain projects did not really work as well as they originally thought; neither dams nor structural adjustment were particularly successful in developmental terms and aid agencies realized this. There is a limited form of reflexivity within development agencies, which means they think about past failures and try to conceive of solutions to problems they encounter. Part of the answer, too, is that circumstances within developing countries changed dramatically over this period. Ghana, for example, experienced a catastrophic economic collapse in the late 1970s and early 1980s (as did quite a number of other developing countries), and development agencies responded to new circumstances with new kinds of development projects and programmes. It is the argument of this book, however, that changes in development policy and practice cannot be understood or explained without reference to the wider global context within which they take place. In other words, the project of international development is situated within, and has been fundamentally shaped by, the changing international order.

A second aim of the book is to uses changes in the project of international development to illustrate and track the broader changes in international order. The project of international development is a significant and in some respects an increasingly significant aspect of global politics. The largest aid donors gave nearly US$120 billion in aid in 2009, double the amount given in 1990 (OECD 2010). As well as the major bilateral donors (of which there are 22) there are many other organizations which form part of the project of international development: regional development banks, other multilateral organizations and many, many private and non-governmental organizations. These agencies operate in the vast majority of the nearly 200 states in the world. It is not just the scale of the enterprise, however, that makes the project of international development a significant part of international politics. Right from its origins as an institutionalized activity in the post-1945 international order, the project of international development was seen as a means to the achievement of significant foreign policy and international political objectives on the part of western states. These ranged from the cultivation of political allies (particularly during the Cold War) to the broader liberal international aims of international security and prosperity. In his 1949 inaugural address President Truman announced 'a bold new program for making the benefits of our scientific advances and industrial progress available for the improvement and growth of underdeveloped areas . . . It must be a worldwide effort for the achievement of peace, plenty, and freedom'. Of course Truman, like many American politicians in the following 40 years, was concerned with the fight against communism, but the idea that international development was an important component of US foreign policy, through its supposed links with security and prosperity, has remained a significant part of the thinking of many western states. In 2003 a United States Agency for International Development (USAID) report argued:

> When development and governance fail in a country, the consequences engulf entire regions and leap across the world. Terrorism, political violence, civil wars, organized crime, drug trafficking, infectious diseases, environmental crises, refugee flows and mass migrations cascade across the borders of weak states more destructively than ever before.
>
> (USAID 2003: 1)

A 2006 Department for International Development (DfID) White Paper argued: 'we believe that eliminating world poverty is not only morally right, but will also create a safer more prosperous world for us all' (DfID 2006: 13). In other words, the project of international development has always been integral to international order since at least 1945, and how it has changed helps us see how international order itself has changed.

Following from this, the third aim of the book is to see how developing countries have been affected by changes in international order since 1945. For almost all developing countries, relations with development agencies have been significant at one time or another, and for some countries it is or has been vitally important. Some countries remain highly dependent on aid resources for the continued functioning of government and the provision of services to their populations. For example, in 2005, fully 28 countries received aid worth more than 10 per cent of their gross national income (World Bank 2007a: 348–50). In some cases and at some times development agencies have had a significant impact on the economic and political policies of recipient states. Beyond this, as the agenda of development agencies has expanded into new areas such as political reform, good governance, participation and gender, so more and more areas of social and political life have come under the influence of external agents. In some countries where large numbers of aid agencies operate, the mere presence of these agencies has a pervasive impact on social, economic and political life. The project of international development is thus an extremely important part of the international relations of very many states, and how it has changed in the context of changing global order is a very important part of the story of developing countries in international politics.

The rest of this introduction does three things. First, it discusses the significance of taking a historical approach to the project of international development (i.e. going back to 1945). Second, it explores the idea of 'international order', which provides the analytical foundation for the examination that follows. Finally, it sketches out the structure of the book and the basic claims it makes.

History and critique

Many contemporary books on international development have a summary chapter on what happened in the post-1945 period, but almost all books written on the subject are focused on the contemporary period, roughly from the rise of neoliberalism during the 1980s. This book takes as a starting point the view that a more thorough historical approach is necessary for several related reasons. The first is that it helps us to reflect on many of the contemporary arguments that are had about development. It has been a regular feature of discussions of aid, for example, that there ought to be more of it, and developed countries are often criticized for not giving enough (J. Sachs 2005). A more historical approach to understanding development gives us some resources for engaging with these arguments, not least because development projects and programmes have quite often failed, sometimes through no real fault of the development agencies themselves, and the aggregate impact of foreign aid on development is unclear. Second, some historical knowledge allows us to reflect on contemporary development policies and projects. Many of the contemporary concerns of development agencies – infrastructure, poverty alleviation, agricultural development – have been priority areas in the past too, again with rather mixed results. It is not that these things are not important – they may well be – but attempts to tackle these kinds of issues should at least recognize that they have a history that might be able to teach us things that would inform these contemporary efforts.

Third, and more significantly, a historical approach to the project of international development allows for a more systematic critique of this project. The term 'critique' here does not mean being 'against' the project of international development. Over the years there have been many commentators who have cast doubt on the project of international development – in terms of whether it is really needed, or whether it has done any good (Bauer 1976; Easterly 2006; Moyo 2008). The aim of this book is not to contribute another such critique, although the book is concerned among other things with where and when development projects and programmes do not succeed. The suggestion here is that, in terms of the study of development, having a significant historical perspective is almost necessarily 'critical' in the sense that it opens up a line of investigation that disrupts and potentially undermines the contemporary self-presentation of those agencies involved in international development. The similarity is with other fields (economics, ethics, political theory, perhaps even science) where a historical approach opens up a series of new and revealing questions and contextualizes what is so often taken as having no context (Kuhn 1962; Macintyre 1967; Tully 1988). It allows us to ask why development agencies thought differently in the past about what was necessary for development, and why development policy and practice have changed. More significantly, it raises the question of what reasons we have for thinking that current development policy and practice is 'right' (and not the product of the forces that made previous development policy and practice different). In this way history has the potential to destabilize current and settled understandings and provide us with the resources for thinking critically about the project of international development.

Finally, a historical approach allows us to see the extent to which the understanding of what development is has changed over time. During the 1950s and 1960s 'development' was generally thought to be the processes of large-scale structural change to something like 'modernity', and it was thought to involve industrialization, urbanization and the destruction of previous forms of social, political and economic organization. In the contemporary period, as evidenced by the Millennium Development Goals, this understanding of development is much less prominent (at the same time as a country such as China seems to be living through just such a transition) and in its place has come a stress on poverty alleviation and the provision of social services, especially in the world's poorest countries. This book makes no adjudication of which of these visions is right, but they are clearly not the same understanding of what development is. An awareness of these differences might help in reflecting on contemporary policy and practice.

International orders and international development

The structure of the book turns on the concept of an 'international order'. It argues that it is possible to identify two different international orders – one that emerged in the aftermath of the Second World War, which is called here the 'sovereign order', and the other that emerged through the 1980s, which is called the 'liberal order'. The term 'international order' and variants of it are widely but sometimes rather loosely used within the discipline of International Relations and beyond. In March 1991, President George Bush famously argued that a 'new world order' was coming into existence (Bush 1991). The idea of a 'post-Cold War order' has been used regularly by commentators, as a counter to the 'Cold War order' that prevailed until 1989 (Cerny 1993; Clark 2001). The term 'world order' has been used by thinkers as diverse as Robert Cox, Samuel Huntington, Anne-Marie Slaughter and Francis Fukuyama (Cox 1996; Huntington 2002; Slaughter 2004; Fukuyama 2004). Even the idea of a 'global order' has been invoked by David Held and James Rosenau (Held 1995; Rosenau 1999). Roughly what all these uses seem to indicate is that it is possible to identify certain concepts (sovereignty, rights), agencies (states, social forces, 'civilizations') and practices (balancing, intervention, institutionalization) that together characterize international politics at a particular time.

Used in this way the concept of an 'international order' has both descriptive and explanatory components. It is descriptive as it identifies the key features of global politics at a given time and distinguishes it from other periods. The concept cannot be anything other than a kind of sketch – a stylized account of the main features of international politics during a particular period. However, it is also explanatory up to a point because these key features 'structure' (shape, condition) the actions and interactions of actors within a particular international order, and as international order changes so we expect the actions and interactions of agents to change too because the structure within which they operate changes. This is so because the basic structures of an international order shape what it is possible to do, what is seen as desirable or undesirable and legitimate or illegitimate. The extensive forms of intervention of various kinds that occurred during the 1990s were made possible because of changes in international order (the collapse of the Soviet Union for example) and were seen as increasingly legitimate (because of changing understandings of sovereignty). This pattern of intervention was less possible and intervention was certainly seen as less legitimate in the international order that prevailed after the Second World War. In this sense George Bush was right that a 'new world order' was coming into existence. It is important to note, however, that the international order that prevails at a given time does not determine the actions of agents – it structures them. In other words, like all (good) structural explanations it does not deny agents the capacity to reflect on their situation and develop new and creative ways of acting. It simply says that what agents do is conditioned by the international order they find themselves in and as this changes so new kinds of actions are made more or less possible, desirable and legitimate.

As the varied accounts noted above show, there are a variety of ways in which any particular international order can be thought to be structured. There are significant differences in what are thought to be the key actors, for example (are they states, 'social forces', 'networks' or global markets?), and significant differences in the role accorded to forms of power (military, economic or 'ideological' power) and the role accorded to ideas or norms. In this way, arguments about what the key structures are in any given international order replicate wider debates within the discipline of International Relations and the social sciences more generally about the basic ontology of international political life: material vs. 'ideational', states vs. mode of production and so on. At the heart of these disputes lie some very knotty problems of social theory and philosophy. It is not clear that any adjudication on these problems is possible, and it may not even be desirable. One reason for this is that any attempt to do so slices the world up into various components and attempts to suggest that one element – states or military power or global markets – is the key, essential, most important or privileged one. This seems implausible given that the concept of an international order describes the interrelationship of various factors that exist together, or at least it requires heroic attempts to make the other elements of the world dependent upon this one key element. It seems more plausible, if less analytically neat, to say that elements of an international order are intimately related to one another in such a way that there is no one single, final, privileged component (Cox 1996).

This book takes the fairly conventional view that international order is created and structured by three interrelated spheres or arenas: power-political agency, economic structures and processes, and structure of meaning – power, the economy and norms. This book is organized around two international orders, a sovereign order and a liberal order, and one of the arguments of the book is that these elements relate to one another to create significant differences between these orders.

The next set of questions relates to how and why international orders change over time. A number of points can be made. First, an international order has tensions, ambiguities and contradictions within it. The shift from one to another is partly about the playing out of these tensions. So, for example, the sovereign order had within it both a significant commitment to sovereignty and self-determination and a significant commitment to the norm of development. There was a tension here that played itself out as international order began to shift during the 1980s. Second, because the elements of an international order are interrelated, shifts in one area impact on other areas. The collapse of the Soviet Union had a significant impact on the normative as well as economic elements of international order. Third, the shift from one international order to another should not be understood as happening overnight. One of the implications of the concept of an 'international order' is that it generates a series of expectations and practices that are unlikely to change rapidly. It is tempting to pick on dates to signal a shift in the character of international order – and this temptation is even stronger in the period under consideration given the very obvious and dramatic changes associated with the end of the Cold War. However, even here there are extensive debates about whether 1989 (collapse of the Berlin Wall), 1991 (collapse of the Soviet Union) or even 1985 (Gorbachev's rise to power and the thawing of Soviet–American relations) should be seen as the definitive date (Lawson *et al.* 2010). There are other possibilities too, including 1979 (the election of Margaret Thatcher, the Soviet invasion of Afghanistan and the Iranian Revolution) and 1980 (the election of Ronald Reagan), both of which might be seen to signal the shift towards neoliberalism, a more expansionist US foreign policy and a renewed emphasis on the problem of managing the 'third world' (Lawson 2010). There is little utility in engaging in extensive debates about which of these dates is more important, in large part because these dates usually serve as shorthand for larger historical processes, and it is these processes we should be interested in, not the dates themselves; and of course these processes are complex and develop over time and cannot be adequately captured under a single date.

Finally, there is a question about the primary causal logic of changes in international order. At basis this is the same kind of question as the question about the primary determinant of the character of any one order, and thus the same kinds of responses can be made. The attempt to say that it is 'really' changes in state power or 'really' changes in global economic process or 'really' changes in norms and ideas that are the primary cause of changes in international order seems to suggest that these elements exist somehow separate from one another such that the causal logic works only in one direction. Given that these elements are interrelated it seems implausible that it would be possible to make this kind of determination, even if it is possible to describe (as Chapters 1 and 5 attempt) the ways in which changes in one area are related to changes in other areas.

The final set of questions here relate to conceptualizing the relationship between international order and the project of international development. In line with the ways in which the explanatory function of the concept of 'international order' must work – as a form of structural explanation – this book does not make a determinist argument that the project of international development can simply be 'explained' by the nature of the international order. The project of international development is itself a dynamic set of social processes and practices that includes a significant element of reflexivity and creativity: western states and development agencies have 'learned' to do different things over time and have responded to new situations with new practices. Nonetheless, and again in line with the concept of an international order, the book argues that the project of international development is structured by the international order within which it operates. It embodies and reflects certain kinds of practices and norms that arise not from within this project but from the broader international order.

Structure of the book

The book combines a thematic and chronological structure. It is divided into two parts that correspond to the two international orders – the sovereign order that characterized global politics from the end of the Second World War to the 1980s and the liberal order that emerged during the 1980s and into the 1990s. Each half of the book has the same structure. It begins by sketching out the salient features of international order in the two periods. In each case we are concerned with the power-political, economic and normative structures and processes that shape the project of international development as it is pursued during these periods. The book then reviews the development theory that dominated the thinking of development agencies during this period, and how this was crucially shaped by international order. Third, the book explores the institutional aspects of the project of international development looking at the policies and operations of development agencies and their relations with one another. Finally, each section concludes with an examination of how the project of international development manifested itself in concrete cases. The cases used here are Ghana, the Philippines and Argentina, and within this we look at the economic performance of these states, aid flows, and a number of development projects and programmes. No selection of three cases is likely to be entirely satisfactory. Nonetheless, taken together, there are some benefits from these particular cases. First, they provide some kind of geographical spread. Second, they are in different ways emblematic of various kinds of developing countries and the various kinds of relationships they have had with development agencies. Third, they can be compared across the two time periods. Of course there are significant limitations to the use of these cases too. They are and must be illustrative only, and the book makes no claims that they are comprehensive (either as individual cases or as a set of cases from which general conclusions could be easily drawn). They are not substitutes for cases of other states in other regions (although they do illustrate some of the issues involved). Despite this, the view taken here is that cases studies are important both for substantiating the arguments of the book about the ways in which the project of international development has changed over time and because they provide an invaluable way of bring the history of international development alive.

Part I

Development and the sovereign order

1   The sovereign order

Introduction

This chapter examines the global context within which, and partly because of which, the project of international development emerged. It begins in the period after the Second World War because it is only then that this project becomes institutionalized in international politics through the regular provision of aid to developing countries and the establishment of permanent aid agencies. This suggests that there is something particular about international order during this period that explains the emergence of the project of international development. This chapter argues that this is US hegemony. 'Development' played an important role in the hegemonic project pursued by the United States after 1945, and there are good reasons for thinking that the project of international development is in important respects an American project. The second aim of the chapter is provide a sketch of international order during this period. Apart from US hegemony, the chapter focuses on the Cold War and superpower competition as the key power-political feature of global politics during this period, which had important implications for the project of international development and for the international relations of developing countries. The chapter then examines the global economy, with a particular focus on the rise and fall of what is known as the 'golden age' of capitalism. The changes in the global economy during this period affected all developing countries (and all developed countries too of course) in significant ways. The 'good times' of the 1950s and 1960s crucially shaped the way development agencies thought about development, and the end of the 'golden age', the extended economic crisis of the late 1970s and early 1980s, was a significant turning point in the history of international development. Finally, the chapter examines some of the norms that emerged and shaped international order, with a focus on the connected norms of self-determination, sovereignty and non-intervention, and on the idea of 'development' itself as a norm.

The elements of international order in this period reinforce one another to produce what is called here the 'sovereign order'. This is an order in which sovereignty crucially structures global politics. This is produced by US hegemony and Cold War competition and by the 'golden age' of global capitalism, as well as by the ideas of self-determination and non-intervention. It is an order in which developing countries are accorded a certain kind of protection, and in which they have a certain kind of autonomy to pursue their own 'development', and where there exists a form of political pluralism.

US hegemony and the Cold War

'Development' and the post-war order

It is commonplace to begin a history of international development with Harry Truman's 'Four Point' speech delivered at his presidential inauguration on 20 January 1949 (Craig and Porter 2006; Easterly 2006). The fourth point of his speech was this:

> We must embark on a bold new program for making the benefits of our scientific advances and industrial progress available for the improvement and growth of underdeveloped areas. More than half the people in the world are living in conditions approaching misery. Their food is inadequate. They are victims of disease. Their economic life is primitive and stagnant. Their poverty is a handicap and a threat both to them and to more prosperous areas . . . I believe that we should make available to peace-loving peoples the benefits of our store of technical knowledge in order to help them realize their aspirations for a better life . . . All countries, including our own, will greatly benefit from a constructive program for the better use of the world's human and natural resources . . . Only by helping the least fortunate of its members to help themselves can that human family achieve the decent, satisfying life that is the right of all people.
>
> (http://www.trumanlibrary.org/whistlestop/50yr_archive/
> inagural20jan1949.htm)

The actual practice of foreign aid was slow to match this vaulting rhetoric. Nonetheless, this speech signals something very important in the history of the project of international development as it provides one of the first explicit articulations of, and justifications for, the project of international development: a deliberate attempt to assist developing countries on the road to 'development' for their benefit and for the benefit of the already developed world.

The significance of Truman's inaugural speech for the history of international development, however, is that a concern with development was only one part of a much larger programme for, in Truman's words, 'peace and freedom'. The first part of this plan was to 'continue to give unfaltering support to the United Nations and related agencies'. The second part was to continue the programme for 'world economic recovery', which meant continued support for the European recovery programme, the Marshall Plan, and plans for 'reducing the barriers to world trade and increasing its volume'. The third part was to 'strengthen freedom-loving nations against the dangers of aggression', which meant establishing the North Atlantic Treaty Organization (NATO) and other bilateral security agreements in the face of potential challenges from the Soviet Union and other communist states. Truman's speech illustrates, then, not just the origins of the project of international development, but the project of US hegemony more generally, within which development was seen as having an important role.

There is no doubt that the United States ended the Second World War in a hegemonic position. The unprecedented nature of US predominance is illustrated by the fact that in 1948 the United States accounted for 48 per cent of global industrial production (Ikenberry 2006: 26). The United States was alone among the 'victors' of the war in having suffered relatively little damage to its economy – the exception was loss of life in the fighting (about 400,000 killed), but even this was relatively small compared with the other 'victorious' states (the UK lost about 450,000 people out of a much smaller population and the USSR a staggering 24,000,000). Britain ended the war in significant debt and had experienced extensive damage to its infrastructure and industrial capacity (Broadberry and Howlett 1998). Britain started the war with an economy about one-third the size of that of the United States, but ended it with an economy about one-fifth as big (Harrison 1998a: 10). The USSR had experienced destruction of its physical capital – by some estimates 25 per cent – to go along with its massive human losses, and had suffered a decline in the relative size of its economy compared with the United States similar to that of the UK (Harrison 1998b: 293). The Axis powers were defeated and occupied, and certainly in the last years of the war experienced significant destruction of both physical and human capital. The United States, then, was in a particularly privileged position at the end of the war (Layne 2006: ch. 2).

More important than the United States' material superiority was the willingness to use this to construct a post-war order that preserved and enhanced US hegemony. In other words, the United States was not just in a position to play the defining role in shaping post-war international politics; it was also very willing to do so. As President Roosevelt said in March 1945, 'there can be no middle ground here. We shall have to take responsibility for world collaboration, or we shall have to bear the responsibility for another world conflict' (Burley 1993: 130). What makes this willingness all the more remarkable was that US planning for the post-war international order started as early as 1939, although it accelerated after the United States joined the war in 1942. Charles Maier quotes a 1942 Council on Foreign Relations report:

> Americans are inclined to believe that the period at the end of the war will provide a tabula rasa on which can be written the terms of a new democratic order. The economic and political institutions of 1939 and before are clearly in suspension and need not be restored intact after the war.
>
> (Maier 1978: 35)

In some respects the basic aims of US planners were the same as those of any other hegemonic state: to construct an international order that served its security, economic and political interests. This is right, but ultimately not especially revealing as it does not explain why the United States thought that certain kinds of specific goals, institutions and practices were ones that would serve its interests. In other words, the crucial thing is not American *hegemony*, but *American* hegemony (Ruggie 1998a). To cast America's hegemonic ambitions simply as another variant of great power hegemony resulting from America's preponderant material power is to radically downplay quite how different America's vision of international politics actually was, and thus how different its understanding was of what would serve its interests. The three defining features of the international order the United States was trying to build were institutionalism, multilateralism and a self-confident assertion of liberal political and economic values.

The United States undertook a great programme of institutional engineering before and after 1945. A simple list makes the point: the United Nations, the International Monetary Fund (IMF), the Bretton Woods exchange rate system, the World Bank (International Bank for Reconstruction and Development or IBRD, as it was originally known), trade organizations (the aborted International Trade Organization or ITO and then the General Agreement on Tariffs and Trade or GATT) and NATO as only the most well known. All these served US interests in various ways and enshrined US power. A relatively open trading system (via GATT) allowed access for US exporters to overseas markets. The Bretton Woods exchange rate system provided exchange rate stability and established the US dollar as a global reserve currency. The United Nations gave the United States (and its wartime allies) veto power through the Security Council and provided some mechanisms for managing international conflict (although they never worked as intended). NATO as well as bilateral security arrangements, particularly with Japan, provided security alliances and helped project US power in Europe and beyond. It seems relatively uncontroversial to say that the great programme of institutional engineering undertaken from 1944 would simply not have taken place without specifically American predominance.

As this programme of institutional creation suggests, however, US hegemony was not of a unilateral kind. Instead it evidenced a significant commitment to multilateralism in at least two ways (Ruggie 1982; Deudney and Ikenberry 1999). First, the creation of these institutions required the agreement and cooperation of other states. Famously, the Bretton Woods Conference of 1944 involved significant cooperation with the UK over the design of the IMF and World Bank, and 44 states attended the conference, of which 19 were from Latin America (Ruggie 1982; Helleiner 2006). But the creation of all these institutions required the agreement of other states, even if this agreement was given in the context of the relative power of the United States. Second, the functioning of these institutions involved extensive and on-going cooperation with other states. The United States was certainly the most important state in these institutions, but they operated only because other states participated in them and because they were based on (albeit unequal) reciprocity. It is important to note that the United States wanted this kind of multilateralism. As Harry White, the leading US negotiator of the Bretton Woods agreements, said: 'the absence of a high degree of economic collaboration among the leading nations will . . . inevitably result in economic warfare that will be but the prelude and instigator of military warfare on an even vaster scale' (quoted in Pollard 1985: 8). This kind of multilateralism was a novel and very important part of the post-1945 international order.

Finally, US planners expressed a series of classically liberal views about international politics. At the broadest level they were convinced that the kind of international political and economic order they were creating would be good not just for them but for other states as well. In making these arguments they drew on the long tradition of liberal international thought that equated economic freedom with peace and prosperity. Cordell Hull, one of the key architects of the post-war order, argued that:

> unhampered trade dovetailed with peace; high tariffs, trade barriers, and unfair economic competition, with war . . . if we could get a freer flow of trade . . . freer in the sense of fewer discriminations and obstructions . . . so that one country would not be deadly jealous of another and the living standards of all countries might rise, thereby eliminating the economic dissatisfaction that breeds war, we might have a reasonable chance of lasting peace.
>
> (Hull 1948: 81)

This stress on the need for open trade (in both America's interests and the interests of other states) was also linked to the desirability of spreading American ideology. As Layne has put it, 'US strategists believed that the nation's core values could be safe only in an international system underwritten by hegemonic US power and open both to US economic penetration and to the penetration of American ideology' (Layne 2006: 9). In this way American policymakers fused a self-interested argument with the spread of liberal economic and political ideas and institutions.

The place of development within this hegemonic order reflected all three of these features: multilateralism, institutionalism and liberalism. During the late 1930s, the United States had begun to support development projects in Latin America through loans from the US Export–Import Bank as part of the 'Good Neighbor Policy' instituted by Roosevelt. These loans were justified on the basis that they would help Latin American economies themselves, but also increase trade and prosperity within the western hemisphere in general to the benefit of the United States (Helleiner 2006: 946–51). In mid-1940, Cordell Hull was stressing America's desire to promote 'methods for improving the standard of living of the peoples of America' (quoted in Helleiner 2006: 952). These ideas were carried over into the US project for the post-war order. There was a general agreement among American planners that 'development' of less-developed countries (LDCs) was important in terms of the security and prosperity of the United States itself, as Truman's speech illustrates, invoking again the classic arguments about the links between prosperity and peace.

The project of international development was institutionalized most importantly through the creation of the World Bank. Article 1(1) of the Articles of Agreement of the International Bank for Reconstruction and Development signed on 22 July 1944 states that the purpose of the Bank was:

To assist in the reconstruction and development of territories of members by facilitating the investment for productive purposes, including the restoration of economies destroyed or disrupted by war, the reconversion of productive facilities to peacetime needs and the encouragement of the development of productive facilities and resources in less developed countries.

(http://siteresources.worldbank.org/EXTABOUTUS/Resources/ibrd-articlesofagreement.pdf)

As we shall see in Chapter 3, actual practice took a few years to live up to this, but it is clear that as early as 1944 the multilateral and institutional basis for the project of international development was being created. Many developing countries certainly saw it that way and lent their support to the agreements (Helleiner 2006: 963). Although it was not established as a development agency the Articles of Agreement of the International Monetary Fund reflect the same kind of concerns. They say that one of its purposes is to:

facilitate the expansion and balanced growth of international trade, and to contribute thereby to the promotion and maintenance of high levels of employment and real income and to the development of the productive resources of all members as primary objectives of economic policy.

[http://www.imf.org/external/pubs/ft/aa/aa.pdf: Article 1(ii)]

This raises the possibility that the project of international development as it manifested itself after 1945 would not have happened without American dominance. Despite Britain's being substantially involved in the negotiations at the Bretton Woods conference, there is no great reason to think that left to their own devices the colonial powers would have enacted anything like this, and in any case they were in no position to do so. There are, as many commentators have noted, a significant set of connections between colonialism and the 'project of international development', and it is possible to read into the colonialism some of the origins of the idea of development. At least some of the justification for European colonialism had always been that it would bring 'progress' and 'civilization' to colonized societies (Pitts 2005; Williams and Young 2009). This idea was enshrined Article 22 of the League of Nations Charter:

To those colonies and territories which as a consequence of the late war have ceased to be under the sovereignty of the States which formerly governed them and which are inhabited by peoples not yet able to stand by themselves under the strenuous conditions of the modern world, there should be applied the principle that the well-being and development of such peoples form a sacred trust of civilisation and that securities for the performance of this trust should be embodied in this Covenant.

(http://avalon.law.yale.edu/20th_century/leagcov.asp)

There are more prosaic connections too. Before the Second World War, for example, colonial officials in Britain were beginning to take the idea of the economic development of their colonies more seriously and, as Uma Kothari has shown, many colonial administrators made the transition to being development practitioners (Hyam 1999; Kothari 2005). There is, however, no evidence at all that Britain or the other colonial powers were concerned with the broader project of international development in the way that the United States was. It seems then that as an *international project*, institutionalized and generalized within international politics, 'development' originated within and significantly because of US hegemony. Over the years since the end of the Second World War, the United States' record on development issues and its relationships with developing countries have been severely criticized, often with good cause. Thus it is easy to forget that the project of international development is itself significantly, if not largely, the result of US predominance in global politics in the period immediately after 1945 when the United States attempted to create a new kind of institutionalized international order that fused liberal idealism with American self-interest.

The Cold War

This project for US hegemony was developed before and independently from the specific threat that the Soviet Union began to pose to US dominance. By the time of Truman's 1949 inaugural, however, the Cold War was becoming a dominant feature of the post-war period. During that speech Truman said that 'the United States and other like-minded nations find themselves opposed by a regime with contrary aims and a totally different concept of life. That regime adheres to a false philosophy . . . that philosophy is communism' (http://www.trumanlibrary.org/whistlestop/50yr_archive/inagural20jan1949.htm). Truman went on to lay out the numerous apparent defects with communism and concluded that 'the actions resulting from the Communist philosophy are a threat to the efforts of free nationals to bring about world recovery and lasting peace'.

The emergence of the Cold War and superpower rivalry had a series of very significant implications for the project of international development. From the US perspective, in particular, it both enhanced the significance of this project and increasingly shaped the way it was practised. The United States did not abandon the liberal belief in the connections between prosperity (development) and peace and security, and so for many US policymakers 'development' was seen as a mechanism for combating communism; as they had done with post-war Europe, so they thought that the lack of development in third world states would provide a breeding ground for communism. In addition, as Wolfgang Sachs has put it, the promise of 'development' would 'engage the loyalty of the decolonizing countries in order to sustain the struggle against communism' (W. Sachs 1992: 2). The promise of 'development' then sat as the US alternative to both communism and colonialism.

In terms of practice the Cold War had a very significant impact on the project of international development. This can be seen as early as 1947, when Truman articulated what became known as the 'Truman Doctrine' in a speech before a joint session of the US Congress on 12 March 1947. The backdrop to the Truman Doctrine was an economic crisis that gripped Europe during the winter of 1946–7.

In the context of increasing tension between the United States and the USSR, American policymakers became concerned that this crisis would present political opportunities to the already strong communist movements in many European states. In the case of Greece this was compounded by a civil war between communist groups and forces loyal to the Greek king, and a fear that if Greece was 'lost' to communism, then Turkey would follow (an early articulation of the 'domino theory') with a loss of control of the Dardanelles Strait, a strategically important link between the Black Sea and the Mediterranean. The British government had been supporting the Greek king during the civil war and had provided some assistance to Turkey, but on account of its own economic difficulties it announced in early 1947 an end to its economic and military assistance to both countries. The Truman administration stepped in and provided military and economic assistance to both countries and established a permanent military presence in the region. Truman's 1947 speech can be seen as the clearest articulation that the United States would use its financial and military assistance in the context of Cold War rivalry:

> One of the primary objectives of the foreign policy of the United States is the creation of conditions in which we and other nations will be able to work out a way of life free from coercion . . . I believe that our help should be primarily through economic and financial aid which is essential to economic stability and orderly political processes . . . If we falter in our leadership, we may endanger the peace of the world – and we shall surely endanger the welfare of our own nation.
>
> (http://avalon.law.yale.edu/20th_century/trudoc.asp)

In other words, foreign aid, and other forms of assistance, would be used explicitly in the fight against communism.

The Cold War had a paradoxical impact on LDCs themselves. On one hand, and most obviously, it exposed some of them to extensive and often violent conflict. The most obvious cases are those of large-scale war – Vietnam, Angola and Mozambique for example – in which the superpowers sometimes overtly and sometimes covertly supported military groups in often extraordinarily destructive wars. It has been estimated that 500,000 people were killed in the Angolan civil war and perhaps 900,000 in Mozambique. Beyond this, both superpowers, but especially the United States, intervened covertly in non-military ways in a number of countries, including Iran, Chile, the Philippines, Panama and Guatemala (Westad 2007). Indeed, as the 'conflict' between the United States and the USSR become more 'stable' during the late 1960s and into the 1970s, so the 'third world' became an increasingly important arena of superpower struggle.

On the other hand, Cold War competition gave some states resources and protection. Many developing countries benefited from military support from one or other of the superpowers, for example. The Soviets gave military and financial aid to a significant number of developing countries in their support for 'national liberation movements' (Porter 1984; Westad 2007). In 1955 Nasser signed a US$250 million arms agreement to obtain Soviet military equipment from Czechoslovakia, setting a precedent for military assistance to other Middle-Eastern states, including Syria, Yemen and Iraq, and over time states in other regions, including Indonesia, Guinea, Sudan, Ghana, Cambodia and Zaire. By one estimate Soviet weapons exports to third world states exceeded US$2.7 billion from 1954 to 1964. From 1965 to 1972 the figure is estimated to be US$6.5 billion, including assistance to states such as Nigeria, Ethiopia, Iran, Pakistan and Uganda. From 1973 to 1977 the figure is estimated to be US$16.5 billion (reflecting the growing importance of superpower competition in the third world), including very significant military assistance to communist groups (and then subsequently the governments) in Angola and Mozambique (Porter 1984: 19, 31). The United States followed a similar pattern. Beginning with assistance to Greece and Turkey, the United States provided military assistance to a significant number of developing-country governments, including those in Iran, the Philippines, Pakistan, Ethiopia and many other states in Africa and Latin America.

Three points are worth noting about this. The first is that significant amounts of assistance went to governments that were certainly not explicitly ideologically allies. This was particularly true of Soviet military assistance, which went to non-communist states including, for example, Nigeria. Second, as the lists above indicate, some countries received military aid from both superpowers. Third, although superpower military assistance gave them some leverage over recipient states, not only was this rather limited in practice, but in fact the relationship enabled third world states to exercise leverage over the superpowers, particularly by recasting local disputes as parts of the great ideological struggle or by playing one superpower off against the other (Porter 1984: 29–30; Sluglett 2005). One example helps to illustrate the point. The United States provided Ethiopia with military assistance during the 1950s and 1960s, partly because the United States operated an important radio station in the country. This, however, did not stop Emperor Selassie negotiating a loan from the Soviet Union, partly in order to 'blackmail' the United States into providing more military assistance to build up the Ethiopian military in order to deter Somali aggression. When Selassie was overthrown in a coup in 1974, a communist government came to power which allied with the Soviet Union and received very significant amounts of Soviet military aid. In so doing the Soviets shifted away from supplying Ethiopia's regional challenger, Somalia, with military aid. As Ethiopia allied with the Soviet Union, the United States began to supply Somalia with aid and equipment, culminating in a deal in 1980 to supply military aid in exchange for the right to establish military bases in Somalia (Lefebvre 1991).

Beyond this military assistance, and the aid given by both superpowers (to be examined in Chapter 3), superpower rivalry benefited developing country government (if not their societies) in two other important ways. Both the USSR and the United States had few qualms about supporting authoritarian governments that were more or less brutal in their treatment of at least sections of their own societies. Of course, as noted above, sometimes the superpowers intervened dramatically in the internal affairs of third world states, but very often they were content to leave the government of these states alone in return for whatever it was that the superpower wanted. This may have been morally dubious, but it had the effect of protecting (some) third world states from extensive concern with their internal affairs. Second, superpower rivalry gave some developing countries a certain kind of protection because it legitimized (or at least helped to sustain) a limited form of political pluralism within global politics. It was simply much easier to be a communist state when the USSR was around to provide support (as Ethiopia after 1974) and when one could join a 'bloc' of states and receive political support as well as financial resources. The consequences of this for the people of many 'communist' states in the third world may have been ambivalent, but it did help to sustain a sovereign international order.

The global economy: from 'golden age' to 'stagflation'

As we have already seen, a very significant part of the US hegemonic project was the construction of a particular kind of international economic order. Whatever the exact causal relationship between the US hegemonic project and changes within the global economy, it is clear the period from 1950 to the mid-1970s was one of remarkable global economic growth: the so-called 'golden age' of capitalism. It was only in the mid-1970s that both the institutional and intellectual consensus that shaped the international economic order began to unravel.

Bretton Woods and 'embedded liberalism'

John Ruggie coined the term 'embedded liberalism' to describe the post-war economic order created by the United States. In doing so he drew explicitly from the work of the historian and sociologist Karl Polanyi. In his most famous work, *The Great Transformation*, Polanyi drew a distinction between 'embedded' and 'disembedded' economic orders (Polanyi 1957). Embedded economic orders were ones in which the 'market' and economic relations were subordinate to and expressions of broader social and political goals. A disembedded economic order was one in which these social and political goals became themselves subordinate to the 'market' and in which the logic and demands of market relations come to play a dominant role in society. For Polanyi, the nineteenth century was a period in which the markets gradually became disembedded, but by the early twentieth century, and particularly after the First World War, more and more states started to try impose direct social control over market relations in order to respond to the social and political consequences of 'market fundamentalism'. As Ruggie argues, 'once this domestic transformation began . . . international liberalism of the orthodox kind was doomed' (Ruggie 1998b: 68). What this meant was that the international economic order established after the Second World War could not be a return to unfettered international economic liberalism but rather would have to balance economic liberalism with the demands of governments for more social and political control of the 'market' (more domestic intervention), and with the international and cooperative management of global economic relations (Ruggie 1998b: 68). 'Unlike the economic nationalism of the thirties, the international economic order would be multilateral in character; but unlike the liberalism of the gold standard and free trade, its multilateralism would be predicated upon domestic intervention' (Ruggie 1991: 203).

This is 'embedded liberalism', and it characterizes not just the broad views certainly of US planners, as well as Keynes, the key British architect of Bretton Woods, but the institutional structures put in place under US hegemony (Ikenberry 1992). This included the IBRD and the IMF, and plans for an International Trade Organization (ITO), which was replaced by the more ad hoc GATT when the United States itself failed to ratify the Havana Charter that established the ITO. The IMF and the Bretton Woods exchange rate system provided a way of multilaterally managing balance of payments problems and, through the provision of support from the IMF, provided a way for countries to overcome balance of payments difficulties without undergoing a severe deflationary process (with its attendant problems of unemployment and social unrest). The general agreement on the desirability of reducing barriers to trade was balanced by a series of exemptions that would enable countries to pursue domestic social policies, particularly full employment, but also the protection of strategically important industries (defence and agriculture for example) and certain preferential trading arrangements. Both the ideas and the institutions established as part of the 'embedded liberalism' compromise dominated the international economy for 30 years.

The Marshall Plan

As with the broader project of US hegemony, so the narrower project of reconstructing global economic relations faced new and immediate challenges that came partly from growing tensions with the Soviet Union. As we have already noted, by 1947 economic conditions in many European states were very poor: production was stagnating, trade reducing, and there were shortages of food and essential inputs, significant government deficits and rising inflation (Eichengreen 1995). This presented three kinds of problems. First, the Bretton Woods system could not really operate as planned as the European states were unable to participate in it because of their dire economic situation. Second, the international economy could not recover without a European economic recovery. Third, this was increasingly seen as a political problem. As economic conditions worsened, so the threat of political instability and rising communist influence in European states increased. Despite the initial plans that the newly created IBRD would assist European countries in their economic reconstruction, the scale of the economic crisis, and inability of the IBRD to raise sufficient capital in a short period of time, meant that more immediate funds were necessary. It was this that motivated the Marshall Plan. Between 1947 and 1951 US$12.4 billion was channelled to European countries (equivalent to US$65 billion in 1989 prices) (Wexler 1983: 25–51; Reichlin 1995: 39). By 1951 the European economies had recovered remarkably well. Overall European gross national product (GNP) increased by 32.5 per cent, industrial production rose by 36 per cent and agricultural production by 16 per cent (Wexler 1983: 94–5).

The first generation of scholarship on the Marshall Plan ascribed considerable causal importance to Marshall Plan aid in the European economic recovery, because of the way it supplemented domestic sources of investment finance, and thus boosted agricultural and industrial production and helped to repair damaged infrastructure (Eichengreen 1995; Reichlin 1995). Subsequent generations of scholars tended to take a more sceptical view of the economic impact of Marshall Plan aid, arguing that European economic recovery was already under way and that in any case Marshall Plan aid only amounted to 10 per cent of investment over the period from 1948 to 1951 (Milward 1984). A more balanced assessment of the impact of the Marshall Plan argues that its primary contribution was in terms of institutions and politics, particularly its role in altering the environment in which economic policy was made. First, the provision of Marshall Plan aid helped to alleviate the tensions between capital and labour by reducing the sacrifices made by both sides. Second, the strings attached to US aid strengthened the hand of those policymakers that favoured a return to a more open economy, and politically centrist parties were able to use Marshall Plan aid to weaken the political position of communist parties. Third, Marshall Plan aid encouraged European economic integration by making the provision of aid conditional on European governments coordinating among themselves about the distribution of aid (Eichengreen 1995). In so doing the Marshall Plan embodied some of the ideas associated with embedded liberalism as it pushed for both a return to relatively liberal domestic economic arrangements *and* increasing governmental cooperation in the management of European economic relations. The Marshall Plan succeeded at least in terms of its political objectives, whatever its exact contribution to the economic recovery of Europe.

The 'golden age of capitalism'

The period from the early 1950s to the mid-1970s was remarkable for the fact that many countries experienced sustained and significant economic growth with high levels of domestic employment and relatively low inflation (see Table 1.1). It seems clear that the international economic arrangements established under US hegemony did make an important contribution to the stability and success of the international economy up to the 1970s. At the very least they provided a series of institutions and practices which ensured that economic relations between the industrialized countries could take place in a more orderly and beneficial manner than had been the case in years before the Second World War. In addition, America was prepared to incur the costs of its hegemonic position in return for longer-run economic and political benefits (Marglin 1990: 11). For example, the Marshall Plan and the reconstruction of Germany and Japan cost money and led to a relative decline in the importance of the US economy as these countries recovered, but this was something the United States was prepared to tolerate as part of its broader multilateral hegemonic project.

Table 1.1 Selected macroeconomic indicators for major industrialized countries, 1950–75 (annual averages)

	GDP growth rate (%)	Unemployment rates (%)	Inflation (%)
France	5.13	2.1	5.5
Germany	5.92	1.6	3.8
Japan	9.29	1.6	5.2
United Kingdom	3.02	2.85	4.6
United States	3.65	4.75	3.1

Sources: Maddison (1989: 22); Glynn *et al.* (1990: 47).

Underpinning this was a dramatic growth in labour productivity and an investment boom of 'historically unprecedented length and vigor' (Glynn *et al.* 1990: 42). There was a dramatic growth in the volume of trade, which was certainly encouraged by the reduction in trade tariffs under successive GATT negotiations. The growing internationalization of the world economy was also paralleled by an increase in capital flows (Glynn *et al.* 1990: 69, 87). While the golden age was certainly felt most in OECD countries, many developing states also experienced sustained economic growth and a relatively favourable international economic environment. Overall growth rates for developing countries were reasonably high – certainly compared with what came after (see Table 1.3 below). The prices of primary commodities during the period were reasonably high, partly as a result of strong demand arising from growth in the global economy, and prices of significant imports, particularly oil, were relatively low; in addition, developing countries operated in an international economic environment with stable currency and interest rates. This generated a huge amount of optimism about the possibilities for the development of less-developed states within the structures of the existing global economy and, as we shall see, played an important role in shaping the way development was understood.

The end of the 'golden age'

By the mid-1970s the 'golden age' was over. Growth rates fell and inflation and unemployment rose – a situation that became known as 'stagflation' (stagnation *and* inflation; Table 1.2).

There is an extensive set of debates about the causes of this decline. One popular view locates the primary cause in the oil price shocks of 1973 and 1979. Clearly these did have an important role in the relative economic decline of the late 1970s and early 1980s. Equally it is clear that at least two other sets of factors are important. First, there were emerging as early as the late 1960s a series of domestic macroeconomic problems within many OECD states (Glynn *et al.* 1990). The productivity slowdown noted above started in the late 1960s, at least in the United States, Germany and Japan, and capital–output ratios were also deteriorating, although both of these show significant further decline after 1973.

Table 1.2 Selected macroeconomic indicators for major industrialized countries, 1973–83 (annual averages)

	GDP growth rate (%)	Unemployment (%)	Inflation
France	2.32	5.9	10.9
Germany	1.72	4.4	4.7
Japan	3.72	2.1	6.3
United Kingdom	1.10	6.8	15.0
United States	2.42	7.45	7.9

Sources: Maddison (1989: 22); Glynn *et al.* (1990: 47).

Second, there was the unravelling of some of the post-war institutional arrangements that had helped maintain stability in the international economy, most notably the ending of the Bretton Woods exchange rate system. This is also related to the oil price rises as the floating of the dollar led to a depreciation the dollar, which meant that oil exporters were receiving less real income because oil was priced in dollars. As Glynn and colleagues put it:

> the institutional and behavioral framework was fraying at the edges . . . [P]roblems of inflation, the funding of rising public sector deficits and expenditures, and persistent unemployment were superimposed upon underlying problems in the organization of the system of production and in the macroeconomic structures.
>
> (Glynn *et al.* 1990: 97)

As the 'golden age' ended so the intellectual and political consensus upon which it had been built started to erode. In particular 'embedded liberalism' and Keynesian demand management started to come under fire for having contributed to the decline of the OECD economies. In many respects 1979 marks the most significant turning point here. In that year Paul Volcker, a committed monetarist, was appointed as Chairman of the Federal Reserve. Margaret Thatcher was elected in the same year and Reagan took office the following year. What this signalled was the start of the neoliberal revolution in public policy in the west, and as we shall see in terms of development theory too.

The end of the 'golden age' had a series of important implications for developing countries. The relatively favourable external environment that had existed through the 1950s and 1960s started to change. Growth rates declined (Table 1.3), and many developing countries experienced a severe economic crisis in the late 1970s and early 1980s.

As OECD economies started to decline so the demand for, and thus prices of, primary commodities started to fall, and of course the oil price rise of 1973 affected some developing countries very badly as their import bills rose dramatically. In the short term, many LDCs were able to finance this through international borrowing, but only at the cost of rising indebtedness. For a while this seemed

Table 1.3 Regional growth rates, 1960–84

	1960–4	1965–9	1970–4	1975–9	1980–4
East Asia	0.75	4.38	7.56	6.88	6.1
Latin America and Caribbean	5	4.9	6.6	4.82	1.46
Middle East and North Africa	n/a	7.27	7.48	5.08	3.62
Sub-Saharan Africa	4.9	3.64	5.62	2.26	1.88

Source: World Bank.

to be sustainable, but the second oil price rise of 1979 and the increase in dollar interest rates pitched many countries, and most dramatically of all Latin American countries, into crisis. In this sense the increase in capital flows that is so characteristic of the golden age had a paradoxical impact. It allowed Latin American states access to private capital, but also exposed them to the volatility of these flows and the risks associated with a sudden increase in the cost of servicing their debts. The economic crises experienced by many developing countries during this period had a number of important consequences. They discredited the development theories that had supposedly underpinned their development strategies and it exposed them to greater scrutiny from developed states, partly because, as the Latin American debt crisis showed, these crises could have an important impact on financial institutions in the developed world.

Self-determination, sovereignty and 'development'

The third aspect of the post-1945 international order is the 'normative' one. Here we are concerned with the kinds of norms – shared understandings about the appropriate ways to act – that shaped international politics in this period. We focus on three: the end of empire as a legitimate form of political organization and its replacement by the idea of national self-determination; the norm of non-intervention in the internal affairs of sovereign states; and the emergence of development itself as a norm in international politics.

Decolonization and self-determination

One of the most striking aspects of the post-1945 international order is the dramatic rise in the number of sovereign states. The original membership of the UN in 1945 was 51 states. A significant portion of these could be classified as 'developing countries', including 19 South American states, three African states (four if South Africa is included) and four Middle-Eastern states (five if Turkey is included) as well as India and China. As the process of decolonization got under way so membership of the UN grew rapidly. By 1955 there were 76 members and by 1965 117. By 1975 membership had risen to 144 and by 1985 to 159. The overwhelming bulk of this increase in membership came in the form of newly independent states as a result of the process of decolonization. In 1960 alone 16 Africa states become independent. The fact that decolonization happened so quickly and almost universally (with a few exceptions) indicates that something important had changed in the post-war international order. Even those countries that tried to resist this process, such as Portugal, succumbed pretty quickly and the Portuguese empire in Africa collapsed in the mid-1970s.

It has been conventional to divide explanations of decolonization into three types (Springhall 2001: ch. 1). International explanations stress the dramatic shifts in the distribution of power in the aftermath of the Second World War and the avowedly anti-colonial stance of the two new superpowers. In this view the United States was instrumental in pushing the weakened European states to withdraw from their colonial holdings. This is evident, for example, in the US response to conflicts in Malaya and Indonesia in the late 1940s. In both states the colonial powers (Britain and the Netherlands respectively) were attempting to reassert their rule in the face of nationalist and sometimes communist-inspired independence movements. The problem with this from the US perspective was not just that the United States was avowedly anti-colonial, it was that, as the political independence of these states was more or less inevitable, so the more the colonial powers resisted, the more likely it was that radical groups would gain political power at the expense of more US-friendly nationalist groups (Westad 2007: 112–14; Shipway 2008: ch. 6). As National Security Council Report 51 (NSC 51) put it: '19th century imperialism is no antidote to Communism in revolutionary colonial areas. It is rather an ideal culture for the breeding of the communist virus. The satisfaction of militant nationalism is the first essential requirement for resistance to Stalinism' (quoted in Westad 2007: 114). The United States was playing a much larger game within which the smaller concerns of the colonial powers were less important. The Soviet Union, too, used its military and financial aid to assist 'revolutionary' and 'nationalist' groups in their anti-colonial struggles.

This shift in the global order is well illustrated by the Suez crisis in 1956 (Halliday 2005: 112–14). In that year Nasser nationalized the Suez Canal, both as a symbol of national independence and as a source of revenue for the Egyptian state. For Britain and France this was the culmination of a series of events that convinced them that Nasser was a threat – including the purchase of Soviet arms from Czechoslovakia. They entered into a secret deal with Israel (whose relationship with Egypt was also deteriorating) to invade Egypt and reassert control of the canal. Crucially, the British did not inform the United States of the plan and seemed to be relying on the logic of Cold War competition to elicit American support in the operation. This was a mistake. Although the United States was indeed wary of Nasser, especially given the Czech/Soviet arms deal, it did not want to see colonial control reasserted in the region in which it itself was trying to play a larger role. The Soviet Union threatened to retaliate against Britain and France but, more importantly, the United States pressured Britain and France to adopt a ceasefire and then withdraw their troops. Indeed, the United States blocked a standby agreement Britain was trying to negotiate with the IMF and threatened to sell a significant holding of UK government bonds (with the potential for a significant currency devaluation) unless Britain complied. Britain did comply and the changes wrought in the post-war order were brought starkly home to British policymakers.

A second line of explanation has stressed the role that nationalist forces within colonial territories played in pressuring colonial states to grant independence. In many colonies there emerged movements agitating for independence. Some of these were well organized and able to mobilize significant numbers of people – in India for example. In Kenya the Mau Mau rebellion, although localized, led to eight years of emergency rule and an extensive and often violent conflict between the Kikuyu rebels and the British colonial army/police (D. Anderson 2005). In a number of other countries, such as Algeria, Indonesia, Malaya and Indo-China, the colonial powers were confronted with violent resistance to their continued rule. In other countries, anti-colonial movements were less violent, but all of these forms of protest created challenges for the colonial powers. First, they increased the costs to the colonial powers of maintaining control of their colonies. Second and perhaps more importantly, they helped to delegitimize colonial rule, in part, of course, because many of these nationalist movements were appealing to the 'liberal' values of self-determination and freedom that the colonial powers often themselves espoused. Increasingly, colonial powers, even before they gave up their colonies, were forced to justify their continued rule on the basis that it was only a temporary period before the granting of independence to colonial territories.

A third line of explanation has stressed the role of domestic pressures within the colonial states themselves. Although this is obviously related to the rising costs of maintaining colonial rule in the face of nationalist rule, it also reflects other factors. There had always been opposition to colonial rule within the colonial states on economic, political and moral grounds. In the face of the rising human and financial costs, however, there was a more widespread questioning of the necessity for maintaining colonial rule. In Britain opposition to continued control of Kenya hardened after 11 Mau Mau prisoners were beaten to death in a prison. There were financial reasons too. Maintaining colonial rule was becoming more expensive, and many colonial governments were facing an increased demand for government spending at home as they tried to sustain the welfare state and full employment. Finally, albeit slowly, the European colonial powers were themselves adjusting to the new international circumstances by focusing more on economic and political relations within Europe. As the empire receded, so the project of European integration became more and more important.

It seems unnecessary to come to definitive conclusion about these debates, in large part because the trajectory of decolonization was rather different in different places and within different empires (Shipway 2008). What does seem clear is that these three kinds of pressures – international, nationalist and domestic – reinforced a normative shift that was already under way from seeing colonial rule as a legitimate form of political authority to seeing it as illegitimate. There are at least two related shifts here. The first is what James Mayall has called 'the nationalization of the concept of self-determination', which he argued undermined the concept of empire as a legitimate political form (Mayall 1989). In the aftermath of the First World War the idea of national self-determination became more widely accepted as a way of thinking about the specific claims to independent statehood made by peoples in Central and Eastern Europe (R. Jackson 1993: 75). In other words, it became legitimate to argue that statehood should be granted to a 'people' because it formed a nation. Nations, as some kind of collective identity, had then a privileged claim. Nationalist movements in colonized states were quick to embrace this kind of language, however fictitious the claim that the people inside colonial borders constituted a 'people' or a 'nation'.

The second shift relates to the ending of 'civilization' as a standard for assessing claims to independence. It had always been one of the justifications for colonialism, particularly in Africa, that the people of colonized states were not ready to govern themselves, and that it was for the colonial powers to bring these people to a 'standard of civilization' when they could become independent entities (R. Jackson 1993: 71; Gong 1984). This was made particularly explicit in Article 22 of the League we noted earlier. This provided some (rather vague) yardstick by which to assess claims for independence, but after the Second World War it was rapidly abandoned (R. Jackson 1993: 74). This shift is clear from the language of the UN Declaration on the Granting of Independence to Colonial Countries and Peoples: 'all peoples have a right to "self-determination"', and no 'inadequacy of political, economic, social or educational preparedness should . . . serve as a pretext for delaying independence' (UN 1960). Taken together these two shifts – the nationalization of the concept of self-determination and the ending of the standard of civilization – meant that colonial holdings were increasingly seen as illegitimate and this helped pave the way for the rapid decolonization that took place after the Second World War.

Sovereignty and non-intervention

Associated with the acceptance of the claim to self-determination of colonized peoples was a switch from a 'positive' to a 'negative' sovereignty regime. In the positive sovereignty regime, sovereignty was not just a norm, but was something that states could actually themselves assert and defend in the face of external threats. With the granting of independence to a large number of former colonies this changed because many of these states were not capable of asserting and defending their sovereignty; they were too weak to do so. Newly independent states were granted many of the trappings of sovereignty such as diplomatic recognition, a seat at the UN and, very significantly, the right of non-intervention. According to Jackson this played a 'pivotal role' in sustaining the political independence of many developing countries:

> despite the enormous inequalities of power . . . and the fact that some states could if they desired forcibly intervene at will in the affairs of other states, it usually has not happened . . . there is evidently a great reluctance on the

part of major military powers to infringe upon the jurisdiction of even the least substantial sovereign state . . . Forcible intervention . . . is construed as bullying and widely condemned.

(R. Jackson 1993: 192)

In David Chandler's words, the result was 'nominal great-power acceptance – however hypocritically – of a law-bound international system' and 'the principle of non-intervention was . . . a constituting principle of the new international community of states (Chandler 2000: 56). This was enshrined in the Charter of the United Nations, which stressed the principles of sovereign equality and non-intervention.

'Development' as norm

The final normative change associated with the post-war order was the rise of 'development' itself as a norm. As the 1969 UN Declaration on Social Progress and Development put it, 'social progress and development are the common concerns of the international community' (UN 1969). This was intimately linked to the idea of self-determination of colonized 'peoples' because one of the purposes of sovereignty was the freedom to undertake a project of national development for and on behalf of these newly independent peoples (Williams 2008a: 36). In other words self-determination and 'development' became intertwined. The idea that one of the purposes of being a sovereign state was to pursue 'development' was enthusiastically embraced (at least in rhetorical terms) by the leaders of newly independent states. As Kwame Nkrumah put it:

> The dependent territories are backward in education, in agriculture and in industry. The economic independence that should follow and maintain political independence demands every effort from the people, a total mobilization of brain and manpower resources. What other countries have taken three hundred years or more to achieve, one dependent territory must try to accomplish in a generation if it is to survive.

> (quoted in Westad 2007: 91)

This was a specific expression of a broader shift in the understanding of the relationship between the government and its society that has affected developed states too. The massive expansion of government activities during the twentieth century, and especially after the Second World War, can be traced to the emergence of the idea that it is one of the government's primary responsibilities to help provide its population with material well-being. As Thomas and Lauderdale have argued, 'the state is chartered with the responsibility for "national welfare" . . . which means a national economic policy that stimulates gross national product and a national welfare program' (Thomas and Lauderdale 1988: 388). The 1986 UN Declaration on the Right to Development said that 'states have the right and the duty to formulate appropriate national development policies that aim at the constant improvement of the well-being of the entire population and of all individuals' (UN 1986).

The other side of this regard for 'development' is that the provision of development assistance to developing states, to assist in their national development projects, also became an international norm (R. Jackson 1993: 112–14). We will look in more detail at the provision of development aid in Chapter 3, but the fact that all developed states give development aid is a sign of how this has become a new norm in international politics. Alongside this, there has been a massive profusion of various kinds of organizations dedicated to 'development', not just bilateral and multilateral development agencies, but very large numbers of private and non-governmental agencies too (Chabbott 1999). The period after the Second World War is characterized by a shared understanding between developing countries and the international community that 'development' was desirable and to be encouraged as far as possible.

Conclusion

The project of international development, development agencies, and indeed most developing countries, were born into a world that was structured in important ways. It was structured by US hegemony and by Cold War competition. It was structured by a series of institutional arrangements and an intellectual consensus about the management of international economic affairs. And it was structured by a series of ideas about self-determination, sovereignty and development itself. As we will see in the next three chapters, these significantly shaped the project of international development. They conditioned the way development agencies operated, they conditioned the way development agencies thought about development, and they conditioned the way development agencies related to developing countries.

These structures sometimes reinforced one another and sometimes did not. That is, they generated certain kinds of outcomes, but they also produced certain tensions and contradictions. The political pluralism sustained by Cold War competition, the provision of aid resources to developing countries, embedded liberalism, the generally benign international economic environment (at least in relative terms) and the norms of self-determination and non-intervention all helped sustain a sovereign international order. However, there were also tensions. Despite the granting of political independence and the norms of self-determination and sovereignty, the major powers did intervene in the affairs of some developing countries, sometimes very brutally. In addition, there was a central tension which became very important by the early 1980s. 'Development' had become a norm in international politics; governments were expected to pursue 'development' for and on behalf of their populace. And the leaders of developing countries embraced this wholeheartedly – at least in principle. In the pursuit of 'development' they would be 'assisted' by development agencies within the general structural limits created by Cold War competition and the norms of sovereignty and self-determination. This 'worked' at least for a while. However, the tension here is obvious – or at least the potential for this series of implicit and explicit bargains to unravel is clear (R. Jackson 1993: 194). What if the international order shifted to reduce the restraints facing development agencies? What if LDC leaders were deemed not to be fulfilling the promise of 'development'? Or, more radically still, what if LDC governments were seen as the cause of rather than the solution to the problem of underdevelopment? These questions were posed more sharply as international order started to change during the 1980s.

2 Development theory in the sovereign order

Introduction

In this chapter we review the dominant ways in which the problem of development was conceived during this sovereign order – roughly from the end of the Second World War to the mid-1970s. The focus is on those 'theories' of development that had most influence on the project of international development. There were other accounts of development, of course, often of a Marxist or quasi-Marxist kind such as dependency theory, that had a very significant impact on the academic study of development, but which were much less important in shaping the policies and practices of development agencies. The two bodies of thought on development we will look at here are 'development economics' and 'modernization theory'. 'Development economics' emerged after the war as an economics specifically about the problems and possibilities of development. 'Modernization theory' was a more specifically American body of thought about development and it incorporated political and social as well as economic elements. The chapter reviews the assumptions and arguments of these two bodies of thought, tries to makes explicit the links and between them, and shows how they were related to the sovereign international order. The last part of the chapter begins to examine the ways these understanding of development were being challenged by the end of the 1970s.

'Development economics'

'Development economics' emerged after the Second World War and was associated with thinkers such as Hans Singer, W. Arthur Lewis, Gunnar Myrdal, Paul Rosenstein-Rodan and Albert Hirschman, among others. It was an economics about the special problems facing developing countries and, despite there being disputes and disagreements between development economists, it is possible to draw out from this body of thought certain shared assumptions and characteristic arguments.

The 'shadow of Keynes'

Development economics was heavily influenced by the work of John Maynard Keynes (Hirschman 1981; Toye 1987). First, as Hirschman stressed, Keynes broke the mono-economics claim. The Keynesian 'revolution' in economic theory had 'established the view that there were *two* kinds of economics: one the orthodox or classical tradition . . . And a very different set of analytical propositions and of policy prescriptions . . . that took over when there was substantial unemployment of human and material resources' (Hirschman 1981: 375–6, emphasis in original). Keynes's analysis suggested that the dominant economics up to then, what he called the 'classical theory', did not and should not apply to such situations as the Great Depression. Once the idea had been established that there was not just one single body of economic theory to analyse and prescribe for all economic situations, the view that there might be a special kind of economics for developing countries – based on their particular characteristics and problems – immediately had more credibility (Lewis 1984). This argument was developed famously by Dudley Seers, who argued that it was the economic conditions of the industrial countries that were a 'special case' and that economics as a discipline ought to take the conditions facing developing countries as their more usual frame of reference (Seers 1963).

The second important influence of Keynes derived from his argument that economies might have multiple equilibria: situations in which supply and demand in the economy were in balance. Keynes's argument challenged the classical view that an economy had a natural tendency to balance at a full employment equilibrium. He said right at the beginning of *The General Theory* that 'the postulates of the classical theory are applicable to a special case only and not to the general case, the situation which it assumes being a limiting point of the *possible positions of equilibrium*' (Keynes 1936: 3, emphasis added). Keynes denied that the economy had any natural tendency to a full employment equilibrium and instead argued that the economy could be in equilibrium at any number of points below the full employment level: where supply and demands in the economy were 'balanced' but also where there were high levels of unemployment. It was just such a low-level equilibrium that Keynes argued characterized the Great Depression. It was precisely because this was an equilibrium position (a balance) that there were no 'internal' pressures for the economy to grow again. For Keynes one of the key reasons for this was the role played by expectations (Keynes 1936: 46–51). As long as producers had no reason to think that the economy would start to grow they would have little reason to invest in more capital or employ more workers. As they did so demand would remain suppressed, reinforcing the negative expectations of producers. In this situation there was a need for some 'external' stimulus in the form of government measures to stimulate the economy (Keynes 1936: 378–9). Increasing demand in the economy through government spending programmes, for example, would in turn stimulate increased supply and the economy could move towards full employment.

This argument was taken by development economists to suggest that developing countries too could be 'stuck' in a low-level equilibrium. That is, there could be a set of self-reinforcing conditions that would keep developing countries poor unless some mechanisms could be found to 'break out' of this low-level equilibrium (Bardhan 1993: 134). This idea was developed by Gunnar Myrdal, who coined the phrase 'cumulative causation' to describe these kinds of self-rein-forcing conditions (Myrdal 1957). One implication of this was that 'development' could be achieved by generating cumulative causation in the other direction; that is, generating a self-reinforcing 'upward' spiral which would produce sustained economic development. The final general implication of Keynes's arguments for the existence of multiple equilibria was that the forces of demand and supply – the 'market mechanism' – could not be relied upon in all conditions to produce desirable outcomes; indeed according to Keynes it was forces of supply and demand that could keep an economy in a low-level equilibrium. This suggested to many development economists that a faith in the market to deliver socially desirable outcomes at all times was misplaced, and instead they adopted a more flexible attitude towards when and where to rely on the market, and when to rely on the government, to distribute economic resources.

A third significant influence of Keynes on development economics related to the role of the state. As noted above, for Keynes the government had an important role to play in pushing an economy out of a low-level equilibrium (Peacock 1993). This it would do by stimulating demand through fiscal and monetary policy: reducing taxes, increasing government spending and reducing interest rates (Keynes 1936: 278). Keynes thought this would involve a 'moderate' level of planning by the state (Keynes 1936: 379). This rather modest argument was developed in a number of ways by development economists, all of whom gave to the government a significant role, particularly in the allocation of investment funds. Beyond the role given to the state by Keynes, development economists were as Hans Singer argued:

> strongly influenced by the experience of successful planning of the economy in the UK during the war, also by the war success of the centrally planned Soviet Union . . . [a]s well as the experiences of Roosevelt's New Deal and the creation of a social welfare state in the UK.
>
> (Singer 1996: 2)

That is, development economists saw what states and planning could achieve and assumed that such precedents could be at least partly replicated in developing countries.

Main assumptions

There are five main assumptions that characterize development economics as it emerged in the 1950s and 1960s. First, it was assumed that 'development' was possible within the existing structure and institutions of the global economy, but it was far from inevitable. This assumption was necessary for there to have emerged a 'development economics' at all, but it distinguished development economics from more radical theories of development such as dependency theory that cast doubt on the possibilities for development within the existing structures of the global economy. That development was not inevitable followed from the

Keynesian arguments about the possibility of low-level equilibrium. Many development economists did argue for certain reforms in international economic relations, particularly the end to protectionism that discriminated against developing country exports, but in general they did not see these relations as a substantial barrier to development success (Hirschman 1958: ch. 10). The one partial exception to this was the so-called 'Prebisch–Singer' hypothesis. Raul Prebisch and Hans Singer both argued that there was a tendency for the terms of trade between primary products and manufactured goods to decline (Prebisch 1950; Singer 1950). In other words primary product exporters would have to sell more and more of their goods to buy the same amount of manufactured goods. In this way, trade was stacked against most developing countries that relied on the production and export of primary commodities. This argument was important, but for both of them the answer was not to abandon international trade; it was to reduce reliance on the production and export of primary products.

Second, development economists usually assumed that development was mutually beneficial. This has been stressed by Hirschman, who argued that the view that 'development' would be beneficial for both rich and poor countries was 'needed if western economists were to take a strong interest in the matter' (Hirschman 1981: 375). Paul Rosenstein-Rodan argued that 'it is generally agreed that industrialization of "internationally depressed areas" . . . is in the general interest not only of those countries, but of the world as a whole' (Rosenstein-Rodan 1943: 201).

A third assumption was that the process of development involved industrialization. The various arguments for the significance of industrialization are reviewed below, but for all development economists the modern industrial economy provided the basic template for development: as Hollis Chenery put it, 'successful development in virtually all countries has been characterised by an increase in the share of manufacturing in total output' (Chenery 1979: 70). In this way development economists all operated with the view that what development was substantially about was the creation of 'modern' economic institutions and practices.

Fourth, development economists all operated with the assumption that developing countries needed (or at least could use) external assistance in the form of expertise (technical assistance), technology and capital for investment. Prebisch talked about the 'need for an enlightened transfer of financial and technological resources' (Prebisch 1985: 179). Hirschman argued that development economists operated with the view that the 'core industrial countries could make an important, even an essential, contribution to the effort of the periphery through expanded trade, financial transfers and technical assistance' (Hirschman 1981: 379). Given the view that development was about the establishment of modern institutions and practices, and given that the 'modern' west was then the model, it followed that economists and others from the modern industrialized countries might be in a privileged position to assist developing countries.

Finally, development economists argued that coordination by the state was necessary for development to be successful. Given the existence of low-level equilibrium and the necessity of some kind of 'external' stimulus to generate 'development' it is almost a necessity that the state plays a significant role in the development process as within a sovereign state it is the only agent capable of administering the appropriate stimulus. There were disagreements between development economists over the extent of planning the developing-country governments should undertake, but all development economists accepted that it was necessary for the state to play a larger role than would be envisaged by classical economic theory.

Arguments for industrialization

It is possible to get a better sense of development economics if we examine a number of specific arguments. The first are arguments for the importance of industrialization. Development economists made a number of specific arguments about the desirability of industrialization and a number of different claims about how this was to be achieved. The most famous argument came from W. Arthur Lewis (1954). He argued that within subsistence (or 'traditional') agriculture there was a high level of underemployment of resources and low productivity, and thus very little surplus was produced. Given this, there were potentially large supplies of labour in the agricultural sector that could move to the industrial (capitalist) sector without any decrease in agricultural production (there were 'unlimited supplies of labor' for the capitalist sector). This in turn meant that wages in the industrial sector would remain low (depressed by the unlimited supply of labour) and thus profits would accrue quickly within the capitalist sector, providing a surplus that could be taxed and invested. In this dualist model the industrial sector would be the dynamic element, sucking labour out of the stagnant subsistence agricultural sector. To complete the picture Lewis argued that as the process of development proceeded there would also be a need to modernize agricultural production through the application of technology that would raise productivity.

A second set of related arguments for industrialization were put forward by Prebisch. He argued that the basic problem of development 'involved raising the level of productivity of the entire labor force' (Prebisch 1985: 177). The possibilities of doing this through raising agricultural production were limited by the low demand elasticity for agricultural exports: people did not consume much more food when it got cheaper. Therefore 'industrialization had a very important role to play in the employment of these large masses of manpower of very low productivity' (Prebisch 1985: 178). Industrialization would also help in the 'overall penetration of technology', which was important for raising productivity. Finally for Prebisch, industrialization would help reduce the vulnerability of developing countries to fluctuations in the demand for and price of primary commodity exports, as well as overcoming the long-run deterioration in the terms of trade between agricultural and industrialized countries (Prebisch 1985: 178).

There were disagreements between development economists over how best to promote industrialization. Lewis for example favoured a programme of what he called 'balanced growth' focused on both industrialization and increasing agricultural productivity (Lewis 2003). Hirschman favoured what he called 'unbalanced growth' whereby the promotion of particular industries in turn stimulated the development of other sectors of the economy (they emerge to provide inputs and services or what were called 'forward' and 'backward' linkages) (Hirschman 1958: ch. 4). Despite these differences there were at least two things that the arguments about industrialization shared. The first was a belief in 'cumulative causation': that the creation of a dynamic industrial sector would help generate a 'virtuous circle' that would lead through linkages and the spread of technology to sustained development. The second was that whatever strategy was pursued the state would have a significant role to play in directing investment. Rosenstein-Rodan talked of a 'scheme of planned industrialization' (Rosenstein-Rodan 1943: 204). Prebisch argued that industrialization would require 'rationality and foresight in government policy' (Prebisch 1985: 180).

Arguments for trade restrictions

A second set of characteristic arguments revolved around the necessity for certain restrictions on trade. These were developed most fully in arguments for what became known as 'import substituting industrialization' (ISI). In line with the abandonment of 'mono-economics' many development economists argued that the classical theory of free trade needed to be amended. The classical argument suggested that free trade was mutually beneficial. If all countries specialized in the production and export of what they were best able to produce this would lead to the most efficient allocation of economic resources and would benefit all countries (a country would be able to import from another country what it itself would have to expend more resources producing). The problem this classical argument for free trade posed for a strategy of industrialization was obvious. Developing countries did not have a comparative advantage in industrial manufacturing, so industrialization was unlikely to take place if the classical argument for free trade were followed. Some forms of restrictions on trade were then necessary if industrialization was to be successful. Some of the arguments were simply ones related to the 'infant industry' argument that had long been recognized as a possible exception to the free-trade argument (Hirschman 1958: ch. 7). The more highly developed arguments linked trade restrictions to a theory of industrialization through import substitution. The underlying premise of ISI was that developing countries imported significant amounts of manufactured goods from industrialized countries. This showed there was a domestic market for manufactured goods. If this was right, the domestic market could be satisfied by the *domestic* production of these manufactured goods. The development of domestic manufacturing, however, required restrictions on the import of manufactured goods in order to develop. As Prebisch put it, 'import substitution stimulated by a moderate and selective protection policy was an economically sound way to achieve certain desirable effects' (Prebisch 1985: 179). In the longer term, the domestic industries developed behind protectionist barriers could be exposed to international competition. The final point to note about ISI is again the important coordinating role for the state. The government would have to allocate investment to selective industries, or at the very least establish the system of import restrictions that would stimulate import-substituting manufacturing.

Arguments for aid

A final set of arguments revolved around the role of foreign capital and development aid. We have already noted the assumption of most development economists that development required various forms of external assistance. An initial set of arguments for the role of foreign assistance came from the adoption and modification of Keynesian-inspired growth models. The most influential of these was the Harrod–Domar model (Harrod 1948; Domar 1957). This model directly linked changes in investment to changes in national income through a number of simple equations. Although highly formalized, the model could be used to make recommendations about the amount of investment needed to achieve a certain growth rate (given a static capital–output ratio). The gap between the amount of domestic savings available for investment and the amount necessary to achieve a certain growth rate came to be known as the 'savings gap'. If such a gap existed then additional domestic savings would have to be mobilized or investment capital would have to come from external sources. Given that developing countries were characterized by low productivity rates and thus the generation of only small surpluses, so domestic savings were low and thus there was a substantial 'savings gap'; thus capital would have to come from abroad (Chenery 1979: 382–455). The necessity for foreign investment or aid then was built in to the basic way the problem of development was understood. In addition to this, there were the more specific arguments related to strategies of industrialization whereby investment capital was needed to develop certain sectors of the economy or certain kinds of manufactured goods. As Prebisch put it, 'international financial resources were to complement and enhance a country's capacity to save, while changes in the structure of trade were necessary to use these savings for capital goods imports' (Prebisch 1985: 180).

There were always thinkers who disagreed with development economics. There were a host of more radical theories that stressed the inevitable constraints developing countries faced from the structures of the international economy and the pattern of relationships between 'core' and 'periphery' (Kay 1989). There were also those who, despite the massive influence of Keynesian economics, remained wedded to some of the arguments of classical economics and thus rejected the idea that developing countries required their own form of economics (Schultz 1964; Bauer 1976). Nonetheless, development economics was very influential and, as we shall see in the next two chapters, the arguments that development economists advanced found their way into the policies of development agencies and developing-country governments. By the late 1970s and early 1980s, however, the arguments of development economists came under sustained attack. In retrospect it is easy to see some of the weaknesses of development economics: its rather mechanical view of the development process and its naïve view of the ability and willingness of the state to engage in 'rational' planning. As Bardhan has argued, 'early development economics often displayed an unquestioning faith in the ability of the state to correct market failures and imperfections and to effectively direct the economic process towards development goals' (Bardhan 1988: 63). But on the other hand, as Hirschman has argued, it is important to recognize the contribution that development economics made to the establishment of the project of international development: 'one historic function of the rise of development economics was to inspire confidence in the manageability of the development enterprise and thereby to help place it on the agenda of policymakers the world over' (Hirschman 1981: 381).

Modernization theory

'Modernization theory' or 'political development theory' had a different set of analytical concerns and a different kind of intellectual genesis from development economics. It was focused on the political, social and psychological aspects of development, as well as the economic. Modernization theory was influenced much more by classical sociology than by economics; in particular a concern with the question of 'modernity'. One of the foremost modernization theorists, Gabriel Almond, argued that 'the political scientist who wishes to study political modernization in the non-western areas will have to master the model of the modern' (quoted in O'Brien 1979: 51). For modernization theorists the transformation to 'modernity' was accompanied not just by economic changes such as industrialization, but by a host of other related shifts in the character and organization of politics, the spread of 'rationalization', the growth in technology, and the diffusion of certain norms, habits and attitudes.

Modernization theory was also a distinctly American theory. Institutionally it was associated with the work of two groups of scholars. It originated in the work of the Harvard Department of Social Relations. From the mid-1950s the centre of gravity for modernization theory shifted to the Social Science Research Council's Committee on Comparative Politics (Higgott 1983: 15–21; Gilman 2003). It was under the auspices of this committee that the most famous modernization theory was produced by Almond, Lucian Pye, Edward Shils, David Apter, Sydney Verba and Samuel Huntington. Second, modernization theory was American in the sense that a picture of a particularly American 'modernity' or 'political development' provided the basic backdrop for theorizing about modernization, especially in terms of the way 'modern democracy' was envisaged. As Rustow has argued, many of the assumptions of modernization theorists reflected the 'assumptions of the Western, and more particularly of the Anglo-American, political tradition since the seventeenth century' (Rustow 1968: 43). For example, Almond's account of what he called 'rule making' certainly reflected the distinctly American legislative and judicial system. In addition, much of modernization theory operated with the view that representative democracy was a central pillar of 'modernity' and that that this form of politics had reached its highest stage of development in the United States (O'Brien 1979: 51–3).

Third, modernization theory evidenced a particularly American set of intellectual (academic) concerns. The first was a shift within US political science away from the study of institutions and towards a 'behavioural' approach to the study of politics (Rustow 1968: 37). As Robert Dahl suggested, the behavioural approached originated in 'dissatisfaction with the achievements of conventional political science, particularly through historical, philosophical and the descriptive-institutional approaches' and 'sympathy towards "scientific" modes of investigation and analysis' (R. Dahl 1961: 766). This meant, according to Dahl, 'an attempt to explain the empirical aspects of political life by means of methods, theories, and criteria of proof that are acceptable according to canons, conventions and assumptions of modern empirical science' (R. Dahl 1961: 767). This more 'scientific' mode coincided with a related development within American social science: the influence of 'grand sociological theory', embodied particularly in the work of Talcott Parsons, a key inspiration for many modernization theorists (and one of the leading figures in the Harvard Department of Social Relations) (Gilman 2003: 74). Parsons was concerned to develop a general theory of society (or the 'social system') that would not only describe the particular features of 'modern' societies, but generate a series of variables that could be used to assess and analyse all societies. Implicit and sometimes explicit in this were two assumptions: an evolutionary one that all societies would eventually become 'modern' (because of the superiority of the modern system in certain of its functions) and a normative one that the modern society was to be preferred over 'primitive' ones (Gilman 2003: 88). These two intellectual strands came together in modernization theory with its attempt to analyse in a 'neutral' and formally rigorous way the entire process of 'modernization' and the relative 'modernity' of various non-western societies (O'Brien 1979: 52).

Main assumptions

There were different strands within modernization theory, and its intellectual centre of gravity shifted over time. It is nonetheless possible to draw out certain common assumptions (Higgott 1983: ch. 2). First, as already suggested, 'modernization' meant the transition from a position of 'backwardness' or 'primitive' society, to a 'modern' society. At its most simplistic the 'transition' was presented in an almost mechanical and certainly linear way as a series of 'stages' en route to modernity (Rostow 1959, 1971). Even when not presented in quite such a mechanical fashion, it was still held that modernization was the 'process of change towards those types of social, economic and political systems that have developed in Western Europe and North America' (Eisenstadt 1966: 1). This is the key central assumption of all modernization theory. A second assumption is that this transition was desirable and, what is more, desired by those in 'backward' or 'primitive' societies (O'Brien 1979: 54). Political leaders in the non-western world were held to 'acknowledge the legitimacy' of democratic politics and a liberal civic culture (Almond and Verba 1965: 4).

A key question these assumptions raised was what exactly constituted the 'modern' to which primitive polities were to move. As we noted above, 'modern' was understood in a broad sense as encompassing political, economic, social and psychological elements. Beyond this, however, modernization theories never came to any collective agreement as to how exactly these spheres were to be understood or about the priorities among them. For Almond the stress was on the political, and he regarded 'modern' political systems as those that exhibited a high degree of functional specialization, a secular political culture, a scepticism towards overly ideological politics (and a concomitant stress on the importance of bargaining and compromise) and a commitment to pluralism (Almond and Powell 1965; Almond and Verba 1965). The basic model Almond was working with was, of course, a particular account of US politics. Pye stressed the commitment to equality, the growth of the capacity of the political system, and the growth of specialization and differentiation within politics (Pye 1965). Apter took a broader focus and argued that 'modernization' could be defined as the growth of complexity in human affairs, as the growth of an attitude of enquiry and a questioning about the sources of political authority, and a growth of organizational complexity and functional differentiation (Apter 1965). For Dankwart Rustow, 'political modernization' involved the growth of centralized authority, the formation of a national identity, the growth of political equality and participation and the 'widening control over nature through closer cooperation among men' (Rustow 1968: 40).

The influence of Parsonian sociology can be clearly seen in the stress on complexity, and on functional specialization and differentiation. Of course, these kinds of definitions were also to serve as the starting point for empirical investigations into the extent to which various polities had achieved political modernization. However, these definitions also served to define their opposite: 'backward', 'primitive', 'traditional' or 'pre-modern'. Indeed, the understanding of this condition was simply an absence of 'modernity'. So, for Apter, for example, 'traditional' societies are simple (rather than complex), sacred (rather than secular), static (rather than changing), and where behaviour is validated by 'reference to immemorial prescriptive norms' (rather than the result of rational reflection and free choice) (Apter 1965: 83).

One other significant strand of thinking about 'modernization' involved a stress on the personal and psychological aspects of 'modernity'. This is exemplified by the work of Alex Inkeles (1969, 1975). The impetus behind his work was to investigate the impact of modernization on 'the individual' and in so doing to investigate the attitudinal changes that accompany modernization (and the sources of these changes). In the tradition of empirical 'science' Inkeles and his colleagues interviewed 6,000 young men in six developing countries to measure a set of attitudes, values and behaviours 'particularly relevant to understanding the individual's participation in the roles typical for a modern industrial society' (Inkeles 1969: 209). Inkeles argued that the evidence 'shows unmistakably that there is a set of personal qualities . . . which identify a type of man who may validly be described as fitting a reasonable theoretical conception of the modern man' (Inkeles 1969: 210). These qualities included 'openness to new experience'; the assertion of independence from traditional authority figures; belief in the efficacy of science and medicine and an 'abandonment of passivity and fatalism'; ambition for oneself and one's children; a belief in the importance of timekeeping and planning in one's personal affairs; an interest and participation in community affairs and local politics; and a desire to keep up with national and international affairs (Inkeles 1969: 201). Again, of course, the 'traditional' man was then defined as one without these qualities.

Policy implications?

Despite the different emphasis of Inkeles, it is clear that both strands of modernization theory cohere around a particular version of what counts as 'modern'. It is essentially an idealized account of a certain kind of American, liberal, secular and rational modernity with a pluralist and democratic politics. The analytical implications are almost breathtaking, as of course are the practical implications. How is such a thing as the 'modern' to be created in 'traditional societies'? Despite the huge amount of intellectual energy that went into it, modernization theory in fact is rather unclear on how these changes might be brought about. Almond argued that, 'in the new and modernizing nations of Asia, Africa and Latin America, the process of enlightenment and democratization will have their inevitable way'; but exactly why this was the case was a lot less clear (Almond 1970: 232).

The first problem of the specifically political development theory was the dependent character of politics itself. In much of this thinking the character and organization of politics was dependent on other social, economic and personal changes (Rustow 1968: 39). This relegated the problem of political development to these other aspects of modernization, but it also seemed to deny the autonomy of politics itself in generating modernization and thus called into question the efficacy of purely institutional approaches to political development (holding elections, instituting democracy). A second problem is precisely the one of explaining change. The analytical drive to develop a 'universal' model that could be used to assess the 'modern-ness' of all societies risked being unable to explain the change associated with becoming modern. It is one thing to say that modern societies are characterized by increasing complexity and functional differentiation, but that does not explain how these emerge or are generated. Indeed, the behavioural revolution and the desire for 'scientific' empirical study militated against the use of historical evidence and, as it were, traditional social theory to actually explain and trace the emergence of the 'modern'.

These problems fatally damaged modernization theory as an actual account of the transition from 'backward' to 'modern'. Rather than any coherent account of how this transition is to occur, modernization theorists identified a gaggle of possible 'drivers' of modernization. These included such things as spread of technology, 'cultural diffusion' and increasing contact with already 'modern' states. Inkeles's work suggested that formal schooling and participation in factory work were major causes of 'modern' attitudes (Inkeles 1969: 212–16). However, although this gave some insight into how these modern attitudes might be generated it did not explain how formal schooling and factory work were themselves to be developed. The problems we have noted so far led many modernization theorists to search for agents who might be able to lead the modernizing charge. The two most usually identified were 'political elites' and the military. Political elites, committed to the modernizing project, could drive the process of modernization in the face of their 'traditional societies'. Alongside this the army could serve as a vehicle for the inculcation of modern attitudes and a sense of national identity (Gilman 2003: 184). Despite its influence modernization theory was in fact surprisingly vague about how the grand transformation to modernity was actually to be achieved.

By the late 1960s some of the optimism of modernization theory was starting to wane. The actual political and social conditions in many developing countries, particularly political instability and civil conflict, called into question the idea that these states would move in any simple way to a 'modern' future (O'Brien 1979: 55). This led to a shift away from political development conceived of as the growth of democracy and towards the idea that, during the process of development, 'political order' might be more important as a way of managing the conflicts that would inevitably arise during the transition. This was represented most clearly in Samuel Huntington's classic *Political Order in Changing Societies* (Huntington 1968). This shift is best understood as an amendment to, rather than a rejection of, modernization theory. It suggests that during the process of modernization strong (rather than democratic) political institutions are necessary to contain and control social conflicts in developing states.

Right from its origins modernization theory was subjected to extensive criticism (Willner 1964; Ferkiss 1966). Like development economics, it is easy to see why this might be the case. In its early years it was certainly overly optimistic about the possibilities of political development. It is certainly American-centric both in its analytical ambitions and in terms of the model of the modern it used. It also contributed relatively little to knowledge about what developing countries were actually like (as opposed to unlike) and it had relatively little to say about how such a process of modernization might take place. Despite this, modernization theory did not really go away. It certainly fell into the background of development thinking in the late 1970s and 1980s, but it re-emerged with a new vigour, albeit with new labels (governance, participation, civil society), in the 1990s.

Development theory and the global order

There are a number of important similarities between development economics and modernization theory. First, they both operated with a view of development as the replication of western modernity. For development economics this was evident in the stress placed on industrialization as the key element of economic development, and for modernization theory it was evident in the entire edifice of modernization theory. Second, both theories were in little doubt about the desirability and achievability of 'development' ('modernization') and about whether political elites and the rest of society both wanted and would benefit from development.

Third, both development economics and modernization theory justified and legiti-mized the activities of the increasing number of aid and development agencies: outside 'help' was needed if the transition to economic and political modernity was to be achieved. The final point to note about both 'development economics' and 'modernization' theory is that, although both were simplistic, and perhaps even naïve, they had at least a grasp of development as a process of social trans-formation and at least some account of how this process might happen. This may seem like a small recompense for all their apparent weaknesses, but as we shall see later the idea of development as a social transformation to something like modernity increasingly drops out of the mainstream of development theory.

Both development economics and modernization theory also have significant connections with the global order described in the previous chapter. Four aspects are particularly clear. First, there are obvious connections between development economics and the kinds of institutional arrangements characterized as 'embed-ded liberalism' that were established under US hegemony at the end of the Second World War. There is a shared Keynesian heritage both in terms of the role of public authorities in the management of economic affairs, but also in terms of the modifications to the traditional liberal arguments for free trade. In this sense, development economics reflected the much broader intellectual and institutional consensus around 'embedded liberalism'. As we shall see, when this broader consensus started to unravel during the second half of the 1970s, so development theory too started to change.

Second, development economics was shaped by the normative shifts within global order – particularly the commitment to sovereignty and self-determination. This was evident in both the role for the state and the role of external assistance. Development economics reflected the idea that states were sovereign entities and that the government was the key political authority charged with promoting the process of development. External agencies were to assist in this process (reflect-ing the emergence of development as a norm within international politics) but not to interfere too much in the internal affairs of sovereign states. It was the governments of developing countries who were to lead the process of economic development as a national project.

Third, and related to this, development economics was clearly shaped by the optimism that characterized the 'golden age' of capitalism. It was not that devel-opment economists thought that development would be easy to achieve; it was that the relatively benign international economic environment helped condition the optimism that characterized development economics.

Finally, and perhaps most significantly, development economics and moderni-zation theory were related to US hegemony more generally and to the Cold War more particularly (Gilman 2003: ch. 5). The newly hegemonic position of the United States, and the demands of Cold War competition, meant that for the first time the United States had to find ways to manage third world states. In this situ-ation, the Keynesian revolution in economic theory reinforced the image of the development economist as an expert with privileged access to knowledge useful to the process of policymaking. The rise of this economic 'expertise' was part of a more general trend in the late nineteenth and early twentieth centuries which saw 'experts' taking an increasingly significant role in public policy debates (Larson 1977; Haskell 1978). The rise of the 'expert' advisor was associated with the increasing number and complexity of the tasks facing governments, and with attempts to introduce a 'neutral' and 'scientific' element into the process of government policy formulation and assessment (Haskell 1984; Critchlow 1985). The view that social science could contribute expert insight to the policy formulation process was based on an 'epistemological optimism' which assumed that 'methodological advances . . . allowed for decisive breakthroughs in explaining and predicting social developments and, thus, achieving a cognitive mastery of society' (Wittrock *et al.* 1991: 52).

In the United States, social science and particularly economic 'experts' were increasingly being brought into government, most obviously under Roosevelt, but also under Hoover (Wittrock *et al.* 1991: 39). The New Deal in America was imbued with the idea that 'the transition to a society of abundance was a problem of engineering, not of politics' (Maier 1978: 31). This was to be accomplished through technically sophisticated officials rationally, and in a politically 'neutral' way, promoting the public interest (Burley 1993). This attitude was thoroughly implicated in the Marshall Plan and in the international institutional arrangements put in place after the Second World War (Maier 1978). Pye said that:

> the increasing academic interest in the problems of the new states . . . has been inspired more by events in world politics than by any indigenous advance in political science theory . . . in large measure, the concept of political development was first defined by statesmen and policymakers and not by scholars.
>
> (Pye 1966: 31)

Conclusion: transformation in development theory

By the mid- to late 1970s development theory was increasingly in crisis. Intellectually, institutionally and politically, modernization theory and development economics ran out of steam and seemed increasingly at odds with national and international changes. The end of the golden age was leading to a reassessment of the Keynesian consensus, which in turn led to a reassessment of development economics. The increasing problems facing developing countries – culminating in the Latin American debt crisis – led to a series of critiques of the arguments of development economics about the role of the state and restrictions on trade. Through the end of the 1970s and early 1980s this led to the triumph of neoliberalism, at least within many of the major development agencies. Modernization theory, too, fell out of favour, if only temporarily, as the social, political and international context within which it emerged started to shift (Gilman 2003: ch. 6 and 7). It was not that the problem of managing America's relationships with developing countries was any less pressing; it was that the confidence in the kind of technocratic liberalism that imbued modernization theory started to wane, partly as a result of its implication in the Vietnam War, and partly as a result of the increasing evidence that developing countries were not treading the path from 'traditional' to 'modern' so often suggested by modernization theorists. The Iranian revolution confirmed that modernization theory had got something seriously wrong, and started to lead American policymakers to think that political elites in developing states not only might not want its picture of an American-style modernity, but might even be actively hostile to American ideas and America's role in the world. As we shall see in Chapter 5, the reanimation of America's hegemonic project in the 1980s utilized a different and altogether more aggressive set of ideas to help guide relations with developing states.

3 Development institutions in the sovereign order

Introduction

In this chapter we turn our attention to the agencies involved in the project of international development from the end of the Second World War through to the 1970s. The chapter looks at two groups of agencies. The first is the bilateral aid agencies. The most important of these is the United States, but the chapter also examines aid given by the Soviet Union and China. One might be tempted to think that these were mirror images of each other: the superpowers using their aid in competition with one another to influence developing countries. There were, however, very significant differences between the aid programmes of the two superpowers in terms of the way they were institutionalized within their domestic bureaucracies, the ways they related to developing states and the kinds of projects and programmes they funded, and in terms of their size the US aid programme dwarfed that of the Soviet Union. To put it rather bluntly, the United States was 'doing' development, whereas the USSR was not. Given the significance of 'development' within the hegemonic order constructed by the United States this is unsurprising, but it does provide additional evidence that in many ways the project of international development is an American project. The chapter also looks at a selection of other bilateral donors: Japan, the UK, France and Sweden. There are some similarities between these donors, but also some very significant differences, again in terms of how aid provision was institutionalized domestically, and in terms of which states they give aid to. There are also important changes over time, particularly in the case of Japan, which went from having a small and regionally focused aid programme driven by economic interests to a large and diversified aid programme which provided aid to a significant number of states outside its region.

Second, the chapter looks at the multilateral development agencies, including most significantly the World Bank, but also the regional development banks and the United Nations Development Programme (UNDP). Many of the regional development banks were modelled on the World Bank, and although they were created for a number of reasons (including economic and political interest) they demonstrate the significance of the multilateral form in the project of international development. Of course, all of them reflect the continued relative power of the

United States, which was instrumental in establishing many of them and continued to have a significant impact on their functioning. In these ways, the United States replicated at a regional level the kind of order it created at the global level, with the same fusion of self-interest with institutionalism, multilateralism and liberalism. The UNDP is in some respects an outlier here. It played an important role within the UN system and in some respects was important for developing countries themselves (which often felt it was an advocate for them) but it suffered from a funding crisis precisely because the United States often viewed it as antithetical to its broader interests.

Taken together, these agencies demonstrate the extent to which the project of international development became institutionalized within international politics. However, a comparative examination also reveals that the form of political pluralism produced and sustained within the sovereign international order is reflected in development agencies. The different agencies gave monies to different states for different kinds of reasons, and developing countries themselves obtained aid from one or other and sometimes both superpowers. This, combined with the significance of sovereignty as a norm, and the respect initially accorded to post-colonial rulers, meant that developing countries (or at least some of them) had a significant amount of autonomy in relations with development agencies. This started to erode in the late 1970s and early 1980s as economic crisis, the rise of neoliberalism and the use of conditional lending (structural adjustment lending) combined to make development agencies increasingly intrusive in their dealings with developing states, and as the 1980s went on so the political pluralism that characterized donors during this period started to decline.

Bilateral aid agencies

An initial working definition of aid is gifts and concessional loans of economic resources, such as finance and technology, employed for economic purposes provided to less-developed countries by the governments of the developed world. There are a number of things to note about this definition. The first is the stress on 'gifts and concessional loans', which means that for monies provided to count as aid there has to be something better about the terms than purely commercial terms – this might be lower rates of interest or longer repayment times. Second, the definition excludes military assistance. Third, aid is money provided by governments and multilateral agencies, so it excludes private financial flows to developing countries. Finally, aid encompasses more than just money and can include the provision of goods, technology and expertise.

United States

In 1960 US aid provision was about four times that of France, eight times that of the UK and 20 times that of Japan (OECD). The total amount provided by the United States rose and fell during the 1960s and 1970s, but it still remained the world's largest aid donor until the late 1980s (Figure 3.1), despite the fact that

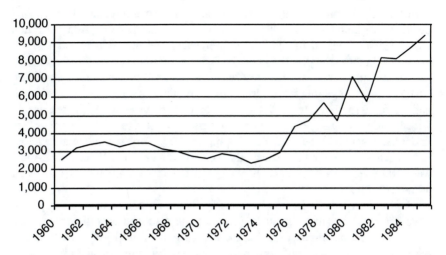

Figure 3.1 US bilateral aid disbursements, 1960–85 (US$ millions at current prices). Source: OECD.

the United States stands out among western aid donors as the one where there is significant domestic political opposition to foreign aid.

We noted in Chapter 1 the dual origins of the US concern with 'development' in both the broad project for US hegemony and the narrower concern with containing communism: the four-point speech and the Truman Doctrine. The Foreign Assistance Act of 1948 (which established the Marshall Plan) created the Economic Cooperation Agency, the first US institution dedicated to aid and development assistance. US foreign aid to non-European countries really got going with the 1950 Act for International Development (McGuire 1952; Amuzegar 1958). The Act said that it was the policy of the United States to 'encourage the flow of technical knowledge and capital to countries which provided conditions under which such technical assistance and capital can effectively and constructively contribute to raising standards of living' (quoted in Amuzegar 1958: 532). This Act created the Technical Cooperation Agency to deliver technical assistance to developing countries. The then Secretary of State, Dean Acheson, said that the 1950 Act was a 'security measure' as the United States' 'military and economic security is vitally dependent on the economic security of other people' (quoted in McGuire 1952: 343). Despite these general sentiments it is clear that both in the United States itself and in the rest of the world this was understood to be in some large part about combating communism (McGuire 1952). This was made clearer by the Mutual Security Acts passed during the 1950s (Amuzegar 1958: 533–4). These acts were intended to unite the military assistance and the foreign aid and technical assistance programmes. The 1951 Act said its purpose was 'to maintain the security and promote the foreign policy of the United States by authorizing military, economic, and technical assistance to friendly countries to strengthen mutual security and individual and collective defences of the free world' (United

States 1951). During the 1950s the US aid programme continued to grow and develop institutionally. In 1954 the International Cooperation Administration (ICA) was established to administer foreign aid and technical assistance programmes. In the same year the Food for Peace programme (sometimes called the 480 programme) was established to channel food aid to developing countries, partly as a way of getting rid of surplus food produced in the United States (Frank and Baird 1975: 142). In 1957 the Development Loan Fund (DLF) was established, which provided loans on more concessional terms to developing countries under the auspices of the ICA. The ICA represents the first real bilateral development agency as we see them today. By the second half of the 1950s the ICA had established field offices in 60 countries and employed over 4,000 staff (Cleveland 1959: 219–21).

By the late 1950s US bilateral aid was firmly established as an on-going part of US foreign policy. However, such assistance was also institutionally fragmented and the subject of on-going domestic criticism (Cleveland 1959). The Kennedy administration did a significant amount to develop the US aid programme. Shortly after taking office, Kennedy announced what he called the 'Decade for Development': 'there exists, in the 1960s, an historic opportunity for a major economic assistance effort by the free industrialized nations to move more than half the people of the less-developed nations in to a self-sustained economic growth' (quoted in Lancaster 2007: 69). The 1961 Foreign Assistance Act reorganized US foreign assistance. It separated military and economic assistance and created a unified agency – USAID – that drew together the ICA, the DLF and the Food for Peace programme. The new agency also started to develop new methods for distributing its aid. Of particular importance was the country programming process, whereby US aid would be conditional on the recipient country's having an economic development plan. This contrasted with the previous method of ad hoc funding of individual projects (Lancaster 2007: 72). The amount of aid given also increased in the first half of the 1960s – particularly to Latin America and increasingly to sub-Saharan Africa both in absolute terms and as a percentage of GNP. Although the containment of communism was an important element of the renewed stress on development assistance, it was also clear that the broader hegemonic objective of economic development was being taken more seriously. Aid was being used not just to buy political support (although it was used for that too) but to encourage 'development'.

In the late 1960s and early 1970s domestic opposition to US aid programmes emerged more forcefully, from both the left and the right of the political spectrum (Frank and Baird 1975: 133). The left was critical of what it saw as the excessive amounts of military assistance being given by the United States while the right argued that the aid programmes were inefficient and did not sufficiently promote US interests abroad. The opposition culminated in 1971 when Congress refused, for the first time, to pass an aid authorization bill (Lancaster 2007: 76). US aid policy was reworked in the wake of this. There was a need to garner political support in Congress, of course, but importantly there were changes taking place within the US development community. As we noted above, the US aid programme had steadily become more institutionalized and professionalized. The staff of USAID, whatever their own political views, tended to be genuinely committed to the project of development as a desirable end in itself for developing countries, regardless of its Cold War rationale. Within this community (which also included at this time influential development think tank the Overseas Development Council) views about development and use of aid were changing (this was reflected in the World Bank and other donors too, as we shall see). Plenty of evidence was emerging that the benefits of growth in developing countries were not 'trickling down' to the poorest sections of those societies. This led to a new concern with 'growth with equity' and to a concern with providing more developmental benefits to those poorest sections of society. Associated with this was a new concern with improving agriculture (the majority of the poor lived in rural areas), health services and education and a downplaying of the role of large capital projects as the key determinants of development.

In 1973 Congress passed new legislation that mandated a shift in the use of US aid towards funding projects for the 'basic human needs' of the poor in developing countries (Lancaster 2007: 73). This change of emphasis signalled two important things. First, whatever the Cold War origins of the US aid programme it had changed to stress more the long-term goal of economic development. Second, it signalled that the aid community within the United States (USAID, think tanks, sympathetic members of Congress) had become a political force in its own right. US foreign aid was still used for political (and Cold War) purposes but it was also being used (and understood to be being used) for genuinely humanitarian and developmental purposes (at least as that was understood by USAID). US aid began to rise significantly in the later 1970s and continued to rise through the first half of the 1980s for reasons that reflected both the political and humanitarian/developmental purposes of aid. The attempt by the Ford administration to encourage a peace settlement between Israel and Egypt led to a significant rise in aid to both countries such that they became the two largest single aid recipients by 1976; by the late 1970s these two states accounted for one-quarter of US bilateral aid. In addition, the United States was providing aid to a number of other states for fairly obvious political/Cold War reasons (Turkey – key NATO ally; the Philippines – US military bases; Nicaragua – to combat left-wing insurgency). However, the United States was also involved in giving aid to a variety of countries – particularly in Africa – where there were no especially clear political interests: Mali, Benin and Burkina Faso, for example (Lancaster 2007: 79). In addition, as a result of famine in Ethiopia and floods in Bangladesh, emergency aid and food aid rose sharply (Lancaster 2007: 178).

Despite the initial scepticism of the Reagan administration towards foreign aid, much the same continued through the 1980s. Aid to Latin America increased for obviously Cold War reasons, but so did aid to Africa. Total US aid to Central and South America rose from $280 million in 1980 to $1,175 million in 1985, while aid to Africa rose from $1,507 million to $2,860 million. By 1989 US bilateral aid was 30 per cent higher than it had been in 1980 (Lancaster 2007: 83). All this was neatly summarized by President Reagan in 1985. Speaking of the 1985

International Security and Development Cooperation Act he said that, 'in helping our allies and friends meet their security, development and humanitarian needs, we directly support US interests and objectives. Our foreign assistance programs, despite any perceptions to the contrary, are manifestly in our own national interest' (White House 1985). The similarities to Dean Acheson's comments 35 years earlier are clear. This continuity of vision confirms the abiding place that 'development' and foreign aid had in post-war US foreign policy; it was a tool for fighting the Cold War, for sustaining and expanding US influence, for spreading American ideas and, at least in part, for genuinely humanitarian action. Despite the domestic opposition, foreign aid had become institutionalized and professionalized and the foreign aid budget had nearly quadrupled in size from 1960 to 1985.

USSR and China

The USSR also had a bilateral aid programme which it too used for political purposes. However, although there is a superficial similarity between the United States and the USSR, their aid programmes were very different. The USSR did not develop a coherent foreign aid programme, it did not maintain country offices dedicated to development, and it did not develop a professionalized aid agency. The Soviet aid programme was also substantially smaller than that of the United States – although accurate comparable figures are hard to establish. The Soviet bilateral aid programme began in the mid-1950s. Part of this was simply a response to the growing US aid programme, but part of it was animated by the idea that Soviet aid could assist newly independent states to make a 'peaceful transition' to socialism (Guan-Fu 1983: 71). It was also driven by the idea that by encouraging reliance on the USSR for capital flows, and by encouraging trade with the USSR, the USSR would benefit economically and be able to exert influence over developing states. In this initial period of Soviet aid, the most important recipients were countries such as India, Egypt, Ghana, Guinea and Mali, whose leadership was deemed to be at least sympathetic to the USSR, as well as Iraq and Indonesia (Guan-Fu 1983: 72, 75). Aid to these countries was used to finance large-scale construction and industrial projects, including, most famously, the Aswan Dam in Egypt (where the USSR stepped in when the United States refused to fund it) and the Bhilai steel mill in India (Goldman 1964). Most of the aid was in the form of machinery and equipment and the USSR often entered into arrangements whereby these would be repaid by the export of commodities to the USSR. During these years too, Soviet economic assistance tended to be very opportunistic – stepping in when western donors did not provide funding – as with the Aswan Dam. One estimate of Soviet bilateral aid during the period suggests that it rose from US$128 million in 1955 to $628 million in 1960 (Guan-Fu 1983: 75). By way of comparison, US bilateral aid in 1960 was $2,580 million. Despite this initial burst of activity there was a significant reduction in Soviet aid in the early 1960s, falling to a low of only $91 million in 1962. This inconsistency in Soviet aid provision was reflected too in aid to particular countries. Bar a few examples, such as India, the USSR did not establish permanent, on-going aid relations with its recipient countries. Indonesia, for example, received a significant amount of aid in 1960 – and then none at all for the next four years (Guan-Fu 1983: 75, 78). The USSR was also discovering that aid did not guarantee compliance and that many newly independent states deeply resented Soviet interference in their domestic politics (Guan-Fu 1983).

Soviet aid started to grow again during the second half of the 1960s. A CIA estimate suggested that Soviet foreign aid to non-communist developing states totalled about US$500 million a year through the second half of the 1960s, but again this was only about one-fifth the total amount given by the United States during the same period (CIA 1970). In the second half of the 1970s the USSR expanded its bilateral aid programme as part of a more concerted attempt to exert influence over developing countries in the context of growing superpower competition in the third world. Soviet aid reached $1,640 million by 1980 – but again this was only about one-quarter that given by the United States in the same year. This expansion – and more general engagement with developing countries – was driven by Cold War competition in the wake of war in the Middle East and the split with China. The Soviet bilateral aid programme then remained very different from that of the United States: it was not 'professionalized' in the way that it was in the United States; there was no permanent development agency like USAID – rather a number of different bureaucratic entities were responsible for foreign aid; and assistance remained on a project-by-project basis heavily concentrated in large-scale infrastructure and industrial projects.

China has assumed a great significance as an aid donor in the last 10 years or so, particularly in sub-Saharan Africa, but as early as the mid-1950s China had a small but significant aid programme, animated by a desire to influence newly independent states, and as a mechanism for competing with the USSR for influence in the developing world (Poole 1966). China began to provide aid to non-communist states in 1956, including Cambodia, Indonesia and Egypt. In the early 1960s a number of sub-Saharan African states received Chinese aid (Guinea, Ghana, Mali, Tanzania, Kenya and Somalia). China also provided aid to Algeria (along with the USSR) (Poole 1966). The amounts were small – China's aid programme was smaller than that of Italy, Japan, France and Belgium, and dwarfed by that of the United States – and mostly comprised concessional credits, the provision of technical assistance in the form of Chinese technicians, support for small manufacturing and infrastructure projects, and support for agricultural development, particularly rice cultivation (Jackson 2007). China's domestic political and economic problems – associated with the 'Great Leap Forward' – led to a decline in aid provision in the middle of the 1960s, but it rose again in the later 1960s, with the most notable project being the Tanzania–Zambia railway: a huge construction project started in 1970, and one of the largest single Chinese foreign aid projects (US$400 million) (Jackson 2007: 3). This was designed to free the Zambian economy from reliance on Rhodesia and apartheid South Africa (Snow 1994). By 1983 China had supplied some kind of aid – sometimes small amounts – to about 40 countries in Africa (Jackson 2007: 9). Foreign aid again dropped in the early 1980s and remained at a relatively low level until more recent years. There are some similarities between Chinese aid and Soviet aid, as China did not establish a single 'development agency', and most support was on an ad hoc project-by-project basis.

Japan

The development of the Japanese aid programme is particularly fascinating. By the middle of the 1980s Japan had become the second largest bilateral aid donor in the world, and had made the transition from lending primarily in its region for largely political and commercial reasons to being a significant member of the club of western donors, shifting its lending to poorer states, particularly in Africa, and stressing 'basic needs' and poverty reduction as explicit aims of its aid programme. In other words Japan's aid programme had become 'socialized': under pressure from the United States, and with a desire to conform to western development norms, Japan changed its bilateral aid programme to be more in line with other western donors.

The Japanese bilateral aid programme has its origins in the reparations it was forced to pay after its defeat in the Second World War (Brooks and Orr 1985: 323–4). During the late 1950s, while these reparations were still being paid, Japan made its first loans, including to Goa, India and South Vietnam. The aid programme that developed in the 1960s had a number of features. First, it was heavily concentrated in providing aid to states in its region. Almost all aid during the 1960s was to states in East and South East Asia (Lancaster 2007: 115). Second, the aid was driven significantly by commercial considerations. Japanese aid went particularly to finance projects in the energy and mining sectors as a way for Japan to gain access to resources (Yasutomo 1989: 492). Third, Japanese aid at this time was heavily tied; loans would be provided on the condition that Japanese firms were employed to build the project. Finally, Japanese aid tended to be offered on relatively harsh terms compared with aid from other bilateral donors. Total Japanese aid grew steadily through the 1960s, from US$77 million in 1960, to $226 million in 1965 and $371 million in 1970 (OECD). Japanese aid was, however, institutionally fragmented. In 1961 an Overseas Economic Cooperation Fund (OECF) was established as a lending institution under the auspices of the Ministry of Finance. In 1962 a separate technical assistance organization, the Overseas Technical Assistance Agency (OTCA), was established under the auspices of the Foreign Ministry. This was later replaced by the Japan International Cooperation Agency (JICA). Apart from these two major organizations, other elements of Japan's aid programme were scattered across other government departments (Brooks and Orr 1985: 324–6).

A number of factors in the mid-1970s led Japan to reconsider the size, scope and practices of its aid programme. The Japanese economy had grown rapidly and as its exports had grown so there was a less urgent need to use foreign aid to expand export markets in the region (Lancaster 2007: 116). The fact that the economy had done so well – combined with economic slowdown in the United States – led the United States to pressure Japan to share more of the burden of managing global affairs. Finally, there were some sharp criticisms of Japanese aid

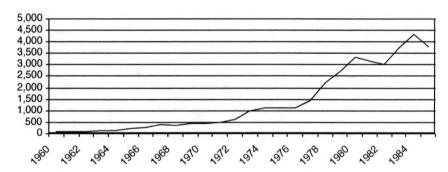

Figure 3.2 Japanese bilateral aid disbursements, 1960–85 (US$ millions at current prices).
Source: OECD.

from both recipient countries (there were riots in Indonesia and Thailand when the Japanese prime minister visited) and other western donors about the excessively commercial, rather than developmental, elements of Japanese aid (Yasutomo 1989: 492–3). In 1977 Japan announced its intention to double its bilateral aid provision (see Figure 3.2).

It also made a number of other changes to its aid programme. It expanded the range of countries it gave aid to (although it still gave the majority of its aid to states in the region) and it announced in 1978 that it would untie its aid loans (although this took some time to implement) (Lancaster 2007: 118–20). In 1981 the Ministry of Foreign Affairs argued that Japanese aid policy had two rationales: economic interdependence and humanitarianism (Yasutomo 1989: 495). In the same year Japan adopted a 'basic needs' approach to its development assistance. This meant giving more of its aid money to poorer states and shifting is finding towards projects in health, water provision and sanitation (Lancaster 2007: 119). To be sure, some of the largest recipients of Japanese aid during the first half of the 1980s remained states in the region – Indonesia, Thailand and Burma for example – but by the late 1980s Japan had also become the single largest aid donor to a number of African states.

France

French aid during this period was in some ways different from that of most other bilateral aid donors. France had a relatively large aid programme, already giving US$783 million in 1960 (more than twice the UK's aid budget) and rising, albeit in fits and starts, to $1,174 million by 1975 (see Figure 3.3).

France's aid programme, however, was almost totally focused on maintaining close relations with its ex-colonies, particularly in Africa. Not only did over 90 per cent of its bilateral aid go to its former colonies, but for many of these states France provided between 80 and 90 per cent of their aid inflows (Lancaster 2007: 147). This allowed France to continue to exercise significant influence over these states, and in so doing pursue what it took to be its interests in these

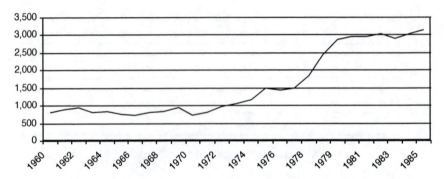

Figure 3.3 French bilateral aid disbursements, 1960–85 (US$ millions at current prices).
Source: OECD.

states. Roughly speaking the provision of aid had three aims (Renou 2002). First, it was an attempt to retain some form of international status in the radically changed post-war world. Second, it provided a way of securing access to strategic resources. Third, it enabled French companies to maintain and exploit privileged monopolistic situations (Chipman 1989).

As Lancaster shows, the organization of French aid was extremely complex and opaque. France did not develop a unified aid/development agency, despite the apparent problems of coordination that emerged within the French aid programme. Underpinning the relationship with its ex-colonies, however, was a system of highly personalized relationships between French political elites and governments in francophone Africa (exploited by both sides for their personal and political gain), military cooperation and French military actions in support of their client regimes, and the Franc Zone, which operated to ensure monetary stability in francophone Africa and enabled France to exercise significant control over franc zone economies (Renou 2002: 9–11). Despite criticisms of both the policies and the organization of French aid through the 1970s and 1980s nothing very much changed. As Lancaster rather politely puts it, that was in large part because portions of the French political class 'had developed . . . less savory stakes in the close relationships and generous aid transfers to African governments' (Lancaster 2007: 154). Essentially then, French aid, until the 1990s, was largely about maintaining French prestige and promoting French commercial interests, often through various kinds of corrupt practices.

Britain

The British bilateral aid programme can be traced back at least to the Colonial Development Act of 1929 and the 1945 Colonial Development and Welfare Act (Little and Clifford 1965: 31–2). Both Acts provided for monies to be spent on 'development' projects in British colonies, and through the 1950s most UK 'aid' was spent in Britain's colonies. By the end of the end of the decade many colonies had become, or were about to become, independent. This necessitated a new kind of aid programme and in 1964 the British government created the Overseas Development Ministry (ODM), with a minister, Barbara Castle, who had a seat in cabinet, and which unified the British aid programme that had been spread between the Foreign Office, the Colonial Office and the Commonwealth Relations Office. Subsequent to this, the British aid programme grew in fits and starts to the mid-1970s (Figure 3.4).

There were several related factors that explain the ups and downs of British aid provision. The first was organizational. The cabinet status of the ODM was short-lived – until 1967 – and then in 1970 it was renamed the Overseas Development Administration (ODA) and became part of the Foreign and Commonwealth Office (FCO). In 1974 it regained its independent status, but in 1979 reverted back to being under the FCO. Second, these organizational changes themselves reflected the relative weight given to overseas aid and development by successive British governments. The periods of Labour government (1964–70 and 1974–9) demonstrated most commitment to foreign aid as demonstrated by the higher political profile given to development and to the larger aid budgets. The periods of Conservative government (1970–4 and 1979 onwards) demonstrate the reverse, and in particular UK bilateral aid fell through the first half of the 1980s under the Thatcher government. Third, Britain's broader macroeconomic fortunes played an important role in constraining aid budgets, particularly in the late 1970s and into the early 1980s, suggesting that, although there was public support for Britain's aid programme, it was also vulnerable to cuts during economic hard times (Killick 2005).

In terms of development policy too there were some significant changes. Until the mid-1970s, British aid provision was informed by the standard view derived from development economics that aid was needed to finance the 'savings gap', and it was provided to fund discrete development projects and technical assistance programmes (Killick 2005: 79–80). In the mid-1970s this began to change. A

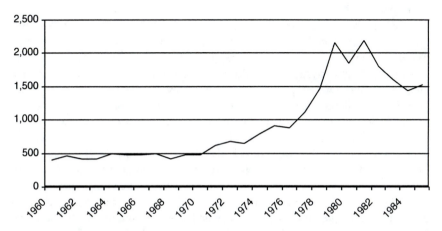

Figure 3.4 British bilateral aid disbursements, 1960–85 (US$ millions at current prices).
    Source: OECD.

White Paper produced in 1975 was entitled *Overseas Development, the Changing Emphasis in British Aid Policies, More help for the Poorest* (Ministry of Overseas Development 1975). This new emphasis on targeting the poorest groups was part of the more general shift in aid policies in the mid-1970s. This was short-lived, however, and was replaced in the early 1980s with explicit support for IMF and World Bank structural adjustment lending. Despite these organizational upheavals there remained a number of continuities in British aid. The first was that the core staff of ODM/ODA remained intact during much of this period and led to the emergence of a professionalized and reasonably highly regarded aid administration that demonstrated a high level of commitment to the cause of 'development' (Young 2001). This was bolstered by the establishment of the Overseas Development Institute, which provided research and advocacy for international development. Second, as the colonial origins of British aid would suggest, much of it remained directed at its former colonies (McKinlay and Little 1978). Even into the mid-1980s over 70 per cent of its aid went to Commonwealth countries (Killick 2005: 65). Third, until the 1990s a large proportion of British aid was 'tied'. This meant that imports funded by British aid were restricted to goods and services originating in the UK.

Sweden

Rather than review all the Scandinavian aid donors we will concentrate on one – Sweden – that exemplifies a different approach to aid and development, which characterizes these donors as well as Canada and the Netherlands (Stokke 1989). It has been the stereotypical view of these states that they are motivated by humanitarian and genuinely developmental concerns, rather than political or strategic interests. This is largely correct in the sense that the bilateral aid programmes of these states are an expression of 'social values' of their domestic society: internationalism, solidarity and assistance for the poor and deprived (Lumsdaine 1993: 135).

Sweden had no aid programme to speak of until 1962. In that year the Swedish government announced a plan to significantly expand Sweden's aid programme. The then prime minister said that Sweden's aid 'was an expression of a feeling of moral duty and international solidarity' (Tage Erlander quoted in Lumsdaine 1993: 173). Sweden's aid programme grew rapidly (Figure 3.5).

Sweden's aid programme was also one of the most relatively generous. In 1965 Sweden gave about 0.2 per cent of GNP in aid; in 1970 0.32 per cent; by 1975 it had risen to 0.8 per cent and by the late 1980s it was nearly 0.9 per cent (Lumsdaine 1993: 133; Noel and Therien 1995). In 1965 Sweden established the Swedish International Development Agency (SIDA) to implement Sweden's bilateral aid programme. In addition to this there are a number of other agencies that played a role in Sweden's aid programme, including a research cooperation agency, an industrial cooperation agency and an export credit board (Karre and Svensson 1989: 257). Sweden's aid programme also had very strong domestic support. Consistently over 70 per cent of respondents to questionnaires said that Sweden's aid levels were about right or should be increased (Karre and Svensson

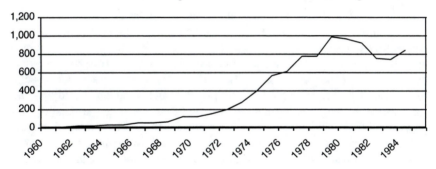

Figure 3.5 Swedish bilateral aid disbursements, 1960–85 (US$ millions at current prices).
Source: OECD.

1989: 259; Lumsdaine 1993: 141). There were no significant moves by any Swedish political party to reduce Sweden's aid programme, and all governments seem to have shared the same basic view that Sweden should have a generous aid programme directed at promoting economic growth and social justice.

There were debates about a number of changes in Sweden's aid practices in the late 1970s and early 1980s, particularly about the increasing 'commercialization' of Sweden's aid programme. Sweden started to give more tied aid in the later 1970s – although this only ever reached about 20 per cent of all aid allocated. This was justified on the grounds that it would help boost employment in Sweden. In 1978 SWEDFUND was established with the explicit aim of encouraging cooperation between Swedish businesses and businesses in its aid recipient states (Karre and Svensson 1989). Sweden also established an 'associate financing' system to help promote Swedish exports. These changes, however, only marginally altered the usual picture of the Swedish aid programme. The final important element to consider is who the main recipients of Swedish aid were. It is here that differences from the other western aid donors become clear. Overwhelmingly Sweden gave its aid to the so-called 'frontline' states in Southern Africa and to socialist states in other regions. Over half of all Sweden's aid went to 'socialist' states (Karre and Svensson 1989: 253). This included aid to Angola, Ethiopia, Mozambique, Cuba, North Vietnam and Nicaragua under the Sandinista government (Lumsdaine 1993: 110). There are some connections here between Sweden's generally centrist/centre-left government and its extensive welfare state and it is clear how different this was from the more Cold War-orientated aid given by the United States.

Theoretical debates

This review of some of the major bilateral aid agencies provides material for reflecting on the theoretical debate about why states give bilateral aid at all and to whom they give it. The literature here is voluminous, but at the broadest level we can see explanations for aid giving clustering around three basic approaches. First, there are varieties of 'state interest' (or 'realist'-inspired accounts) that place the political, strategic and economic interests of the aid-giving states as the key determinants of aid (Kaplan 1967; Wittkopf 1973; Maizels and Nissanke 1984;

Schraeder *et al.* 1998). In this view, aid is simply another foreign policy tool, to be used in the pursuit of national interest, and the developmental needs of aid recipients are not a major consideration in the distribution of aid. The problem with this argument is that it is far too unspecific, as states pursue different kinds of interests and perceive their interests in different ways. As we saw in Chapter 1, the United States has an 'interest' in development and, although US aid was used for a variety of purposes beyond the developmental, we might also expect it to provide aid for development as part of its broader hegemonic project. Similarly, France's aid provision to its former colonies in sub-Saharan Africa served its economic 'interests', but there was also clearly something more going on to do with French culture and international prestige. Again, in a similar fashion, we can see that Japan's aid programme initially reflected in a fairly straightforward way its regional economic concerns, but as it broadened out so different kinds of 'interests' were served to do with its international reputation. At one level all aid can be thought of as reflecting the 'interests' of donor states but, unless some more effort is put into specifying what those interests are and how different states can perceive their interests differently, the argument is uninteresting.

Second, there are accounts that examine the impact of domestic political and social conditions, again in the aid-giving states, as key drivers of aid (a kind of 'liberal'-inspired approach) (Noel and Therien 1995). Here the focus has been on the policymaking process and the impact of different domestic political systems and institutional structures on aid. Here too the developmental needs of recipient countries are not considered a key determinant; rather aid reflects domestic bureaucratic and political concerns and priorities. Again, there is a sense in which this argument is true. Clearly changes in government have had a significant impact on aid programmes (as with Kennedy, for example, and in the UK), as have spending cuts and the relative weight of pro- and anti-aid lobbying groups. Similarly, the ways in which aid provision becomes institutionalized within the domestic bureaucracy has mattered for aid provision – the extent to which there is a single professionalized aid bureaucracy, for example, and the relations between this and other government departments such as the foreign affairs or finance ministry. However, although these factors are important they have to be seen in the context of 'national interests' and the broader global context, and taken by themselves these kinds of arguments do not help explain why there was a general increase in aid provision during this period, especially from the mid-1970s onwards.

Finally, there are a variety of more 'norm-based' ('constructivist'-inspired) accounts (Lumsdaine 1993; Hattori 2003). Here the focus has been on the moral and humanitarian vision that underpins aid giving, and the idea of aid giving itself as a 'norm' of international politics. These are two slightly different accounts. The first stresses that aid provision is sometimes given for genuinely humanitarian reasons – that aid-giving states care about poverty or malnutrition, for example. There seems little doubt that this happens, as aid to Ethiopia during the famines in the mid-1970s and mid-1980s shows. The second stresses the idea that aid giving itself is a norm of international politics. The very fact that all 'developed' states give foreign aid, despite their being very different in many ways, is a sign that aid giving has become a norm and a standard practice within international politics. However, in this argument again, it is not so much that states are motivated by the needs of recipient countries, but that giving to 'needy' states is something they feel they ought to do. This kind of argument helps to explain the widespread practice of aid giving, but like many 'norm-based' arguments it can only operate at a fairly high level of generality and ignores the role of domestic and international political factors in determining aid provision.

The theoretical debate about the motivation of for aid giving is inconclusive in the sense of getting anywhere near a single answer to the question of why states give aid. In that sense Hans Morgenthau was right when he said that of the 'innovations which the modern age has introduced into the practice of foreign policy, none has proven more baffling . . . to understanding . . . than foreign aid' (Morgenthau 1962: 301). There just are a variety of factors that help explain the aid giving of different states at different times. Sometimes there are clear political interest motivations for aid on the part of some states, something that was obviously clear during the Cold War. For other states, though – the Scandinavian donors, for example – the 'interests' that are served by aid giving are less clear cut and the significance of, for example, their domestic welfare system and political culture seems more important. For some donors the relationship with ex-colonies has been particularly important – France and Britain most obviously – but this applies only to the relatively few European colonial powers. Some states give more to their 'region' – Japan, for example – whereas others do not. Finally, the aid-giving agencies are located in different institutional and political structures that condition their aid, as well as having different degrees of domestic support for their aid programmes. Given these differences it seems unlikely that any general answer to the question of why states give aid is to be found.

Two final points about bilateral aid are worth noting. First, despite ups and downs in the provision of aid from individual donors there was a general upward trend in bilateral aid provision during this period (Figure 3.6) (although a decline in aid as a percentage of gross national income). Second, an increasing share of

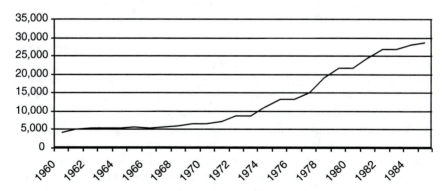

Figure 3.6 Total OECD Development Assistance Committee (DAC) bilateral aid disbursements, 1960–85 (US$ millions at current prices). Source: OECD.

bilateral aid was given to the world's poorest states, particularly in sub-Saharan Africa. In 1960 only about 8 per cent of bilateral aid was given to the least developed countries, but by 1975 this had risen to nearly 18 per cent and by 1985 to almost 20 per cent (OECD).

Multilateral agencies

In addition to the emergence and consolidation of bilateral aid, this period also witnessed the emergence of several multilateral aid agencies (Figure 3.7). The most significant multilateral development agency, in terms of money and of influence, was and remains the World Bank. It was the only multilateral development agency until 1959 when the first regional development bank, the Inter-American Development Bank (IADB), was founded. This was followed by the African Development Bank (AfDB) in 1964 and the Asian Development Bank (AsDB) in 1966. These three are the most important regional multilateral development agencies, although there are a number of others.[1] The most important UN development agency, the UNDP, is not a development bank; rather it undertakes a number of functions within the UN system (particularly coordination of the numerous UN specialized agencies at work in developing countries) as well as providing technical assistance and grant aid to developing countries. Taken together these multilateral agencies demonstrate the centrality of the multilateral form in the post-war era and the power of the United States in establishing this form.

The World Bank

The World Bank (or IBRD to be more exact) was founded in 1944. Its articles of agreement state that its purpose was to:

> assist in the reconstruction and development of territories of members by facilitating the investment of capital for productive purposes, . . . the reconversion of productive facilities to peacetime needs and the encouragement of the development of productive facilities and resources in less developed countries.
>
> [Article I(i)]

The World Bank differed from the emerging bilateral development agencies in that it was established as a particular kind of bank and this crucially shaped the way it approached the problem of development in the years after 1945. First, it was founded to provide loans for discrete development projects, rather than general budgetary support. Second, the World Bank was expected to raise investment capital through the sale of its own securities (bonds) in the financial markets. Though these bonds were to be guaranteed by the member governments, the Bank was nonetheless established as a financial institution with obligations to those who purchased its bonds. The facts that it was established as a particular kind of bank,

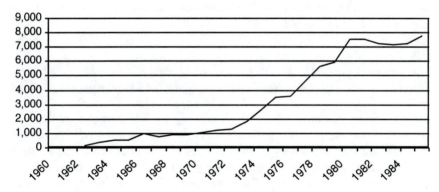

Figure 3.7 Total multilateral aid disbursements, 1960–85 (US$ millions at current prices).
Source: OECD.

and that it was run by bankers, influenced its lending practices. Until the establishment of the International Development Association (IDA), the World Bank loaned money at or near market rates of interest. The rationale for World Bank lending was that, as the loans were backed by capital from its member states, it was able to provide finance for projects which private investors would not provide and loans tended to have a long repayment schedule. In the early years of its operations prospective loans were assessed using procedures followed in the private investment community. The expected values of gross benefits were compared with expected gross costs over the life of a project and the annual net benefits were compared with the proposed amount of investment (Mason and Asher 1972: 241). This, combined with the rate of interest, limited both the potential number of borrowers and the potential number of projects the Bank could finance. Almost from the beginning of its operations the World Bank was criticized for the fact that it could not provide 'soft' loans to countries which were not in a position to borrow at market rates of interest. Calls for the provision of financing to developing countries on more liberal terms than those provided by the Bank started in earnest in the 1950s. The creation of IDA in 1960 was in part designed to counter these criticisms and forestall the creation of a proposed UN agency which would provide soft loans to many of the newly independent states (Mason and Asher 1972: 385). However, although this agency could provide loans at much lower rates of interest it was still established as a project lending institution and project preparation was undertaken by World Bank staff.

The World Bank was also founded on the principle that it would be 'non-political'. Article III5(b) of the World Bank's Articles of Agreement states that loans shall be granted with 'due attention to considerations of economy and efficiency and without regard to political or other non-economic influences or considerations'. Eugene Black, president of the World Bank from 1949 to 1962, said that:

> the professional job of the economist is . . . to make the politician [and] civil servant . . . aware of the economic consequences of their decisions, and to

provide evidence on which the decision-makers can weigh the benefits and costs of alternative courses of action.

(Black 1963: 24)

This supposed non-political stance, however, clashed with the decision-making procedures, which gave developed countries significant formal power through the system of weighted voting on the Board of Directors. In general the number of votes a country has on the Board is determined by the amount of capital that countries pay into the Bank. The Board is charged with the day-to-day running of the Bank, and approves all loans, policies and Bank reports. There are also more 'informal' mechanisms for the United States in particular to exercise influence and there is evidence that the US government has influenced various aspects of the Bank's operations (Gwin 1997). There is good evidence that the Bank was pressured by the United States to suspend lending to Chile after Allende's election in 1970, to Vietnam in 1977, to Nicaragua in the 1980s and to Iran in the 1980s and 1990s (B. Brown 1992). There is also evidence of a direct attempt by the Reagan administration to pressure the Bank into adopting a more 'market friendly' approach to development (Ayres 1983: 230–2). More generally, however, most of the time the United States does not explicitly exercise the power it has over the Bank because it does not have to: the Bank promotes the broad hegemonic project of the United States simply though its day-to-day operations – as it was designed to do.

The vast bulk of Bank lending until the 1970s was for infrastructure projects. In 1969, for example, lending to the power and transportation sectors accounted for 69 per cent of total Bank lending (Mason and Asher 1972: 134, 200). The rationale for this was made clear in the Bank's *Sixth Annual Report*:

An adequate supply of power, communications and transport facilities is a precondition for the most productive application of private savings in new enterprises. It is also the first step in the gradual industrialization and diversification of the underdeveloped countries. These basic facilities require large initial capital outlays, which, because of the low level of savings and the inadequate development of savings institutions, cannot be financed wholly by the countries themselves . . . Therefore the resources of the Bank are called upon to provide the foreign exchange necessary for the building of these vitally important facilities.

(IBRD 1951: 14)

Social sector lending such as that in health and education was debated within the Bank, but, at least until the late 1960s, was rejected on the basis that these were not sectors in which sound investments could be made, and on the basis that the provision of infrastructure was the most pressing developmental task (Mason and Asher 1972: 152, 154; Caulfield 1997: 63–4). As the first official history of the World Bank put it, the Bank 'was slow to break away from its early devotion to capital infrastructure' (Mason and Asher 1972: 468).

By the early 1970s under the presidency of Robert McNamara, however, the Bank's policies were beginning to change. Most striking was the new stress on poverty alleviation. In his 1973 address to the Board of Governors of the World Bank, McNamara said that 'the basic problem of poverty and growth in the developing world can be stated very simply. The growth is not equitably reaching the poor. And the poor are not significantly contributing to growth'. He also said that 'the data suggest that the decade of rapid growth has been accompanied by greater maldistribution of income in many developing countries and that the problem is most severe in the countryside'. This, he argued, meant a need to 'design development strategies that would bring greater benefits to the poorest groups in developing countries'. In particular he emphasized the need to focus on agricultural development as a way of improving the livelihoods of the large numbers of rural poor (McNamara 1973). This was a significant reworking of the basic development theory underlying the Bank's work, and was part of a more general shift among development agencies. At the same time lending by IDA grew rapidly, from $131 million in 1968 to $1,543 million in 1980 (OECD).

Inter-American Development Bank (IADB)

The first regional development bank was the Inter-American Development Bank (IADB), created in 1959 alongside the Organization of American States (Tussie 1995). Latin American states were very keen to establish a regional development bank. Although they had a significant presence at the Bretton Woods conference, and had made up nearly half of the original members of the World Bank, they felt increasingly neglected by the Bank as it turned its attention to newly decolonized states (Krasner 1981: 305; Tussie 1995: 18). They knew that any regional development bank would be funded in large measure by the United States, but they hoped to exert some influence over the structure of the bank and the direction of its lending. For the United States the establishment of the IADB, and more generally the Organization of American States, was part of a renewed engagement with Latin American states for both developmental and Cold War reasons.

Its lending grew rapidly, from US$87 million in 1969 to $208 million in 1975 and $567 million in 1980. A number of points about the IADB are worth noting. First, it had a 'soft loan' arm right from the beginning. This was originally directly funded by the United States. Second, and again right from the beginning, the IADB tended to lend in different areas from, for example, the World Bank. During the 1960s it lent much less in areas such as transport and relatively more in areas such as agricultural development, water, sewerage and education (Krasner 1981: 313). In that sense it anticipated some of the changes that would take place in the policies of other donors in the 1970s, although it also followed these changes when, in 1978, it was mandated that at least 50 per cent of its operations must benefit low-income groups. Third, the IADB encouraged and also limited US power. It encouraged it in two ways. First, the IADB was overwhelmingly reliant on US capital for its operations. Second, there is a degree of proportionality in voting rights at the IADB (proportional on provision of capital) that gave the United States over one-third of votes and thus provided it with an effective veto over amendments to the Articles of Agreement (Tussie 1995: 18). On the other hand the extent of proportional voting was limited by the stipulation that at least 50 per cent of voting rights lay with the borrowing members, so that at least in principle the bank remained under the control of the Latin American states (another good example of the multilateral character of US hegemony).

African Development Bank (AfDB)

The AfDB was established in 1964 (English and Mule 1996). It was different from the other regional development banks in that it was originally established without the participation of developed countries. It emerged out of the rapid decolonization of the continent and the impact of pan-African ideology. Its original membership comprised 23 of the newly independent states. The lack of participation by developed states had two fairly obvious implications. The first was that the bank was wholly controlled by its African member states. The second was that it was relatively poorly resourced. Its initial capitalization was only US$300 million, split between callable capital (money not actually paid to the organization, but which backs bonds issues by the organization) and paid-in capital (money actually provided to the organization). In the years after its founding the AfBD found it difficult to raise money on the international financial markets, as investors were unconvinced that the callable capital provided an effective insurance against default, and members states did not fulfil their obligations to provide money to the organization (it was not until 2003 that the ADB received an AAA rating from bond-rating agencies).

The financial problems came to head when the AfDB wished to create a soft-loan arm. This simply could not be done without money from developed states. As a result of this developed states were invited to participate in what became known as the African Development Fund in 1973. The structures put in place to govern this entity are in some respects extraordinary as there was a tremendous imbalance between financial contributions and voting rights (Krasner 1981: 324). Despite providing the overwhelming majority of the funds, developed states had less than 50 per cent of the voting rights, thus preserving the control of African states. In 1982, developed states were allowed to participate in the AfDB itself, thus providing a much-needed boost to its capital, but again only on the proviso that its African member states retain a majority of voting rights. Thus the AfDB had significant autonomy from developed states, and remained a significantly African bank with the majority of its staff being African, but also as a result of that a relatively small regional development bank, both in absolute terms and in terms of a percentage of aid flows to the region. In 1973 it lent only about US$20 million, rising to just under $100 million by 1980 and to $200 million by 1985. In the early years of its operation the AfDB concentrated its lending in infrastructure development and, although it did lend more for agricultural development, even the soft-loan facility still lent over one-third of its money for transport projects (Culpeper 1994: 464).

Asian Development Bank (AsDB)

The AsDB was established in 1966 (Kappagoda 1995). Japan had been pushing for the creation of a regional development organization since the early 1960s (Wan 1995: 511). It felt that its own economic and political interests in the region were not well served by the World Bank, and as it was emerging from the immediate post-war period it wanted to exert more influence in the region. The United States was keen to establish a regional institution to support its increasing involvement in the region, and to draw Japan into aid giving in the region (Krasner 1981: 317). As a result of this, the AsBD was different from the IADB and the AfDB in that right from the beginning it had a strong presence of developed countries – notably Japan and the United States, but also Australia and New Zealand. At its founding there were 17 developed states out of a total of 43 members. This was also reflected in the distribution of voting rights; again unlike the IADB and AfDB, developing country members never had a majority of the voting rights. It was agreed that *regional* members should have a majority of voting rights, but as this included Japan, Australia and New Zealand this did not affect the overall balance of voting power between developed and developing states. In 1974 a soft-loan area of the bank was established – the Asian Development Fund – to which Japan contributed nearly half the capital (Wan 1995: 513). The lending programme of the Bank started small, but grew rapidly. It lent US$15 million in 1970, $263 million in 1975 and $327 million in 1980. Lending for infrastructure development (energy production and distribution, transport and communications) made up the bulk of AsDB loans for the first 10 years of its operations. In the second half of the 1970s more loans were made in agricultural development, but it was really only in the late 1970s and into the 1980s that the bank started lending in social sectors such as health and education (Krasner 1981: 319; Culpeper 1994: 464).

It has long been argued that Japan was the most powerful state in the AsDB (Wan 1995). By tradition the president of the bank was Japanese and apart from contributing money the Japanese government collaborated closely with the bank. In the early years of the bank's operations, it served Japan's economic interests well. Countries such as South Korea, Thailand, Malaysia, Indonesia and the Philippines with which Japan has strong trade ties received nearly 80 per cent of all loans, and Japanese firms received over 40 per cent of the total procurements associated with bank loans (Krasner 1981: 319; Wan 1995: 415). By the late 1970s and into the early 1980s, however, the obvious connection between bank lending and Japanese economic interests started to decline, even as its share of financial contributions to the organization rose. More loans went to countries where Japan had no significant economic interests (such as Bangladesh and Pakistan) and Japan's share of procurements also fell (Wan 1995: 517–18). This change reflected the broader changes in Japan's bilateral aid programme.

The United Nations and the United Nations Development Programme (UNDP)

Development issues in the broadest sense are covered by a whole range of UN agencies and the broad project of development is one that has had a high profile at the UN – which is unsurprising given its membership (Jolly *et al.* 2004; Stokke 2009). The UNDP is not strictly a multilateral aid agency, although it does distribute some funds to developing countries. It does, however, serve a number of other functions that make it worth examining in this section. It was founded in 1965 out of the amalgamation of two previous UN organizations, the Expanded Programme of Technical Assistance (EPTA) and the UN Special Fund. The first of these was established in 1950 to provide funding for technical assistance in the form of western experts to developing countries. The programme expanded rapidly and by the time UNDP was formed it had representatives in over 70 countries (Murphy 2006: 55–7). The UN Special Fund has its origins in the late 1940s. It emerged out of a long campaign for the provision of more concessional financing to developing countries. In the end the debate about such an organization was resolved when IDA was created – indeed it has often been suggested that IDA was created to head off the creation of a concessional lending entity within the UN (Kapur *et al.* 1997: 155). At the UN the Special Fund was established in 1958 to provide finance for 'pre-investment' activities, essentially identifying countries and projects for funding. It was these two organizations – the EPTA and the UN Special Fund – that were merged to create the UNDP. The new organization's activities combined the technical assistance and pre-investment activities with a growing role as coordinator for the development activities of other parts of the UN system through its country field offices. US support for UNDP was patchy through the late 1960s and especially into the 1970s. UNDP had become associated much more closely with developing countries themselves than, say, the World Bank, and subsequently the US funding for the organization was often less than promised, leading to a major financial crisis in the mid-1970s (Murphy 2006: 155–62). In place of declining support from the United States, other donors did step in – notably the Scandinavian donors and the Netherlands. Through the 1970s the UNDP's focus was different from that of other donors as it particularly sought to engage with national liberation movements and 'revolutionary' states, such as China, Vietnam and Iran (Murphy 2006: ch. 7).

Theoretical debates

As with bilateral aid there is an extensive theoretical debate about why the multilateral form has been so significant within the project of international development. The big question is: why is not all aid distributed in the form of bilateral aid? After all, this would seem to allow aid-giving states to exercise more control over who gets the aid. Yet all of the western aid donors gave at least some of their aid directly to the multilateral development agencies, although some gave a larger percentage than others. There have been roughly two kinds of answers to this question. The first answer to the question of why there are so many multilateral development agencies has been to search for some kind of comparative advantage in the multilateral form itself that would explain why it is so significant (Rodrik 1995; Buiter and Fries 2002). Various arguments have been given, including that multilateral aid might be less 'political' and thus more developmentally useful; that multilateral agencies have a closer relationship with recipient governments than bilateral donors; that multilateral agencies are repositories of knowledge and expertise; and finally that multilateral agencies are better able to provide conditional lending. There may be something to all these arguments, although they apply in different ways to the different agencies, but all of them are rather technical and non-political. As we have seen, there was always a more political element to the founding and operation of these multilateral development agencies. This suggests a second kind of answer. One of the characteristic features of US hegemony during this period was the creation of a variety of multilateral organizations as part of its broad hegemonic project, and it is little surprise that development organizations were established in this mould, particularly as the United States played a significant role in establishing most of them. The multilateral character of these organizations gave them a certain kind of legitimacy, but there were also political benefits to be gained from participation in these organizations on the part of other developed as well as developing states. Developed states gained some form of influence (and a seat at the table) at the same time as they benefited from the United States' absorbing a considerable portion of the burden of financing these organizations. For developing countries the creation of these organizations gave them a certain, though limited, influence, but also created an institutionalized commitment from the United States to development financing.

Conclusion: pluralism, power and sovereignty

A number of important themes emerge from this review of the origins and functioning of these aid agencies. During this period there were a variety of forces at work that shape aid provision. Cold War competition was obviously important for both the United States and the USSR, and in a different way for China, but certainly for the United States there was both a broader hegemonic ambition to do with constructing a liberal-capitalist international order and, as time went on, an increasingly important domestic development community whose ambitions cannot be reduced to the logic of the Cold War. For Japan its regional and economic interests were initially important, but over time it too shifted its aid programme to be more in line with emerging international norms. France is probably the simplest case; its post-colonial ambitions and commercial interests dictated its aid programme. For Britain we see a mixed set of issues. There is the colonial heritage that does shape British aid giving, on the other hand, and, like the United States, there are also other motivations at work and an increasingly vocal development community. Sweden, as a representative of a set like-minded aid donors, represents a different set of issues again. Despite these differences, however, the broader picture is one of aid becoming increasingly institutionalized within international politics and, generally, one of rising aid provision, particularly to the poorest states. In addition, it is clear that 'development theory' did play an important role in shaping aid provision during this period, although, of course, it was also shaped by many other factors too. In particular there was a stress on infrastructure lending, and later in the 1970s a switch to more of a focus on basic needs, poverty alleviation and increased lending for social sectors. Despite this, however, there is evidence of a form of pluralism among development agencies that reflects the wider pluralism of the sovereign international order. There were a variety of different donors which gave aid to different kinds of states for different kinds of reasons. Also, some states received aid from a number of these different donors. This, combined with the Cold War, gave to developing countries a certain kind of autonomy when dealing with development agencies: there were often other sources of funds and there was a limit to how much the superpowers could pressure developing countries. In addition, of course, many developing countries received quite significant resources from these aid donors. The next chapter looks in more detail at how this all played out in specific developing countries.

4 Development practice in the sovereign order

Introduction

In this chapter we look at how the project of international development actually worked in developing countries themselves. The first part of the chapter looks at some of the problems associated with assessing the impact of aid. These problems are well known but often overlooked in much of the contemporary debate about aid and development, partly because they suggest there are real limits to our knowledge about the impact of aid but also because what knowledge we do have suggests that aid has a very mixed record. Next it examines aggregate aid provision during this period and examines the rather limited evidence for the success and failure of development projects in general. The chapter then turns to the development experience of three sample countries: Ghana, the Philippines and Argentina. For each country we look at their developmental performance over time, aid flows and some World Bank projects. The sample projects give us something simply looking at aggregate flows cannot give us: a real sense of what the project of international development actually looked like on the ground. Projects have been chosen for which there is a detailed description of the project, some kind of evaluation undertaken by the World Bank, and sometimes a significant secondary literature. The chapter concludes by examining how development practice during this period reflects both development theory and the broader sovereign order.

Assessing aid

One of the great questions surrounding the project of international development, of course, is whether aid 'works'. In fact it is hard to know for sure for a number of reasons. First, there is the vexed issue of what 'works' might mean. Should this be understood in narrow terms as an assessment of whether a particular project or programme achieved its stated objectives? Or should it be understood in terms of longer-term sustainable impact? This is important because projects can deliver their stated benefits in the short term, but fail to maintain this over the longer term. Alternatively, should 'works' be understood in terms of the impact on broader developmental or macroeconomic objectives, such as economic growth or poverty reduction? This is important because discrete projects, even if successful, can have little impact on, say, economic growth rates, which tend to be determined by a complex set of factors and relationships, both internal and external (Kenny and Williams 2001). In other words there could be lots of successful individual projects, but this might not necessarily add up to 'development'. Second, there is the obvious but deeply problematic issue of counterfactuals ('what would have happened in the absence of . . .'). The difficulty is of 'controlling' for the numerous factors that can influence development outcomes so as to assess the specific success of one particular project or programme. Clearly there are a host of exogenous factors (changing terms of trade, oil price rises, fiscal crises) that can have a profound impact on the success or failure of a particular development intervention (which might have been more or less successful in the absence of these factors). In other words, a project may be 'good', but still not deliver because of other factors. In addition, of course, developmental or macroeconomic indicators can improve even with a host of 'bad' projects and programmes. A benign external economic environment can boost growth rates even with lots of poorly designed development projects. Third, there is the issue of fungibility. The difficulty here is in assessing the opportunity cost of aid resources. This cuts both ways: in the absence of a particular aid project or programme what resources would have been spent, on what, and with what effects, by the government and other development agencies? In the presence of a particular aid project or programme, what resources are freed up to be spent by the government, on what, and again with what effects (Lancaster 1999)?

This is a daunting list of analytical problems which by themselves suggest that assessing whether aid works is likely to be a difficult and imprecise exercise. This is compounded by another set of problems relating to the available data. First, there are questions about the quality of the macroeconomic and socioeconomic data available in many developing countries, especially in the world's poorest countries (Riddell 2007: 166–7). Second, there are serious gaps in the data that would show the relationship between particular projects and development outcomes. There have been relatively few attempts to generate accurate baseline data and then systematically monitor the impact of projects over time (Riddell 2007: 167–8). This is essential if we are to accurately assess the impact of development interventions. Third, many donors have not undertaken systematic evaluations of their own projects and, even if they have, have often been reluctant to make these publicly available. The institution that has gone furthest in this regard in the World Bank; whatever criticisms can be levelled at the Bank, other donors have not gone anywhere near as far in making easily available their own internal assessments of project failures and successes. Finally, even when donors do evaluate their own projects they often use different evaluation methodologies and use different ways of classifying project impact. Given these difficulties it is not surprising that assessing the impact of aid is hard. Taken together these two sets of problems ought to give advocates of aid pause for thought. Certainly these problems do not mean that aid does not 'work'; it is just that it is often hard to be terribly confident in making general claims about the impact of development projects and programmes.

Aggregate aid provision

In the last chapter we looked at total aid flows from the bilateral and multilateral aid donors. When we look at changes in the sectoral composition of this aid several things become clear (Figure 4.1). First, these figures confirm the general upward tend in aid giving, especially the spike in aid provision during the 1970s. Second, it is possible to see the rapid growth in lending for agricultural development again during the 1970s and a relative decline in the importance of aid provision for energy sector development that in turn reflects some of the changes in development thinking we noted in Chapter 3.

There are some, but actually rather few, aggregate data on the successes and failures of development projects during this period (there are more data available for the period covered in Part II of this book). At the very broadest level it seems that by the mid-1980s the overall success rate of World Bank projects was about 60 per cent (Riddell 2007: 181). This may be lower than the success rate during the 1960s and early 1970s, as it seems clear that there was a decline in project success rates after the mid-1970s. This is an aggregate figure and disguises variations between countries and across sectors. In more recent evaluations of its projects the Bank has recorded lower success rates for projects in sub-Saharan Africa (World Bank 2005a). This lower success rate in sub-Saharan Africa is confirmed by figures from the AfDB. An evaluation of its projects that ended in the late 1980s found that only 23 per cent of its projects were 'very successful' while another 18 per cent were 'marginally successful' (African Development Bank 1991). These are summary results for individual projects undertaken by the donors themselves and it is likely that this is the best possible interpretation of project outcomes.

As noted above, the issue of whether an individual project 'works' is not the same as the issue of whether aid contributes to economic growth or 'development'.

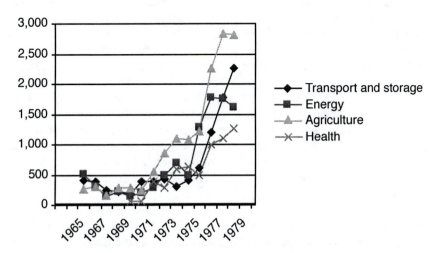

Figure 4.1 Total sectoral aid commitments, 1965–80 (US$ millions at current prices).
Source: OECD.

The summary of an assessment undertaken in the mid-1980s is worth quoting at length:

> In the broadest sense, this report finds that most aid does indeed 'work'. It succeeds in achieving its developmental objectives . . . contributing positively to the recipient countries' economic performance . . . That is not to say that aid works in every count. Its performance varies by country and by sector. On the criterion of relieving poverty, even the aid which achieves its objectives cannot be considered fully satisfactory . . . And there is a substantial fraction of aid which does not work – which may have a low rate of return, or become derelict shortly after completion, or never reach completion, or have positively harmful effects.
>
> (Cassen and Associates 1986: 11)

This is about the most positive assessment that could be given about aid during this period, although even the authors of the report concede that this conclusion is 'not a demonstrable fact', but a 'well-educated assessment' (Cassen and Associates 1986: 11). A recent evaluation of the overall macroeconomic impact of aid has concluded that 'most of the econometric studies of the relationship of aid to growth have found that aid has no significant impact, either positive or negative, on economic performance' (Lancaster 1999: 44). This very mixed record is reflected in the experiences of our three case study countries.

Ghana

As the first sub-Saharan state to gain formal independence from colonial rule in 1957, and with a charismatic leader, Kwame Nkrumah, Ghana was an emblem for the future of Africa. Unfortunately, the tremendous optimism that greeted independence was shattered in the years that followed, culminating in a dramatic economic and political crisis in the late 1970s and early 1980s. For many commentators Ghana remained emblematic, but only as a paradigm case of what went wrong with development in Africa (Killick 1978; Jeffries 1989). Until the early 1970s, Ghana's economic performance was characterized by modest but stable gains, although serious problems were being stored up. Nkrumah did not consistently follow any development strategy, and embraced in various ways a number of ideologies, including pan-Africanism and African socialism. Like many people at the time, however, Nkrumah associated 'development' with industrialization as part of a national project of modernization, which had as its counter-points both colonialism and 'backwardness'. Ghana received increasing amounts of foreign aid, although aid volumes fluctuated with the political instability that characterized Ghana during this period (Figure 4.2).

Ghana also became independent at a time when Cold War competition in the third world was increasing. Given this it received aid from a number of different donors over this period, including both the Soviet Union and China. The logic of Cold War competition was particularly clear in the case of the first project

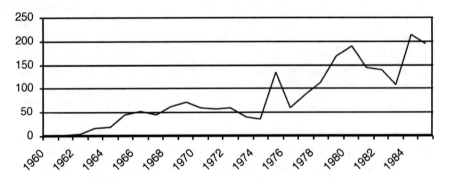

Figure 4.2 Aid disbursements to Ghana, 1960–85 (US$ millions at current prices). Source: OECD.

examined here: the *Volta River Hydroelectric Project*. This was the first project approved by the World Bank for the newly independent Ghana. It was and still is a highly controversial project. In many ways it is emblematic of the kinds of projects undertaken by development agencies in the 1960s. It was a large-scale and ambitious infrastructure/industrialization project of the kind suggested by development economics and it was very enthusiastically supported by Nkrumah, who was convinced that this kind of large-scale project would help to trigger a process of structural transformation (Hart 1980). As it was one of the most important (at least symbolically) of the newly independent states the United States had reasons to remain on good terms with the Ghanaian government. This was particularly the case after the Aswan Dam, when a US refusal to finance the building of the dam had led the Egyptian government to turn to the Soviet Union for aid. The World Bank was also keen to establish good relations with Ghana, again as one of the first newly independent African states.

The project consisted of several elements, all of which were expected to produce significant economic benefits (IBRD 1961a). At the heart of the project was the construction of a dam and hydroelectric power station at Akosombo on the Volta River. The idea of building a dam at this location was not new, but previous studies ruled out the possibility on account of the large costs and the fact that the electricity produced by the power station was far in excess of demand in southern Ghana: hence the desirability and viability of the project hinged on the establishment of a large power-consuming industry. It was here that another long-standing idea was reanimated: establishing an aluminium-manufacturing plant to take advantage of the extensive bauxite deposits in the area. This was to be constructed at the port of Tema about 40 miles away from the dam (thus making it easy to export the aluminium). This in turn required the construction of power lines from the power plant to the aluminium smelter in addition to other lines to serve towns and cities in southern Ghana.

It is worth quoting extensively from the World Bank project document to see the kinds of benefits it imagined flowing from the project. First, it argued that 'the project would make available to Ghana the abundant supply of power *which is necessary for the economic development of the country*' (emphasis added). Then:

> in addition to the direct benefits of the project . . . there are other ancillary benefits. Ultimately tax would be collected from the smelter. In addition, the national income would benefit from the expenditures associated with the project . . . There would of, of course, also be required ancillary investment.

Also, there would be 'non-monetary indirect benefits' from the project: 'for example, the availability of substantial quantities of power might attract new industries. Some related industries and services would most likely grow up around the project area'. In particular it was thought that the new reservoir would boost the fishing industry and could be used for irrigation – thus boosting agricultural production. Finally it was argued that 'the project probably would result in an increase in the general level of labor skills in the country' (IBRD 1961a: 18). It is all there: infrastructure, industrialization, forward and backward linkages, modernization of the economy and the labour force, and so on.

By the standards of the early 1960s this was a very costly project. Its total cost was just under US$190 million. The IBRD lent $47 million at an interest rate of 5.75 per cent for 25 years. The United States lent $37 million and the UK $14 million. The government of Ghana itself was to contribute $35 million, with the rest of the monies being raised on international capital markets. To put the numbers in some perspective, the World Bank did not lend this much money to Ghana in a single project until the mid-1980s. An American industrial company, Kaiser International, had a very important role in the project in the form of a 90 per cent ownership of the Volta Aluminium Company (VALCO), which would use the electricity to power an aluminium smelter and would establish a bauxite refinery (to 'refine' bauxite into a useable form for the smelter). One final point is worth noting about the project documents produced by the Bank. Although the construction of the dam and the creation of the reservoir would necessitate the resettlement of about 80,000 people, almost no mention is made of this at all in the staff appraisal report. Although this project was one of the most high-profile, there were other similar kinds of projects funded during this period. Between 1962 and 1980, for example, the World Bank funded 10 other large infrastructure projects and a number of industrial projects in Ghana.

So what happened? The dam, the hydroelectric plant and the smelter were certainly built and the reservoir, Lake Volta, was created – the largest man-made lake in the world. The dam was built quickly and the hydroelectric plant began to produce significant amounts of electricity in 1966, and continues to produce a significant portion of Ghana's energy needs, and the smelter began operations in 1967. In some ways then the project was a success. Although the energy produced by the project was in excess of demand at the time, as Ghana's electricity consumption has risen so the power station has become more and more important – so much so that it was upgraded in 2006. The smelter has produced significant amounts of aluminium exports and at peak capacity employed over 2,000 workers – 99 per cent of whom were Ghanaian. The smelter also paid significant tax revenue and sold about 10 per cent of its output to the Ghana Minerals Commission, which provided the basis for an indigenous aluminium industry estimated to be worth about $50 million a year. In addition there has been some development of a fisheries industry as a result of the creation of the dam (Hart 1980).

Despite this, the project has generally been viewed as having several downsides. First, Kaiser International never built a bauxite refinery to take advantage of Ghana's bauxite deposits; the company found it cheaper to import bauxite powder, mostly from Jamaica. This meant that one of the key justifications for the project, the development of backward linkages in the form of bauxite mining and refining, never materialized. Second, VALCO negotiated extremely cheap rates for the electricity produced by the power plant as well as certain tax privileges, especially on the import of bauxite powder. In effect the company benefited enormously from cheap electricity produced from a power station and dam funded by western aid agencies. Although rates were subsequently renegotiated, the smelter still had access to electricity at rates below that of other users. Third, some of the expected benefits of the project did not materialize. In particular the irrigation plans never really took off. Fourth, and in what would become a familiar story of big dams, there was a series of environmental and other problems. The resettlement programme was criticized for being insensitive to the needs of the displaced persons and suffered from a series of problems compounded by a coup in 1966 (Lawson 1968). As a result of the creation of the reservoir (and thus stagnant water) the incidence of water-borne diseases increased, including malaria and most seriously schistosomiasis (a particularly nasty disease) (Gyau-Boakye 2001). Finally, there have been a series of problems with the hydroelectric plant itself. When lake levels fell through the 1980s and 1990s the plant produced less electricity – it was operating at below 50 per cent capacity by 1998 – which led to electricity shortages throughout Ghana.

As with many development projects, coming to some kind of final adjudication is difficult. There have been benefits to Ghana and there have been problems. Perhaps this is what we should expect. What we can say is that the World Bank and the other donors were far too optimistic in their assessment of the expected benefits and far too little concerned with the impacts on local communities and the environment. Certainly Kaiser International benefited from what most commentators agree were excessively generous terms. In a final twist to the story the smelter was shut down in 2008, after Kaiser International sold its 90 per cent stake to the Ghanaian government in a joint venture with a Russian aluminium company. Its future remains uncertain.

As we saw in Chapters 2 and 3, development thinking was changing during the 1970s. There was a shift of emphasis away from large-scale infrastructure projects towards projects that explicitly targeted the poor, especially in rural areas. One product of this was what were called 'Integrated Rural Development Programmes' (IRDPs). These were aimed at improving the livelihoods of large numbers of rural people through projects that covered several sectors at once. They typically included agricultural extension services, health service improvements, transport improvements, local infrastructure development and educational programmes (Ruttan 1975, 1984).

The Upper Region Agricultural Development project in Ghana was a classic IRDP. It was approved in 1976 and was to cover an area supporting 10 per cent of Ghana's population. It had a number of components. It supported the establishment of 90 agricultural extension centres to improve the provision of fertilizers, insecticides, animal vaccinations, seeds and farm equipment to rural farmers. It also supported training and education services and the establishment of a functional literacy scheme with a view to improving farming techniques and improving output. It also supported the building of a radio transmitter for the Ghana Broadcasting Corporation network to enable the broadcasting of educational programmes. In addition, the project funded the construction of over 100 new small dams to improve irrigation, and 700 village wells, as well as grain stores and two cotton-processing plants. Finally, the project included institutional support for the Ghanaian agencies charged with delivering these elements of the project (World Bank 1976). The World Bank loaned US$21 million and the UK $11 million with the Ghanaian government and Ghanaian banks contributing the rest. The aim of the project was to improve agricultural production and thus farmer income by a projected 32 per cent. It was exactly designed to target small farmers in the Upper Region, who were seen to have been bypassed by previous agricultural development projects in the region (World Bank 1976: 5). It was predicated on two basic assumptions. First, that the farmers in the region were willing and able to embrace new techniques and new farming technologies. Although it was recognized that literacy rates were low (hence the functional literacy element of the project) it was thought that the basic issue preventing improved agricultural output was the lack of appropriate inputs. Second, it assumed that the kinds of extension services envisaged could in fact be delivered in a timely and effective manner and that improvement in the dams and stores could be sustained.

In many ways this is obviously a very different kind of project with a different kind of developmental logic from the Volta River Hydroelectric Project. Yet there is a similarity in that they are both very large interventions designed to achieve significant change in a short time. They both evince the kind of confidence with which problems of development were approached by the large donors at the time. They seemed to have a high level of confidence in their ability to get the project delivered and for the project to deliver sizeable benefits. Unfortunately neither occurred. As the Bank report written at the end of the project noted, 'the project was not successful in having a demonstrable impact on crop and livestock production' (World Bank 1987a: v). Some of the problems included inadequate supply of insecticides, fertilizers and seeds, lack of adequately trained agricultural extension staff, overly complex procurement procedures, lack of equipment for well-building (as of 1984 only three new dams had been built), that the upgrade to the broadcasting network did not happen, and pervasive management and administration problems. The project, of course, like all development interventions, did change some things and, at least according to the Bank, it did make some contribution to the welfare of farm communities in the region, but this impact was nothing like what had been imagined (World Bank 1987a: 29). The evaluation of this project is in many ways consistent with assessments of IRDPs undertaken during this period in other countries (Ruttan 1984).

Some of this is explained by project design and the very complex nature of the project itself. The Bank noted that project design failed to take proper account of the geography and farming practices of the region, that it failed to recognize the limited administrative and management capacity that existed in the region and in central government, particularly given the complexity of the project, that it had an overly ambitious implementation schedule, that it relied too heavily on expatriate technical expertise, and that in some cases it simply did not fully understand what was involved (in one case the fact that earth compactors were needed to build new dams was not considered during project design) (World Bank 1987a: 13). However, some of the failures can be attributed to the circumstances in Ghana during the period of the project. As the Bank said:

> the project was implemented during a period of considerable political change and steady decline of the country's economy and infrastructure. The effect on the project was that supply of agricultural inputs and raw materials was unpredictable, management did not always enjoy the support of central and local administration, and farmers could not count on consistent incentives to raise production.
>
> (World Bank 1987a: v)

This rather glosses over the most turbulent period in Ghana's history and the cataclysmic economic collapse that accompanied it. Growth rates collapsed, export volumes fell and inflation soared (Table 4.1).

This goes some way to explaining the chronic shortage of project inputs and the terrible administrative and management problem. Runaway inflation led to a collapse in the purchasing power of civil servants, who were forced to moonlight in second jobs, and political uncertainty led to a lack of continuity and political commitment. It also goes some way to explaining the lack of improved agricultural output, as there was a precipitous decline of food production in general

Table 4.1 Ghana: selected indicators, 1960–84

	1960–4	*1965–9*	*1970–4*	*1975–9*	*1980–4*
GDP growth rate (%)	3.52	1.3	4.44	−1.44	−1.18
Inflation (%)	3	6.95	13.66	47.1	62.4
Exports annual growth (%)	3	0	1.6	−5.6	−8.8
Interest payments on external debt (% of export earnings)	n/a	n/a	n/a	2.2	9
Life expectancy at birth (years)	46.3	47.8	49.8	52	53.7
Under-5 mortality rate per 1,000	212 (1960)	200 (1965)	183 (1970)	165 (1975)	149 (1980)

Source: World Bank.

during the period as a result of government policies and a rapidly deteriorating macroeconomic context. There are two obvious points to make. One is that even well-designed projects would struggle against the backdrop of economic and political crisis. The second is, of course, that it is very easy to undertake badly designed projects that would struggle in even the most propitious circumstances.

The Philippines

The economic performance of the Philippines during this period was dominated by a political and economic formation, under the government of Ferdinand Marcos, that prevented the emergence of dynamic export-producing sectors in the economy, prevented the rapid growth of internal demand and the modernization of agriculture, and gradually enmeshed almost all areas of economic life into a wide-ranging and complex pattern of patrimonial rule. This meant that no coherent development strategy was followed. No serious attempt was made to develop the agricultural sector, which remained dominated by a small number of powerful landowning families. Land reform was resisted, which had the effect of preventing any significant reduction in the high levels of rural poverty (B. Anderson 1988; Mosley 1991). The government used an increasingly arbitrary system of trade restrictions and expanded ownership of economic enterprises as a way of dispensing political favours (Hutchcroft 1991). Economic growth rates slowed in the 1970s, and in the early 1980s the Philippines was plunged into an economic and political crisis (Table 4.2).

In addition, and very importantly, the Philippines had a close relationship with the United States that had its roots in the early twentieth century, but developed subsequently in the context of the Cold War. The Philippines hosted two strategically significant US military bases, which not only employed many people, but from which the government was able to extract significant rents, and which provided the Philippines with leverage over the United States (Mosley 1991: 44). In important respects this helped to sustain the Marcos government in power, although after it enacted martial law in 1972 the US government scaled back

Table 4.2 Philippines: selected indicators, 1960–84

	1960–4	1965–9	1970–4	1975–9	1980–4
GDP growth rate (%)	5.2	4.1	5.4	5.0	1.3
Inflation (%)	5.7	4.7	17.1	10	20.4
Exports (annual % growth)	11	−1.8	8.2	8.6	9.2
Interest payments on external debt (% of exports)	n/a	n/a	n/a	7	24.4
Life expectancy at birth (years)	54.3	56.3	57.9	59.9	61.9
Under-5 mortality rate per 1,000	97 (1960)	93 (1965)	89 (1970)	85 (1975)	80 (1980)

Source: World Bank.

its development aid. During the 1970s, however, World Bank lending to the Philippines increased dramatically, with the suspicion that this too was directed more by a Cold War logic than by a developmental one (Figure 4.3; Bello *et al.* 1982).

The two projects examined here form part of the dramatic expansion of World Bank aid to the Philippines in the 1970s. They are rather more mundane than the projects in Ghana, but they help illustrate the range of projects that were funded during this time, and the range of problems, as well as successes, that these projects had. The first is the *Fisheries Training Project*, a US$70 million project to establish a national fisheries training system (World Bank 1979a). This was one of a series of projects designed to develop commercial fishing in as a key sector that would contribute to economic development in the Philippines. In the early 1970s, for example, the Asian Development Bank had helped fund the construction of a new fisheries port. The World Bank itself had been involved in a project to provide credit to fisherman and fishing companies, and had been involved in lending for agricultural education in the Philippines (World Bank 1990).

From the available documentation it seems the government of the Philippines was keen to improve fisheries education and research. At the time – the early 1970s – fisheries were seen as having the potential for significant growth. Fishing had been growing at 5 per cent a year and it was thought that there was significant potential for this to continue, given the possibilities of introducing more commercial fishing. The larger goal of developing the fisheries sector was to better exploit the abundant natural resources so as to become self-sufficient in fish production and contribute to increased export earnings. The Fisheries Training Project

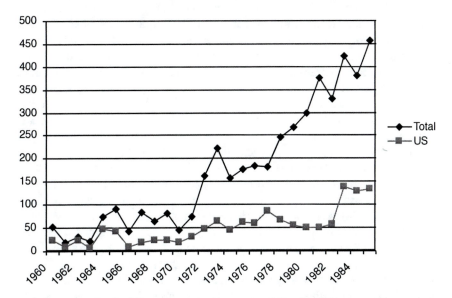

Figure 4.3 Aid disbursements and total US bilateral aid disbursements to the Philippines, 1960–85 (US$ millions at current prices). Source: OECD.

had a number of components. First, it involved the building of a new College of Fisheries, which would be the central body in developing and coordinating fisheries education. Second, it involved the establishment of a number of regional training institutes, which would train fishermen. The project funded the construction of new buildings, buying furniture, training vessels, textbooks and learning materials, the recruitment of specialists to help with curriculum development, and research activities at the College of Fisheries, including a fellowship scheme.

As the Bank noted at the end of the project, the achievement of project objectives was mixed (World Bank 1990). The construction of the buildings and the purchase of the equipment did happen, albeit four to five years later than planned and with some problems. There were costs overruns and delays in the procurement of equipment and furniture, with as the Bank put it 'attempts to manipulate' the procurement process (World Bank 1990: viii). The fellowship scheme had been established and curricula for training and degree programmes had been established. As a result of the project there existed 'a stronger fisheries training capacity' and thus a major objective of the project had been achieved (World Bank 1990: ix). However, the institutions developed by the project remained (at 1987) seriously underutilized. Only one-fifth of the expected students enrolled at the College of Fisheries and fewer than half of the expected students enrolled in the regional trading institutions. Enrolment numbers were also skewed towards inland fisheries, whereas one of the main project objectives was to improve training and education in marine fisheries.

The basic reason for this was that the fisheries sector did not develop as anticipated at the time of project design. 'Project expectations for sectoral performance were overoptimistic . . . in essence a growing economy creates the demand for a technically competent workforces, not vice-versa' (World Bank 1990: ix). The Bank should have realized this, of course, but it illustrates a number of points. First, of necessity projects rely on projections about the future that often turn out to be wrong. In this case there was a boom in inland fisheries and a decline in marine fisheries due to over-fishing; in other words the natural resources were not there to be exploited as the project had imagined (the Bank admitted that knowledge of the resource base was 'inadequate'). Second, projects are sometimes derailed by events out of the straightforward control of development agencies. In this case the government's own fisheries agencies 'remained in a state of upheaval', thus reducing investment in the sector, and there was very lax enforcement of conservation laws (World Bank 1990: 15).

The second project is the *Sixth Power Project*. As the project name suggests, this was the sixth project supported by the Bank to help build electricity-generating capacity (World Bank 1974). This is a sign of how important these kinds of infrastructure projects were. This particular project was driven by a number of concerns. The Philippines president announced in 1972 a policy of 'total electrification' (Government of Philippines 1972). Given that at the time only 30 per cent of the population had access to electricity, this was a sizeable task. In addition, the Philippines was not rich in mineral resources and thus relied heavily on imports of oil, coal and gas. The project consisted of a loan to the National Power Company

(NPC) principally to build a hydroelectric power station and new transmission lines. Both the World Bank and the Asian Development Bank contributed funds and the total cost of the project was US$390 million.

In almost all respects this was a classic infrastructure project of the time and typical of the kinds of projects funded in the Philippines and elsewhere at the time. And in many ways the project worked (World Bank 1983a). The power plant was constructed on schedule if a bit over budget. The transmission lines were completed – but five years later than anticipated and with some significant cost overruns. According to the Bank's evaluation of the project this was the result of poor planning and cumbersome procurement procedures. Apparently not enough soil testing had been done to establish whether certain areas were suitable for building transmission lines, and the rights of way necessary had not been established, leading to extensive negotiations of rights of way with landowners. Nonetheless, and despite the almost inevitable delays in large infrastructure projects, it can be seen as a success. This conclusion is in line with the Asian Development Bank's assessment of its lending to the Philippines power sector, whereby nearly 90 per cent of its projects were rated as successful or partly successful (Asian Development Bank 2005). These projects have contributed to reducing reliance on fuel imports and increasing the electrification rate to nearly 80 per cent by 2000.

What makes this project interesting is that, despite the extensive level of development assistance given to the Philippines power sector, it was beset by a series of crisis from the mid-1980s onwards. Even by the end of this project the NPC was under financial stress as a result of its expansion programme and government caps in electricity prices. By the end of the 1990s there was a major financial crisis in the sector as the NPC had accumulated a cash deficit of US$1.5 billion (World Bank n.d.). Second, there was a power crisis in the late 1980s and early 1990s with demand outstripping supply, partly as a result of the failure to bring online a nuclear power station. Problems of electricity supply continue to this day. Third, electricity continues to be relatively expensive in the Philippines compared with other countries in the region. None of these issues bears on the assessment of this project – or others at the time – but they do illustrate that even successful projects, or even a series of successful projects, do not necessarily fix the problem even in the short to medium term.

Argentina

The development experience of Argentina during this period has become defined by what happened in the early 1980s: an economic and political crisis associated with an unmanageable external debt crisis and the Falklands War. In some ways this is unfair, as the performance of the Argentinian economy was respectable, if erratic, for at least some of this period, although it had started a more serious decline by the mid-1970s. Nonetheless, the type of development strategy pursued by Argentina, a form of ISI, and the ways in which it was pursued, came for the World Bank and IMF to symbolize what was wrong with development strategy in the 1960s and 1970s. As was noted in Chapter 2, ISI as a development strategy was seen as a way of reducing reliance on primary product exports and diversifying the national economy. As early as the 1930s, Argentina enacted a kind of proto-ISI with increased government intervention in the economy and government-led investment in infrastructure. ISI as a strategy for industry-led development really took off after the Second World War with the Peron government, which pursued a policy of nationalization and economic independence. Peron was ousted in 1955 but the basic thrust of ISI continued until the mid-1970s, with a focus on infrastructures, the steel and cement industries, car production and consumer durables. The economy was not without its problems, with persistent high inflation, and there was further political instability, but until the early 1970s ISI sort of worked.

With the first oil price rise this developmental strategy started to unravel. This was to do not just with ISI itself, but with the ways in which certain groups – newly created industrial interest groups and labour in particular – had become politically important. These groups had benefited from ISI and the government was unwilling to take measures that might harm their economic interests. Although some liberalization was undertaken, successive governments resorted to increasing borrowing to maintain economic growth. When world recession hit and dollar interest rates rose the economy was plunged into crisis as growth rates declined, inflation rose dramatically, and the external debt burden became enormous. The Falklands War compounded these problems (Table 4.3).

Although the United States was wary of the Peron government, which it viewed as being of a quasi-fascist kind, there was significant support from development agencies for this strategy of industrial development (Figure 4.4).

Much of this lending was for infrastructure projects. The significance of infrastructure is demonstrated by both of our sample projects. The first is the *Highway Construction and Maintenance Project*. This was a project approved in 1961 to help finance a road building and maintenance programme (IBRD 1961b). It would finance the construction and improvement of over 2,500 km of road and the purchase of road maintenance equipment. The World Bank argued that the country's transport system was seriously hampering its development,

Table 4.3 Argentina: selected indicators, 1960–84

	1960–4	*1965–9*	*1970–4*	*1975–9*	*1980–4*
GDP growth rate (%)	2.3	5.5	3.7	2.1	–0.1
Inflation (%)	25.9	18.8	39.5	221.6	242.8
Exports (annual % growth)	6.5	7.8	1.4	11.2	0.0
Interest payments on external debt (% of exports)	n/a	n/a	n/a	9.75	47.8
Life expectancy at birth (years)	65.4	66	67.2	68.6	69.9
Under-5 mortality rate per 1,000	71.7 (1960)	70.5 (1965)	69 (1970)	55 (1975)	43 (1980)

Source: World Bank.

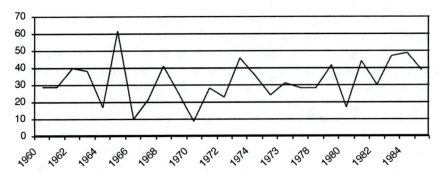

Figure 4.4 Aid disbursements to Argentina, 1960–85 (US$ millions at current prices). Source: OECD.

as only one-third of roads were useable in all weathers, the rest being dirt or gravel roads which were often impassable. The economic benefits of the project were thought to be several. The primary benefits derived from savings in present and future transportation costs. These included less wear and tear on vehicles, and faster turn-around times for road transport. In addition, it was expected that there would be indirect benefits to agricultural production by allowing easier transportation of valuable crops and perishable goods (IBRD 1961b: 10–11).

Again this is a classic project: infrastructure as a constraint on economic development and the use of large projects to stimulate further development. This particular project, however, suffered from a series of problems. First, changes of government and in the management of the highways agency created severe management problems for the project. External consultants were not used properly and road construction took twice a long as expected at increased costs and with 'questionable quality' (World Bank 1969). In addition, the local counterpart funds were not made available, and an additional loan had to be negotiated with USAID. In 1965 the scope of the project was reduced, as was the Bank loan. The situation improved somewhat with the new government in 1966 and in the end the construction works were completed by 1968.

Between 1969 and 1983, however, the World Bank made four more loans to fund highway construction and rehabilitation in Argentina, all of which suffered from the same kinds of problems stemming from political and macroeconomic instability. The Third Highway Project was affected by the political instability that followed the death of Peron as well as rampant inflation, which made it difficult for local contractors to obtain financing, and import restrictions that made it very difficult to obtain the parts and equipment needed (World Bank 1983b). The Fourth Highway Project was delayed by two years because the highways agency lacked funds to start the work and high inflation caused the renegotiation of contracts and in some cases led to contractors going bust. At the same time the economic crisis dramatically reduced transport growth rates to levels well below that estimated at the time of project appraisal, thus meaning that the roads which were built were initially underutilized (World Bank 1989b). The Highway Sector

Project was affected by the deterioration in the financial situation of provincial governments, drastic reduction in budgetary allocation to the transport sector and hyper-inflation (World Bank 1993a).

Despite these problems, many roads were indeed built and in the end one can argue that this was a desirable outcome. Beyond this, these projects illustrate two important things. First, as with Ghana, it is very difficult for development agencies to work effectively in countries undergoing political and economic turmoil. This is not a surprise but it is worth noting, partly because, as we shall see, the experience of this had a profound effect on agencies such as the Bank, which began to take much more notice of these macroeconomic conditions. Second, the fact that the Bank financed five road projects in Argentina during this period tells us something about these agencies themselves: when confronted with failure and difficulty they do not give up.

The final project we will look at here is the *Yacyreta Hydroelectric Project*, another large dam project, and like the Volta River Hydroelectric Project it was high-profile and controversial. Primarily it funded the construction of a dam and hydroelectric power station on the Parana River on the border between Argentina and Paraguay (World Bank 1979b). It emerged out of the Treaty of Yacyreta signed by both countries to establish an agency (YACYRETA) to build and operate a hydroelectric power station. The total cost of the project was estimated to be US$2,261 million – a massive sum – of which the Bank lent $201 million and the Inter-American Development Bank lent the same sum. The rest of the money was to come from loans from the Argentinian government to YACYRETA and from borrowing by YACYRETA on the international capital markets (backed by revenues from the sale of electricity). Apart from increased electricity-generating capacity, the project was expected to have other benefits. It would improve the navigability of the river at a particularly difficult stretch, thus reducing transport costs and opening up the river to different kinds of vessels. It was also envisaged that the irrigation made possible by the dam would allow for more intensive agricultural production in both countries. Finally, it was expected that the reservoirs created by the dam would allow for more intensive fishing.

The project documents indicate that the Bank was aware of the possible environmental risks of the project, and they at least discuss the fact that over 30,000 people would need to be resettled as a result of the creation of the reservoir. However, the environmental risks and the problems of resettlement were not deemed sufficiently high to prevent the project from going ahead. Indeed, as the project documents state:

> the major foreseeable risk is of a financial nature, namely the availability of local funds and the capability of Argentina to obtain the necessary loans from the international banking community. If the economic situation of Argentina were to deteriorate in the future . . . the project might be delayed, and as a result have important cost overruns and in general enter into difficulties in its execution.

> (World Bank 1995a: 24)

At least the Bank was more aware of the risks involved in this project than it was, for example, with the Akosomobo Dam project in Ghana. However, as a report written by the Bank in 1995 says, the Bank failed to secure adequate safeguards to deal with these risks (World Bank 1995a). As a result serious and varied problems arose with this project, associated with the economic and political crisis that occurred in the early 1980s.

First, construction of the dam and power station took eight years longer than planned and was significantly over budget. This delay in completion was the result of a dispute between the Bank and YACYRETA over procurement (YACYRETA preferring a more expensive bid than the Bank), the war over the Falkland Islands in 1982 (which in turn caused political turmoil in the wake of the Argentinian defeat), the difficulties YACYRETA had in raising finance on the international capital markets in the wake of the Latin American debt crisis, poor management of YACYRETA, and the more general macroeconomic crisis in the country (World Bank 1995a). The project was originally justified as the least-cost solution to Argentina's growing energy needs, but in fact the economic and political crisis significantly reduced the growth in demand for energy and the Bank admitted that, 'had this sharp downturn in demand been foreseeable during the 1979 appraisal, Yacyreta would probably have been replaced by smaller sized projects' (World Bank 1995a: iv).

Second, the environmental and resettlement aspects of the project have proved highly controversial. Despite there being a resettlement plan, the Bank admitted that it did not address some important issues such as the provision of replacement housing. On top of this, during the extended crisis of the 1980s the resettlement programme was virtually at a standstill, and, again as the Bank has admitted, YACYRETA did not have the skills or interest to oversee the resettlement programme (World Bank 1995a: vii). The Bank subsequently tried to deal with the resettlement problem in the early 1990s under another loan programme, but, although as many as 40,000 people were resettled in some form, the resettlement programme still seems to be highly problematic. Complaints to the World Bank and to the Inter-American Development Bank by affected communities detail problems with flooding, contaminated water supplies, inadequate housing and local infrastructure, and increased incidence of water-borne diseases as well as general economic hardship (World Bank Inspection Panel 2004; Inter-American Development Bank 2004). The construction of the dam has been the subject of numerous corruption allegations and the affected communities continue to campaign against their treatment. As we shall see in Chapter 7, dam projects such as this became the focal point for a high-profile campaign by non-governmental organizations against the World Bank. The outcome of these sample projects is matched by aggregate assessments of aid to Argentina during this period. For example, a World Bank evaluation of its lending to Argentina 1968–90 found that only 39 per cent had what it called a 'satisfactory' outcome. The success of Bank lending varied across sectors from only 22 per cent in agriculture to 88 per cent in urban development/water supply and 97 per cent in education. The success rate for infrastructure was 42 per cent (World Bank 2000a: 26).

Development practice in the sovereign order

The experiences of these countries and the examples of project lending during this period help illustrate how the project of international development operated during this period. It is clear how lending and the sample projects flow from the dominant ways in which development was understood during this period. There is an emphasis on infrastructure (power, roads, dams) in particular, which was commonly thought to be one of the main constraints on development. We can also see with the Upper Region Agricultural Development Project how the emerging concern that large-scale development projects were not having a significant impact on poverty, particularly rural poverty, led to new kinds of interventions targeting poorer groups.

These projects also demonstrate the kinds of relationships that existed between development agencies and developing countries. Although project documents do contain criticisms of government policies or decisions, development agencies did not target a country's political system or even its macroeconomic environment in their lending (Cold War calculations notwithstanding). In other words, lending remained project based with a view to assisting countries on the road to development understood as a form of modernization. In this sense, this project lending entirely reflects the norms of the sovereign international order of the time.

The projects also demonstrate some of the problems that the project of international development encountered. Some are to do with project design: projects being too ambitious, too complex, or not based on adequate knowledge of local circumstances. However, some are obviously to do with what was going on in developing countries, from political instability to macroeconomic crisis. Given the norms of the sovereign order, development agencies in fact had relatively little leverage over these issues – and there would have been an outcry if they had tried to exercise any such leverage. By the early 1980s, however, development agencies started to take a more confrontational and interventionist stance towards developing countries. It was the start of the era of structural adjustment that itself paralleled the decline of the sovereign order and the emergence of a liberal order.

Part II
Development and the liberal order

5   The liberal order

Introduction

In this chapter we begin our examination of the project of international development in the period from the late 1970s to the mid-2000s. Following the structure of the first part of the book, it starts with an examination of the international order during this period. At the most general level this can be characterized as a liberal international order and it results from a series of changes that start in the late 1970s and run through the 1980s, culminating in the end of the Cold War. The chapters that follow trace the relationships between the emergence of this liberal international order and the project of international development by examining changes in development theory, changes within development agencies and changes in their relations with one another, and the impact of these on developing countries themselves.

This chapter begins by looking at how we might understand the processes involved in the emergence of the liberal international order. It then moves to examine the three areas that make up international order: power-political agency, the global economy and the normative structure. The argument is that this liberal international order is significantly different from the sovereign order that characterized international relations in the years after the Second World War. In turn this makes a significant difference to, though it does not determine, the way in which the project of international development operated during this period. Development theory shifted significantly; the emergence of neoliberalism as a basis for development thinking was followed, especially after the end of the Cold War, by a more expansive liberal account of development that stressed political reform, good governance, in some cases human rights and democracy, and integration into the global economy. The limited form of pluralism that had characterized development agencies vanished. This is particularly obvious in terms of the end of Soviet aid to communist/socialist states and within the western donors there was increasing convergence in terms of policies and operations. By the end of the 1990s it made much more sense to talk about a 'development community' that also now included non-governmental organizations (NGOs), which had become increasingly important development actors. These shifts had a significant impact on developing countries, as they found themselves the subjects of increasingly intrusive development interventions pursued by an increasingly unified group of agencies. In that sense the end of the Cold War and the rise of a liberal international order had profoundly ambiguous consequences for developing countries.

The changing international order

It was argued earlier that the concept of an 'international order' can be used to describe the arrangement of norms, agencies and practices that characterize international politics during particular periods. These structure international politics by defining what is possible, what is desirable and what is legitimate. They do not determine everything that goes on in international politics, but rather they help to generate what happens by structuring the environment within which international actors operate. In terms of the shift to a liberal international order two obvious questions arise: the first to do with dating (when did this happen?) and the second to do with how this shift is to be explained. The temptation to pick on a key date to mark the transition from one international order to another is very strong given the obvious and very dramatic changes associated with the end of the Cold War. In many ways the events associated with particular dates such as 1989 do matter a great deal. On the other hand, the shift from the sovereign international order to the liberal international order is better understood as a more extended process that involves several elements that over time come to change the character of international politics. So there were processes of political, economic and normative change occurring before 1989, and in turn the events of 1989 (and 1991) reinforce these changes and enable new ones that taken together generate a new international order. The liberal international order is certainly in place all through the 1990s and into the first half of the 2000s.

In explaining this shift we can make a number of general points. The first is that not everything changes. Indeed, one of the features of the liberal order is how many of the basic features of the sovereign order remain in place. The most important of these is US hegemony: in many respects the liberal international order can be understood as at least in part a product of the hegemonic order established after the Second World War, and the liberal international order is characterized by overwhelming US predominance. In the move to the liberal order, however, there are two related changes. The first is the one we are more familiar with: the end of the Cold War. This certainly freed the United States and its allies in a host of ways as new kinds of practices became possible and the end of the ideological divide reinforced the broadly liberal economic and political ideas that emerged out of US hegemony. The second is one that is less remarked upon, largely because of the significance accorded to 1989: the reanimation of the United States' hegemonic project during the 1980s, *before* the end of the Cold War. In response to the ending of the 'golden age' of capitalism, being anxious about the decline of US hegemony and driven by what became known as the 'Reagan Doctrine', the United States pursued a more confrontational and interventionist stance towards the Soviet Union and its allies, and towards developing countries that were deemed a 'threat' to US interests. This more self-confident and muscular US stance continued through the end of the Cold War, and arguably reached its pinnacle in the early 2000s with the invasions of Afghanistan and Iraq.

A second feature of the sovereign order that survives is the broad institutional architecture established under US hegemony: the UN, the World Bank, the IMF, GATT/WTO (the World Trade Organization), the EU, NATO and the western alliance more generally. Not only do these survive but in many ways they play a more important role as their geographical reach expands to include Eastern Europe and the states of the former Soviet Union (and China) and as they are given a more prominent role in the management of global affairs under US leadership. One important change, however, is in the guiding principles of the economic institutions, where, partly as a result of the ending of the 'golden age', the embedded liberalism compromise was overturned and a process of 'disembedding' took place as these institutions drove a process of economic liberalization under the guiding principle of neoliberal economics. These factors – the reanimation of the American hegemonic project, the end of the Cold War, the end of embedded liberalism and the reworked mission of the global financial institutions – were the foundations for the emergence of a process of economic globalization. 'Globalization' is not some kind of 'external' force that just 'happened' during the 1990s; it is rather the product of a series of broader shifts in international politics, and 'globalization' can be read as the ultimate expression of US hegemony as it evokes the triumph of free trade, open markets and, in some way at least, American ideology.

A second preliminary point about explaining the emergence of the liberal international order is that it also arises from certain tensions within the sovereign order. The first is that between the broad US hegemonic project and the demands of the Cold War. 'Fighting communism' was a necessary part of US hegemony, but the Cold War also limited US hegemony geographically and ideologically (in ways that helped produce the sovereign order) and it very often involved making a host of compromises in terms of its stated ambitions – be that promoting democracy or multilateralism. These compromises still happen in the liberal order, but with the demands of the Cold War gone America is much freer to pursue its broad hegemonic project, including the export of its own ideology. A second set of tensions involve the normative elements of international politics, and in particular the tension between non-intervention and other ideas and norms in international politics – such as 'development' or human rights. With the emergence of the liberal order this tension is increasingly resolved by downgrading the significance of non-intervention in ways that legitimize a host of new kinds of interventions.

What is clear from these preliminary points is that the emergence of a liberal international order is in some ways already a possibility residing within the sovereign order. Its basic building blocks are there – US hegemony, international institutions, normative tensions – and these merge with neoliberalism/globalization, the reanimation of the US hegemonic project and the end of the Cold War to produce a new kind of international order. This change has a profound impact on the project of international development and on the experiences of developing countries themselves.

The end of the Cold War and the 'unipolar concert'

In the 15 or so years before the end of the Cold War many academics and policy-makers were worrying about the *decline* of US power. The economic problems of the 1970s, such as the end of the 'golden age' and the collapse of the Bretton Woods exchange rate system, the ignominious withdrawal from Vietnam and the economic growth of Japan and Europe, led many to speculate that US hegemony was waning, and it was often argued that this would have a significant impact on international politics as the institutional and cooperative arrangements established under US hegemony would unravel. This had a significant impact on the discipline of International Relations too as academics debated the possibilities or impossibilities for cooperation between states in the absence of a hegemonic power (Krasner 1983; Keohane 1984). This assessment turned out to be radically wrong as the 15 or so years after the end of the Cold War was a period of unparalleled US dominance in global politics. The various terms coined to describe this – unipolar moment, 'hyperpower', lone superpower – all point to the overwhelming significance of the United States in global politics during this period – military, economic, political and ideological (Kapstein and Mastanduno 1999; Cohen 2004). There were several reasons why the concern with US decline turned out to be so wrong.

Structural power and American hegemony

The first was clinically exposed by Susan Strange, who argued that the 'declinist' thesis had misunderstood the nature of US power and US hegemony (Strange 1987, 1988). Certainly data could be provided to show that as other states had grown economically so the United States' share of the global economy had experienced a relative decline, and the defeat in Vietnam did seem to expose the limits of US military power. In addition, the United States was itself experiencing a period of economic recession and structural realignment of its economy (particularly the relative decline of US manufacturing), and the internal political and social upheavals of the 1960s and 1970s seemed to indicate a nation that was fraying at the edges. What this account missed, according to Strange, was that the United States still overwhelmingly possessed what she called 'structural power': the power to 'choose and to shape the structures . . . within which other states, their political institutions, their economic enterprises and (not least) their professional people have to operate' (Strange 1987: 565). This power resulted from the role that the United States had played in establishing a hegemonic order after the Second World War. For Strange it comprised four elements or inter-related structures: the ability to exercise control over – that is, to threaten or to defend, to deny or to increase – other people's security from violence; the ability to control the systems of production of goods and services; the ability to determine the structure of finance and credit; and influence over knowledge, whether it is technical knowledge, religious knowledge or leadership in ideas and who control or influence the acquisition, communication and storage of knowledge or information (Strange 1987).

Strange used this to show that in none of these areas could it be said that the United States was 'losing' power. In the military sphere the USSR was a rival in terms of the possession of military power and nuclear weapons, but among other western states the United States was militarily far superior. In terms of the production of goods and services it was true that America had experienced a relative decline in the production of consumer goods and some industrial products (steel, for example) but it had not experienced a significant overall decline as the production of high-technology goods had increased, as had its share in the production of services. On top of this, US multinational corporations were still the most important and most influential in the world. In terms of finance and credit, the dollar remained the reserve currency of the global economy, US banks were the largest and most important in the western world, and that fact that the United States could unilaterally abandon the Bretton Woods system was a sign not of weakness but of the power of the United States in the global financial system. Finally, Strange argued that America continued to dominate the world's knowledge structures through being the leading producer of high-technology products and through having the largest military research and development budget. She concluded that since each of these four elements of power 'interacts with the other three, and the European and Japanese are so far behind militarily, it seems likely that America will enjoy the power to act as hegemon for some time to come' (Strange 1987: 571). In other words, even during this period of supposed 'decline' America remained the great hegemonic state.

The 'Reagan Doctrine'

The continuing structural power of the United States was a testament to the durability of the hegemonic order it established after the Second World War, and with the end of the Cold War these elements of its dominance became more obvious. Even before the end of the Cold War, however, there is evidence of a globally resurgent United States, particularly under Reagan. After the Soviet invasion of Afghanistan in 1979, the Carter administration started to provide covert military assistance to the Mujahedeen groups fighting Soviet occupation. The use of covert assistance to groups 'opposing communism' really accelerated under Reagan and is usually captured under the label of the 'Reagan Doctrine' (Scott 1996). It has been argued that this marked a significant departure from previous US foreign policy towards the Soviet Union. Rather than focusing on 'containment' it stressed the desirability of 'rollback': actively confronting Soviet influence with the aim of making Soviet foreign policy more costly and ultimately reducing Soviet influence and promoting western liberal capitalism. Much of the practice of rollback actually focused on developing countries, rather than in Europe. Apart from Afghanistan, the other high-profile (and highly controversial) examples of this policy were in Nicaragua (with the funding of the Contra 'rebels') and in Angola with support to UNITA (the National Union for the Total Independence of Angola) (Scott 1996: ch. 4 and 5). The administration also intervened in the Iran–Iraq war, supporting both sides at various times, but largely siding with Iraq owing to the threat the Iranian revolution was thought to pose to other states in the region. The Reagan administration also engaged in a dramatic build-up of US military capability, culminating in the plan for the so-called 'Star Wars' missile defence system (Fitzgerald 2000). This more confrontational stance led some scholars to refer to the early 1980s as the 'second Cold War' – a renewal of more open hostilities after several decades of relative stability and even détente (Halliday 1983).

The end of the Cold War

The extent to which the policies associated with the Reagan Doctrine actually precipitated the end of the Cold War itself is much disputed. Some scholars have argued that by increasing the costs to the Soviet Union of extending its influence, and dramatically raising the costs of competing militarily with the United States, the actions of the Reagan administration were crucial in economically exhausting the USSR, thus forcing it to seek a renegotiation of its relations with the United States (Wohlforth 1994). Others have disputed this, focusing instead on the long-run economic decline of the Soviet Union or on the ideas of Gorbachev as the most significant factors (A. Brown 1996).

There are in fact a number of related dynamics involved in the varying 'ends' of the Cold War that cannot be reduced simply to one factor. The first 'end' of the Cold War took place during the second half of the 1980s with a dramatic rework-ing of superpower relations. It seems clear that Gorbachev did want to establish a new kind of relationship with the United States so as to concentrate on domestic political and economic renewal. This renewal was thought to be necessary in large part because of the increasingly stagnant Soviet economy. This not only made competing militarily with the United States relatively costly (by one esti-mate the USSR was devoting 25 per cent of GDP to military spending compared with about 6 per cent for the United States), but it also threatened the ideological legitimacy of communist rule. This combination of factors led Gorbachev to offer significant reductions in Soviet nuclear and conventional weapons in Europe and started a process of summits and negotiations that led to a dramatic thawing of superpower tensions. This period also saw the winding down of Soviet support for communist and socialist regimes in the developing world, notably in Angola, and the Soviet Union withdrew from Afghanistan in 1988–9 (Halliday 2010). The domestic side of this was the well-known ideas of *glasnost* ('openness') and *perestroika* ('restructuring') through which Gorbachev hoped to rejuvenate the Soviet economy and polity.

The second and most emblematic 'end' of the Cold War, the breaching of the Berlin Wall and the collapse of communism in Eastern Europe, was related to these developments but also contained other factors. Communist rule in almost all of Eastern Europe had never achieved a significant degree of legitimacy among the populations of these states. Indeed, to some significant degree this rule was ultimately guaranteed by Soviet military and political power, which had been used to brutally quash dissent and domestic reform in Hungary in 1956 and Czechoslovakia in 1968. Although the Soviet Union did not use its military power in Poland in the early 1980s it seems clear that it might have been prepared to if the Polish government had not managed to clamp down on the domestic opposition led by the Solidarity movement (Mastny 1998). Given *glasnost* in the USSR there were increasing demands for political reform in Eastern Europe and when Gorbachev decided not to use Soviet power to prop up these regimes (the so-called 'Sinatra Doctrine') they fell victim to various forms of popular uprising very quickly (Schopflin 1990; Weigle and Butterfield 1992).

The third and final 'end' of the Cold War came two years later with the collapse of the Soviet Union itself (Strayer 1998). *Glasnost* led to the exposing of myriad social and economic problems in the USSR. This further eroded the legitimacy of the Soviet government. After the 1989 revolutions in Eastern Europe, popular discontent and protest at Soviet rule spread through many of the constitutive republics of the USSR. At the same time *perestroika* did not deliver noticeable economic benefits to most of the population, and in some cases made the economic situation worse. This was clearly an explosive situation. In February 1990 the Soviet Communist Party agreed to give up its monopoly of political power and, in the elections that followed in the constitutive republics, nationalist and radical reformers won many seats. There followed a period of considerable turmoil, protest and violence as many of the republics (especially the Baltic states) attempted to assert their autonomy. In June 1990, Boris Yeltsin won nearly 60 per cent of the popular vote for President of Russia. In response to the growing separatism, Gorbachev proposed the New Union Treaty, which would create a looser union among the republics, but maintain a single presidency, a single foreign policy and a unified military. For communist hardliners this was the last straw: on 19 August they attempted a coup to displace Gorbachev and roll back the reforms. This was met with significant popular resistance and the coup plot collapsed. Gorbachev was restored as leader, but his position in relation to the republics and particularly in relation to Russian President Yeltsin was fatally weakened. The Baltic states were recognized as independent states in September 1991, and the final end of the Soviet Union came in December 1991 when the leaders of Russia, Ukraine and Belarus declared the Soviet Union dissolved.

The end of the Cold War had a number of very obvious implications. First, it created new demands for forms of global management, including, as a matter of urgency, integrating the post-communist states into the hegemonic order. As with the end of the Second World War there were political/security and economic reasons for this. Stabilizing the post-communist states would help entrench democracy and reduce the possibility that nuclear materials would not be controlled, and the newly open markets of Central and Eastern Europe provided fertile new ground for western companies. Second, the United States and its allies were relatively less constrained in their actions. Despite the Reagan Doctrine the existence of superpower rivalry, both military and ideological, had provided a check on the hegemonic actions of the United States. With this gone, the United States and its allies were freer to project their military power and pursue their hegemonic ambitions. Third, the thought that the United States had 'won' the Cold War, and the thought that the revolutions in Eastern Europe and the collapse of the Soviet Union had vindicated the liberal values of democracy and human rights, significantly bolstered the ideological self-confidence of US and western policymakers.

All this was encapsulated in a famous speech that President George W. Bush made to congress in September 1990. The occasion for the speech was the Iraqi invasion of Kuwait in early August of that year. He said:

> We stand today at a unique and extraordinary moment. The crisis in the Persian Gulf, as grave as it is, offers a rare opportunity to move towards an historic period of cooperation. Out of these troubled times, our . . . objective – a new world order – can emerge: a new era – freer from the threat of terror, stronger in the pursuit of justice and more secure in the quest for peace.
>
> (Bush 1991)

He also said that 'recent events have surely proven that there is no substitute for American leadership' and that 'for American to lead, America must remain strong and vital'. Cutting through the rhetoric it is possible to see here exactly the kind of possibilities offered to the United States from its emerging predominance – a chance to reassert its hegemonic position and continue to fashion an international order in line with its vital economic and political interests and its ideology.

The 'unipolar concert'

Although the end of the Cold War certainly gave the United States new opportunities, the institutions and multilateral character of US hegemony did not change a great deal, and although the United States was certainly the most powerful state in this new international order it is important to recognize that the it was the leader of a broader alliance of western states, what Ayoob and Zierler (2005) call the 'unipolar concert'. They developed this idea in response to the anxiety over the future of the transatlantic alliance in the wake of the invasion of Iraq in 2003. The invasion occasioned significant disagreements between the United States and some of its European allies, particularly France and Germany, and a number of commentators suggested that this had exposed deep-seated disagreements that threatened the future of transatlantic cooperation (Cox 2005). Some suggested that this was the inevitable result of the end of the Cold War: the collapse of the common enemy that had held the alliance together led to the expression of divergent rather than common interests (Mearsheimer 1990; Waltz 2000). Ayoob and Zierler do not dispute the existence of disagreements, but they argue that these should not blind us to the 'dense web of interlocking security and economic interests that bind industrialized Western Europe and American together' (Ayoob and Zierler 2005: 31). This is itself the product of the hegemonic order established by the United States at the end of the Second World War, and they suggest that the relationship between the western states was not fundamentally altered by the end of the Cold War. They argue that one of the key factors holding this alliance together, even during the Cold War, was the recognition that 'potentially serious threats to the economic and security interests of the powerful and affluent states come . . . from the more recalcitrant states in the South' (Ayoob and Zierler 2005: 31; see also Krasner 1985).

With the collapse of the 'threat' from the Soviet Union, the 'unipolar concert' increasingly identified the South as a source of challenges, whether these be in the form of 'rogue' states, 'failed states', political Islam, resistance to economic globalization, or a host of other 'security' threats, such as transnational crime, terrorism, refugees or infectious diseases. The 2002 White House Security Strategy said that 'the United States today is threatened less by conquering states than we are by weak and failing ones' (White House 2002: 61). Ayoob and Zierler quote a Council on Foreign Relations study which concludes by stating that:

> there is a consensus within the transatlantic community on the numerous challenges facing common interests. These include terrorism, authoritarianism, economic incompetence, environmental degradation, and the kind of misrule that exacerbates poverty, encourages discrimination, tolerates illiteracy, allows epidemics and proliferates weapons of mass destruction.
>
> (Ayoob and Zierler 2005: 32)

As Ayoob and Zierler argue, 'this is a polite way of saying that the major threats to international order as conceived in the capitals of the North come from the South, particularly from those forces that major powers cannot control' (Ayoob and Zierler 2005: 32). It is this that leads them to argue that the dominant geopolitical feature of the post-Cold War era is not simply US dominance, but rather the existence of a unipolar concert: a concert of like-minded states that share common interests and common ideas, led by a globally resurgent United States. These common interests and ideas include a common interest in using the multilateral regimes established during the Cold War (NATO, UN, IMF, GATT/WTO, World Bank) to maintain western hegemony, a basic agreement about the necessity of containing 'rogue' states (even if there are disagreements about how this should be done), and a basic consensus about 'prying open world markets under the guise of free trade and liberal investment policies' (Ayoob and Zierler 2005: 36).

There is then a significant amount of continuity between the Cold War and post-Cold War eras. What made the post-Cold War era different was that the United States and the unipolar concert more generally were very much less constrained as a result of the collapse of the communist bloc, and that the south had become a very much more urgent problem for the unipolar concert. In this way the limited form of political pluralism that characterized the sovereign order declined, not so much in the sense that there were no regimes opposed to the power and ideology of the unipolar concert, but in terms of where the power and resources resided. There was no longer any systemic rival to the western alliance, and this had very important consequences for developing countries and the project of international development.

Globalization, inequality and crisis

A lot of the rhetoric about the global economy during this period was one of transformation by means of 'globalization'. Particularly during the second half of the 1990s it was common to come across claims that the character of global economic relations had changed profoundly and that this in turn would affect political, social and cultural life. There were some very important changes in the global economy during this period, but the more dramatic claims about the transformation of global politics were unfounded. Indeed, not only that, but they often operated to gloss over some of the other obvious features of global economic life. In this section we look at the debates about globalization and then stress two of these often neglected elements: first the growing inequality within the 'globalizing' economy and, second, the regular occurrence of economic crises.

'Globalization' and the global economy

Much of the academic and public policy discourse of the 1990s was taken up with debating the meaning and significance of 'globalization'. As Nick Bisley has said, 'it is hard to find a university that has not established a centre for the study of globalization or some variation on the theme, nor a government that has not invoked reform in its name' (Bisley 2007: 1). In retrospect it is easy to see that some of this was rather faddish; the product of the easy availability of research funds, the willingness of publishers to publish almost anything with the word 'globalization' in the title (see Figure 5.1), the desire of academics to mark out a new territory and the ease with which the term could be put to use by politicians to justify a host of economic policy reforms (Naim 2004).

In addition to the faddish character of some of the discussion of globalization, debates over its meaning and significance were severely hampered by other problems. First, there was an on-going issue of evidence. Lots of evidence was of course provided to show that the world was changing radically, but at least some of it was disputable and it clearly varied according to the time-frame used and the ways in which the data were collected (Hirst and Thompson 1999). Second, there were severe definitional problems (Scholte 2002). These included distinguishing 'globalization' from other related terms such as 'internationalization', 'liberalization' and 'westernization', all of which might be understood to

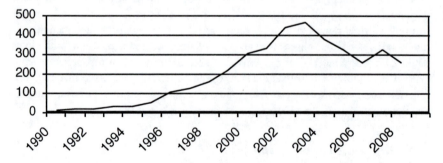

Figure 5.1 Books published in English with 'globalization'/'globalisation' in title, 1990–2009. Source: British Library catalogue.

be part of something called 'globalization', and there was the perennial issue of whether what might be called 'globalization' was really anything new. Of course there were lots of definitions provided. For example, David Held and colleagues argued that globalization was a 'process (or set of processes) which embodies a transformation in the spatial organization of social relations and transactions . . . generating transcontinental or intraregional flows and networks of activity, interaction and the exercise of power' (Held *et al.* 1999: 16). For Anthony Giddens, 'globalization can . . . be defined as the intensification of worldwide social relations which link distant localities in such a way that local happenings are shaped by events occurring many miles away and vice versa' (Giddens 1990: 64). For Jan Art Scholte, 'globalization' referred to processes of 'deterritorialization' in which social relations become delinked from territorial geography and human lives are increasingly played out in the world as a single place (Scholte 2000). It is possible to identify from these quotes some kinds of common ideas about the ways in which our individual lives were increasingly being shaped by global rather than national processes. However, it is hard not to be struck by the suspicion that some of this represents partly a description and partly an aspiration for the affluent middle classes in western states, and by the fact that, as the history of global capitalism, war and empire attests, people have always been profoundly affected by processes and events in other places. A third problem was that definitions of 'globalization' did not go very far in explaining why it was happening (what its causes were) and any attempt to do that generally fell back on some more established theories of the drivers of social and economic transformation (capitalism, for example), raising questions about the utility of the term in the first place (Rosenberg 2000). Certainly some of the more outlandish arguments have not stood the test of time. It is far from clear, for example, that globalization has produced a 'fundamental shift in the constitution of world politics' (McGrew 2005: 38). And it seems that the idea that globalization would lead to the 'eclipse' of the nation-state was deeply flawed (Evans 1997; Weiss 1998). Despite this, it is also clear that during the period under consideration there were important changes in the structure and organization of the global economy, although some of them were simply accelerations of existing trends.

First, there was a significant growth in global trade both in absolute terms and more importantly in terms of the percentage of global output. Trade volumes had been increasing since the end of the Second World War, but the percentage of global output that was traded rose through the 1990s (Hirst and Thompson 1996: 70). Figures for some individual states indicate that exports as a percentage of GDP rose significantly. For the UK, for example, they rose from 13.3 per cent in 1987 to 21 per cent in 1997 and for the United States from 6.3 per cent to 11.4 per cent during the same period (Held *et al.* 1999: 180). It should be noted, though, that this was not true of all countries, and that the majority of global trade took place between developed countries. Second, there was some globalization of production as firms took advantage of cheaper transport and communications costs to relocate production to areas which had lower labour costs or more favourable (profitable) tax and regulatory environments (Held *et al.* 1999: 170). Foreign direct investment rose rapidly through the second half of the 1980s and through the 1990s, although again it was heavily concentrated within the already developed world (Hirst and Thompson 1996: 71; Held *et al.* 1999: 242). Multinational companies also grew in size and significance and many individual industries became internationalized as a result. As Anastasia Nesvetailova and others have argued, the most dramatic change in the global economy came through 'financialization' (Nesvetailova 2007). Global financial flows grew dramatically and there was an explosive growth in new financial products. All global financial markets (bonds, foreign exchange and derivatives, for example) grew at a rate far in excess of the rate of global GDP growth or even the rate of global trade growth (Held *et al.* 1999: 203). Cross-border equity trade grew dramatically, and derivatives markets grew to a size measured in the hundreds of trillions of dollars (Held *et al.* 1999: 208). Again, a great deal of this was concentrated in the already developed world, but it does indicate a significant change whereby finance played a more and more important role in the global economy. This was dramatically confirmed during the 2008 global financial crisis.

The actual economic performance of states, both developed and developing, during this period is mixed in significant part because, as we shall see in a moment, this period was characterized by periodic financial and economic crises. For developed states it is clear that inflation was generally low, but for some unemployment remained stubbornly high and growth rates uniformly lower than in the 'golden age' (Table 5.1). For developing countries it is clear that growth rates in East Asia remained high, but for most other developing regions the picture is much more mixed (Table 5.2).

Inequality

Despite the changes in the global economy during this period, there is no great evidence of a macroeconomic miracle. Instead it is better to see the changes associated with a globalizing economy as generating significant distributional effects. The era of globalization was characterized by increasing income inequalities, both within and between countries. The IMF, for example, has noted that labour's share of national income fell in many developed countries, while that of profits

Table 5.1 Selected macroeconomic indicators for major industrialized countries, 1985–2005 (annual averages)

	GDP growth rate (%)	Unemployment rate (%)	Inflation (%)
France	2.1	9.56	1.78
Germany	2	7.1	1.89
Japan	2.33	3.06	0.71
United Kingdom	2.64	7.35	2.66
United States	3.12	5.37	3.01

Source: World Bank.

Table 5.2 Regional growth rates (%), 1985–2004 (developing countries only)

	1985–9	1990–4	1995–9	2000–4
East Asia	5.98	8.8	6.94	7.98
Europe and Central Asia	n/a	−5.88	1.12	5.94
Latin America and Caribbean	2.24	3.22	2.06	2.46
Middle East and North Africa	1.04	4.2	3.62	3.76
Sub-Saharan Africa	2.64	0.62	3.4	4.06

Source: World Bank.

rose (Guscina 2006). More generally there is a good case to be made that in many countries, developed and less-developed alike, the share of national income of the richest 20 per cent has been rising (Cornia 1999). There has also been rising inequality between countries. A World Bank estimate suggests that in 1960 the per capita GDP of the richest 20 countries was 18 times that of the poorest 20 countries, and by 1995 this had grown to 37 times (World Bank 2000b). It might be argued that rising inequality is not all by itself a problem if the incomes of the poorest are also rising – in other words if poverty rates have been falling. A number of claims have been made to this effect. The World Bank, for example, argued that the number of people living in 'absolute poverty' fell by between 200 billion and 400 billion between 1980 and 1998 (Kiely 2004). Yet there are reasons to be sceptical about this. Much depends on the definitions of poverty used and the particular ways in which poverty rates are to be measured (Kiely 2004; Wade 2004a). Ray Kiely concludes by arguing that, 'if poverty reduction has occurred, then the reason for the downward trend in the last twenty years is the economic growth and poverty reduction in China and India. If these are excluded then all the evidence points to an upward trend' (Kiely 2007: 420). Of course, the growth and poverty reduction in these counties are important, but they are not a generalized experience and thus there is no very good general argument to the effect that globalization has had a significant impact on poverty rates.

This also has a bearing on development strategy. Poverty reduction in China has followed from policies and practices that the major aid agencies and the IMF would not approve of, particularly extensive government direction of the economy. In addition, it also suggests that development strategies pushed by the major donors that increasingly stressed integration into the global economy were, whatever else their effects, not justified on the basis of their ability to deliver significant reductions in poverty.

Crisis

The era of globalization was also associated with periodic economic and financial crises in both developed and less-developed states. During the period under consideration there were at least three significant financial crises that affected global financial markets. First, there was a significant stock market crash in October

1987 ('Back Monday'). By the end of that month stock market values had fallen over 20 per cent in the United States, the UK and Canada, and by significantly more than that in Hong Kong, Australia, New Zealand and Spain. In 1998, Long-Term Capital Management, a US hedge fund, collapsed with enormous losses. In order to prevent a systemic collapse, the fund was rescued by Wall Street banks and other investment funds. Between 2000 and 2002 the 'dot-com' bubble burst spectacularly. The tech-heavy NASDAQ exchange fell from a peak of about 5,000 in March 2000 to not much more than 1,000 by the end of 2002.

There were also a series of regional financial and economic crises. In the late 1980s and early 1990s the 'Nordic crisis' affected Norway, Sweden and Finland (Honkapohja 2009). This was triggered by a banking crisis that was the result of deregulation of financial markets that had led to a variety of speculative bubbles, particularly in the property sector (Honkapohja 2009: 10–14). The effects of the bursting of these bubbles were significant. Finland's real GDP, for example, fell 14 per cent between 1990 and 1993 (Honkapohja and Koskela 1999). The experience of Sweden and Norway was less severe, but all three states had to provide public support for their banking systems (Honkapohja 2009: 20–4). In Japan there was a similar, though much more profound, experience. In the late 1980s Japan experienced a significant asset price bubble as a result of substantial current account surpluses and the too easy availability of credit from Japanese banks. The bursting of this bubble resulted in very significant bank losses, collapsing asset prices (particularly in property and the stock market), generalized deflation and low growth rates. This led many to label the 1990s as the 'lost decade' for Japan. It should be noted that to this day Japan is still suffering from the problems the bursting of this asset bubble caused. Beyond the developed world, there were a number of crises in developing states. In 1994 Mexico experienced a major currency crisis, which necessitated a nearly US$50 billion rescue package from the US Treasury and IMF (Edwards and Savastano 1998). The crisis spread to a number of other Latin American countries, including Argentina and Brazil. In 1997, perhaps the most famous crisis of this period occurred: the East Asian financial crisis. This was followed by the Russian crisis in 1998 and the Argentinian crisis in 2000–2.

The point of this is that there was a great deal of financial and economic volatility during this period. There is some reason to think that this was not in spite of globalization, but *because* of it, particularly the changes in the size and significance of global financial markets. The rapid growth in cross-border financial flows made countries more vulnerable to financial crises, and this increase in global financial mobility was driven by the deregulation of financial markets and the reduction in capital controls in both developed and developing countries – a reduction pushed by the World Bank, the IMF and the US Treasury as part of a broad package of economic reforms (Stiglitz 2002). Increasing financial integration also made crises more likely to spread to other countries – as both the Mexican and East Asian financial crises demonstrate (Claessens and Forbes 2001). More generally there is some evidence that those countries that went furthest in integrating with the global economy were more likely to experience financial and economic volatility (Walton 2004; Weyland 2004).

A great deal of the discussion of globalization, then, was distinctly one-sided in the sense that it stressed the great economic benefits to both developed and less-developed countries alike from integration into the globalizing economy (Rodrik 2001). Much of the story of globalization suggested a relatively harmonious and continuous process of increasing global economic integration. In fact, however, the experience of both groups was distinctly mixed. Despite being largely ungrounded, however, the rhetoric surrounding economic globalization was important. It was used to justify a host of economic policies and, as we shall see in the next chapter, the idea that economic globalization held great possibilities for developing countries became incorporated into the policies and practices of many development agencies. Indeed, in a final irony, many of the developing countries that experienced economic crisis were accused of not doing enough to integrate properly into the globalized economy – although with the most recent financial crisis this kind of sentiment may be disappearing.

Liberalism, sovereignty and intervention

There were also significant changes in the normative structure of international politics during this period. First was the triumph of liberalism in both its economic and political guises. This is obviously related to the end of the Cold War and the establishment of the unipolar concert as the dominant force in international politics, but it has some of its origins before the end of the Cold War, including the abandonment of the embedded liberalism compromise that had shaped the post-Second World War economic order. Second, and related, were a set of changes involving the reworking of the idea of sovereignty, a downgrading of the norm of non-intervention and the rise of various forms of intervention.

The triumph of liberalism

In the summer of 1989 Francis Fukuyama wrote what became a famous (or infamous) article in *The National Interest* entitled 'The End of History?' (Fukuyama 1989). He followed this up with a book-length argument, *The End of History and the Last Man* (Fukuyama 1992). In both pieces he argued that a remarkable consensus had emerged that liberal democracy was the best system for organizing social, political and economic life and that it had 'triumphed' over rival systems such as hereditary monarchy, fascism and communism. Fukuyama went beyond what might have been taken to be a descriptive point to argue that liberal democracy was the 'end point of mankind's ideological evolution' and that it was the 'final form of human government' (Fukuyama 1992: xi). This was what he meant by the 'end of history': not that events, sometimes significant and tragic, would not happen, but that the achievement of liberal democracy was the end of the ideological and political development of mankind. This argument unleashed a tidal wave of critical commentary, and as Fred Halliday said it became 'fashionable to denigrate Fukuyama' (Halliday 1994: 229). Fukuyama's argument was inspired by Hegel and Marx. He argued that both thinkers proposed two important arguments: first, that there was a coherent (not random) trajectory in the develop-ment of human societies from simple (slavery and subsistence agriculture) through to more complex (liberal democracy and capitalism); and, second, that there was some 'end point' where this development would cease – a point at which a form of society had been achieved that satisfied 'the deepest and most fundamental longings' of mankind (Fukuyama 1992: xii). For Fukuyama, it was the 'liberal revolution' in both politics and economics that represented such an end point.

This is not the place to engage in Fukuyama's reading of Hegel or Marx. What is important for us is that, whether or not liberal democracy is some kind of end point, there was some truth in his argument about the triumph of liberalism. The period under consideration witnessed a remarkable and significant ideological resurgence of liberalism. By this is not meant that it was unchallenged; rather that political and economic liberalism became the dominant language through which political and economic issues, both international and domestic, came to be analysed. From a very different political position, Perry Anderson has argued that 'for the first time since the Reformation, there are no longer any significant oppositions – that is, systematic rival outlooks – within the thought-world of the west; and scarcely any on a world scale either' (P. Anderson 2000: 13). That this has happened in the period of US, and more generally western, dominance is not surprising – and casts doubt on at least some of Fukuyama's arguments about the necessary quality of the liberal triumph. However, it is the most important norma-tive shift during this period.

It would be a mistake to think that this emerged solely as a result of the end of the Cold War. The resurgence of economic liberalism, often captured under the label of neoliberalism, started in the late 1970s and early 1980s. In response to the supposed inability of the broad Keynesian consensus to explain the ending of the 'golden age', neoliberal or 'supply-side' arguments became more prominent in the public policy discourses of western states (Johnson 1971). The election of Thatcher and Reagan gave a significant political impetus to neoliberalism. In the next chapter we will look in more detail at some of the neoliberal arguments, but for now we can say that it had both domestic and international elements. Domestically it manifested itself in a variety of projects, such as increasing the 'flexibility' of labour markets, reducing taxes on wealth and wealth creation, privatization of state-owned enterprises (in Britain at least) and liberalization of markets, perhaps most importantly financial markets. Associated with these strategies, at least in rhetorical terms, was a downgrading of the role of the state. This took several forms. The first was that high government spending crowded out the private sector and was thus inimical to wealth creation. Second, there were perverse effects associated with welfare provision (it reduced the incen-tives to work). Third, government bureaucracy was 'inefficient' compared with organizations operating in the private sector because it was not exposed to 'market discipline'. In both the United States and Britain this kind of economic reform programme was wrapped up with a programme of national renewal that also had its international elements – the Reagan Doctrine and the Falklands War – but more generally the international aspect of neoliberalism manifested itself in the end of 'embedded liberalism'. Economic liberalism was increasingly institutionalized in the mechanisms and practices of global economic governance, exemplified in the creation of the World Trade Organization, and as we shall see in the next chapter it is a fundamental element of the reworking of development theory during this period.

In the post-Cold War period this kind of economic liberalism was joined with a more muscular – self-confident and assertive – political liberalism. Again here, though, there were precedents in the 1980s. In particular the Reagan administration started a more concerted effort to support democracy in Latin America. This was initially related to the more aggressive anti-communism associated with the Reagan Doctrine, and was institutionalized through the creation of a number of organizations such as the National Endowment for Democracy, created in 1983 (Carothers 1991, 1994). However, in the later 1980s the promotion of democracy had become somewhat divorced from its anti-communist origins, to the extent of supporting democracy against a number of right-wing authoritarian governments, notable in Argentina and Chile (Carothers 1999: 29). Almost immediately after the collapse of communism in Eastern Europe most western states were quick to assert the superiority of liberal democracy and the values of human rights more generally, which many thought were vindicated by the end of the Cold War. This was not just rhetoric, as western states, and particularly the United States, spent considerable resources promoting and consolidating democratic regimes around the world. The immediate targets of these efforts were the former communist states. The United States established a number of programmes, some under the wonderfully entitled Freedom Support Act (Freedom for Russia and Emerging Eurasian Democracies and Open Markets Support Act) of 1992, to channel funds and technical assistance to these 'transition' states (Carothers 1999: 40–2). As the White House said:

> the collapse of the Soviet Union provides America with a once-in-a-century opportunity to help freedom take root and flourish in the lands of Russia and Eurasia . . . Their success in democracy and open markets will directly enhance our national security . . . [and] the growth of freedom there will create business and investment opportunities for Americans and multiply the opportunities for friendship between our peoples.
>
> (White House 1992)

US democracy assistance also expanded to include significant resources for sub-Saharan Africa, and a diversification of work in Latin America.

The language of the Freedom Support Act mirrored in many ways the language used by US policymakers at the end of the Second World War and George W. Bush's speech in 1990. The institutionalization of American liberal values in the rest of the world was good for them and good for the United States – the classic liberal position that sees mutual interest in the achievement of liberal ideals. Of course, as a number of commentators have pointed out, the commitment to political liberalism was hedged around with both a commitment to economic liberalism and an attempt to bind countries into regimes of global economic governance that generated numerous conditionalities that effectively limited the scope for domestic political and economic reform (Abrahamsen 2000). Nonetheless, it would be wrong to suggest that the United States and other western states were not serious about democracy promotion – although there were practical limits to what they could achieve. It is better to see this kind of work as a logical extension of the particular ways in which the United States understood its hegemonic ambitions.

Another classically liberal idea that gained increasing prominence during this period was human rights. Again here there are precedents in the 1980s, with the more expansive use of human rights rhetoric in American relations with the Soviet Union, although of course the idea of human rights as a matter of international concern had been around longer than that, as manifest in the UN Universal Declaration of Human Rights. Through the 1990s, however, the language of human rights became more important. Regional human rights regimes in Europe and Latin America were strengthened and human rights issues became more prominent in NGO campaigns. There were limits to what could be done but, as Rosemary Foot has shown, even such countries as China did feel pressured by the increased significance of human rights during this period (Foot 2000). In addition, the international human rights discourse expanded significantly to include new kinds of issues and new kinds of rights: indigenous peoples' rights, women's rights and even children's rights. Whether any of this really made sense is beside the point as 'rights' became a dominant language to discuss political, social and cultural questions. Even 'development' came to be talked about in terms of 'rights' (UN 1986).

Sovereignty and intervention

One very important corollary of the triumph of liberalism was a reworking and a downgrading of the norm of state sovereignty and non-intervention. This has two related aspects: first the increasingly intrusive actions of western states and other agencies and second a discursive reworking of the value of sovereignty. The promotion of democracy and of human rights, and neoliberal economic reform programmes, entailed more intrusive actions on the part of western states and international organizations, as we shall see in the next few chapters. Over this period these agents eroded the idea of a realm of 'internal affairs' over which only the domestic (sovereign) governments would have authority. These more mundane interventions were accompanied by a growth in the use of and the perceived legitimacy of (at least within the western alliance) forms of intervention – military and other – by the unipolar concert (Wheeler 2000). These are manifest most obviously in 'humanitarian' interventions in places such as Somalia and Serbia/Kosovo. They are also manifest in the rise of international administrations in places such as Cambodia, Bosnia-Herzegovina and Kosovo, themselves fundamentally shaped by the commitment to liberal political and economic thought (Chandler 1999). On top of this there were a host of other forms of interventions through peace-keeping and peace enforcement missions. The more interventionist actions of the western powers culminated in military actions in Afghanistan and Iraq (Dodge 2005, 2007). It is hard to overstate how different this was from the sovereign order, in which the western powers were constrained by the presence of the Soviet Union and other communist states, and interventions were seen as a great deal less legitimate (Wheeler 2000: part II).

Accompanying this, and in important ways providing the legitimacy for it, was a discursive reworking of sovereignty. At the most general level there is an obvious sense in which liberal values threaten the norm of sovereignty. Liberalism's theoretical universalism generates a kind of 'geographical universalism', and this cosmopolitan element of liberal thought always threatens sovereignty because in the end the achievement of liberal ends trumps the value of sovereignty. It is in this sense that Beate Jahn is right when she argues that liberal thought has always been imperialist (Jahn 2005). More specifically, during this period there emerged a new kind of discourse about sovereignty in which it is seen as conditional upon certain kinds of liberal values. This is evident in phrases such as 'sovereignty as responsibility' (ICISS 2001; Keren and Sylvan 2002). Taken together, the triumph of liberalism, the rise of interventionism and the downgrading of sovereignty provide the normative structure of the liberal order.

Conclusion: development and the global order

The project of international development did not change simply as a result of these shifts in international order. However, as with the project of international development during the sovereign order after 1945, this project was profoundly shaped by these changes. Development theory came to represent one of the best examples of the triumph of liberalism. Development agencies changed the focus of their work to reflect this and they became more unified – a kind of unipolar concert within the project of international development. And the kinds of projects development agencies funded and the kinds of relationships they established with developing countries were similarly different.

By the end of the period under consideration here the so-called 'war on terror' had emerged as a significant element of US (and more broadly western) policy. Despite the dramatic language, in fact the higher profile given to issues of terrorism, radicalization and political Islam did not change the fundamental elements of this new liberal international order and in some ways it reinforced them. It certainly consolidated the view of the developing world as a source of threat and thus as an arena for western intervention. It also increased the legitimacy and urgency of intervention (at least in the minds of western policymakers). Finally, in some respects it reinforced the liberal turn, as the ultimate solution to the problem of terrorism and fundamentalism has often been thought to be the instantiation of liberal values and practices in developing countries. As Larry Diamond put it:

> if we are serious about getting at the roots of international terrorism . . . we
> must get serious about fostering development that gives people hope and

dignity and improves the quality of their lives . . . Unless we help to develop states that collect taxes, limit corruption, control crime, enforce laws, secure property rights, provide education, attract investment and answer to their people, countries will not develop and the violent rage against the west will not subside.

(Diamond 2002: 14)

6   Development theory in the liberal order

We have already hinted at the ways in which development theory changed during the liberal international order. In this chapter we explore these changes more fully from the late 1970s through to the beginning of 2000s. Intellectually, politically, and economically these changes reflect the changing international order. They represent an obvious example of the triumph of liberalism in both its neoliberal economic and its political forms. They are shaped by the resurgent US hegemony and the end of the Cold War which provides new possibilities for more interventionist development strategies. And, finally, they are shaped by the discourse of globalization. The first part of this chapter explores what 'neoliberalism' is and what the main assumptions and arguments of neoliberal development theory were. It pays particular attention to the ways in which neoliberal development theorists understood the relationship between politics and economic development, as it is this understanding that provides the key to understanding neoliberal development theory. Neoliberalism became embodied in probably the most controversial development strategy ever undertaken – structural adjustment lending (SAL): the attempt on the part of the World Bank and the IMF to use conditional lending as a mechanism for neoliberal policy change. Despite the significance of neoliberal arguments, development theory changed through the late 1980s and 1990s. The two most important changes are first a growing concern with institutions and then good governance, which emerges very forcefully in the 1990s, and second a stress on 'participation', 'ownership' and 'partnership'. To put it rather crudely, the first of these concerns emerges out of the recognition that neoliberal reform programmes were not producing the expected economic benefits, and the second emerges out of the recognition that conditional lending was not a terribly effective way of ensuring sustainable policy reform. One final and perhaps more subtle shift takes place under the impact of 'globalization' where the standard neoliberal economic model and a concern with institutions and governance became increasingly justified on the basis that these were necessary in order for developing countries to benefit from the globalizing circuits of finance and investment.

The neoliberal 'counter-revolution'[1]

As we saw in Chapter 2, mainstream development economics was heavily influenced by Keynesian economics. However, just as Keynesian economics did not monopolize the discipline of economics (the most famous counter-example being Milton Friedman), so within the study of development there were always those who did not agree with development economics. Peter Bauer, for example, was a long-standing critic of some of the central arguments of development economics, including about the utility of state planning, the necessity of capital transfers to developing countries and the scepticism about the ability of the market mechanism to generate development (Bauer 1976, 1984). These arguments, however, remained marginal, to say the least (Desai 1982). Through the first half of the 1980s, however, what had been marginal became mainstream. Neoliberal arguments came to dominate the policy prescriptions of the World Bank and the IMF and some of the largest bilateral aid donors – particularly the United States and the UK.

Neoliberal development theory emerged in a particular set of contexts. The story here is complex but for our purposes we can identify several obvious factors. The first is the economic problems associated with the end of the 'golden age' of capitalism. In response to this there emerged an intellectual backlash against 'Keynesian' economics and its attendant policies, which led to a resurgence of neoliberal (neoclassical) economics within the discipline of economics more generally (Johnson 1971). Not only did the rise of the 'new right' in the United States and the UK give neoliberal arguments a higher political profile, but as major shareholders of the World Bank and the IMF these countries were important in shifting the intellectual foundations of these institutions (Howe 1982; Ayres 1983). In particular, A. W. Clausen, who was appointed President of the World Bank in 1981, was much more sympathetic to the arguments of neoliberalism (Clausen 1982). Finally there is the broader development context. Many developing countries experienced economic crises during the late 1970s and early 1980s, suggesting that some new kinds of policies were necessary. In addition, certainly within the World Bank, there was increasing concern that the success of individual projects was dependent upon the wider macroeconomic and political context within which they were implemented. These varied strands came together and reinforced one another to produce the neoliberal counter-revolution in development theory.

Defining neoliberalism concisely is difficult, as it has a number of elements and few of them on their own can be considered 'new' ('neo'). Nonetheless, the view taken here is that the characteristic feature of neoliberalism in the development context is the yoking together of a series of specifically economic arguments, drawn from the classical liberal tradition of economic thought, with a series of political (or political-economic) arguments into a single approach to thinking about development policy.

Main assumptions

The main assumptions of the more specifically economic element of neoliberalism are fairly easy to summarize. First, neoliberal economists often explicitly rejected the claim that the economic conditions of developing countries required a different kind of economics and reasserted what Hirschman had called the 'mono-economics claim' that 'economics consists of a number of simple, yet "powerful" theorems of universal validity' (Hirschman 1981: 374). Second, the basis of this reassertion of mono-economics was that there existed a universal economic rationality. In other words the theorems of economics were universal because the account of behaviour that underpinned these theorems was also universal. People in developing countries responded to price changes in just the same way as people in developed countries. As early as the mid-1960s T. W. Schultz famously argued that peasant families in poor countries were 'efficient but poor', and Harry Johnson argued that even the poorest producers were susceptible to price incentives (Johnson 1964; Schultz 1964; Ellis 1988: ch. 4). These arguments were taken up and generalized as one of the founding assumptions of neoliberalism in development theory. Deepak Lal, one of the most famous advocates of neoliberal development theory, argued in 1983 that 'there is by now a vast body of empirical evidence from different cultures and climates which shows that uneducated peasants act economically as producers and consumers. They respond to changes in relative process much as neo-classical economic theory predicts' (Lal 1983: 105). The key implication of this was that 'incentives' were the key driver of economic behaviour. Some of these incentives came from the broad macroeconomic environment – inflation and exchange rates, macroeconomic stability – and some from the microeconomic environment – relative prices. This claim was also important in rhetorically selling neoliberalism, as it enabled its advocates to criticize development economists and developing country governments for assuming that they knew better than the poor.

The third assumption follows from the first two. It is that markets can produce socially desirable outcomes. By responding to changes in relative prices, economic agents ensure that scarce resources are directed to producing what consumers actually want in an efficient manner. This argument applied to markets inside developing countries as well as to trade relations. Fourth, and a corollary of this, is the claim that individual economic actors have better 'knowledge' than governments and indeed 'development experts': economic knowledge (that is, knowledge of what is demanded by consumers and of what the costs of producing are) is held by individual economic agents who have a much better understanding of their local economic environment than the government could ever hope to have. As Lal put it, 'behind most arguments for government intervention, particularly those based on directly controlling quantities of goods demanded and supplied, is the implicit premise of an omniscient central authority' (Lal 1983: 74). It is this which forms the basis of the neoliberal critique of planning. Finally, and again following from this, is the claim that interventions in the operation of the market, however well intentioned, very often have socially undesirable impacts as they change the incentives facing economic agents and lead to an inefficient allocation of resources.

The basic element of the political economy of neoliberalism took the idea of economically rational actors and applied it to politicians, bureaucrats and 'interest groups'. This approach was sometimes called the 'new political-economy' and had its roots in the work of people such as Anne O. Krueger, Mancur Olson and Robert Bates (Krueger 1974; Bates 1981; Olson 1982). The basic idea was that the world of politics should be understood as composed of self-interested agents interacting with one another in an attempt to maximize their own political and economic benefits. The implication of this view of politics was first that governments (and politicians, bureaucrats and government departments) would do things that systematically benefited themselves, such as increasing their power (patronage), income or political support, and second that society was composed of 'interest groups' which were also self-seeking, concerned to maximize the benefits that flowed from the bureaucracy and the political process.

This new political economy of development was important for a number of reasons. First, it provided a way of explaining why developing-country governments had pursued what neoliberals saw as economically misguided policies: they had done so because it was economically or politically beneficial to particular groups or individual politicians. This might happen in a number of ways. One of the most important examples the new political economy gave was what Robert Bates and others identified as 'urban bias' (Bates 1981). They argued that government policies, such as price controls and high levels of taxation on agricultural products, were having a seriously detrimental affect on the agricultural sector in many developing countries. Because many of these countries relied on agricultural exports to earn foreign exchange, these policies were ultimately detrimental for the whole economy. The answer to the question of why this happened when it was economically damaging was that urban groups, which benefited from these policies (price controls on staple goods), were better organized (and thus politically more important) than rural groups. Second, these arguments implied that changing these economically damaging policies would be very difficult, as politicians and bureaucrats would be unwilling to undertake changes that would harm organized interest groups or their own political and economic interests (Toye 1992). Again as Lal put it, 'the process of gaining fiscal control by reducing public expenditure to a sustainable level, and the subsequent liberalisation program, must inevitably entail either confronting these vested interests or buying them out' (Lal 1987: 293). This was to prove very difficult, as we shall see.

An additional line of argument put forward by neoliberal political economists was supposedly more pragmatic. At the end of his polemic against development economics, Lal argued that, whatever view one took on the economic arguments for the liberalization of markets, there was, in many developing countries, a very strong practical case for reducing the scale of government intervention, which was that governments in these countries were severely lacking in the appropriate *capacity* to engage in these kinds of interventions. Worse still, they were not doing even the barest minimum required of governments at all well (Lal 1983: 108–9). He ended by quoting Keynes himself: 'but, above all, the ineptitude of public administrators strongly prejudiced the practical man in favour of *laissez-faire*' (Keynes 1926: 12). Bauer argued that there were some necessary minimum tasks any government has to undertake – foreign affairs, defence, maintaining a legal system, administration of the monetary and fiscal system – but that 'the adequate performance even of the barest minimum of these tasks would fully stretch the human, administrative and financial resources of the great majority of Third World governments' (Bauer 1984: 28). In other words, even if there was a case for extensive government intervention (which such economists obviously thought there was not) governments in development countries lacked the capacity to undertake it all effectively; and attempts to do so distracted governments from the performance of more important basic tasks. In this view an imperfect market was preferable to imperfect planning (Lal 1983: 106).

Taken together these three lines of argument (from economic theory, from political economy and in terms of capacity) add up to a substantial attack on the role of the state in the process of economic development: that government intervention was unnecessary and counter-productive, that it was self-serving, and that in any case governments were incapable of doing it at all effectively.

The argument against price controls

One can get a better sense of the logic (and, up to a point, the persuasiveness) of neoliberalism by looking at some of the specific arguments neoliberal development theorists made. First, consider the argument against price controls. Price controls might be enacted for a number of reasons: as a genuinely well-intentioned attempt to ensure access to staple goods or as a result of the self-interested actions of politicians, bureaucrats and interest groups. Whatever the reason, neoliberals argued that price controls had a number of damaging effects. If the set price was below the price that would exist in a free market, a number of things would happen. Initially this would lead to a reduction in supply, as the producers (being economically rational) produce less, leading to shortages. To counter this situation, the government may make up the difference between the set price and the market price by paying a subsidy to producers. This might maintain supply (assuming the subsidy can be administered effectively) but only at the costs of a drain on the scarce fiscal resources of the state (which might be spent on other things). At the same time, and inevitably according to neoliberalism, a black market would develop as some people are willing to pay a price above that set by the government (and producers would be willing to sell at a higher price). This is likely to be especially acute if there are shortages of supply. In other words, producers, and those consumers who can afford to pay, circumvent the price controls by operating in the black market. In some circumstance producers may also sell in neighbouring countries if the price is high enough – further exacerbating shortages. This in turn reduces government tax revenues. The government may try to counter this situation by rationing access to staple goods. However, this only creates further opportunities for black market and corrupt activities, as an illicit market for ration coupons develops which creates a significant rent-seeking opportunity (buy ration coupons at the government-controlled price and sell at the black market price). None of the outcomes of price controls has the desired effect of maintaining access to staple goods; indeed they are likely to make matters worse for the poorer groups as they experience shortages and do not have the resources to operate in the black market.

In addition, they encourage black market and corrupt activities and are a drain on the resources of the state.

Arguments against trade restrictions

As we saw in Chapter 2, development economics argued that restrictions on trade were necessary as part of an ISI strategy. These restrictions might come in a number of forms, but often involved direct quotas on imported goods, taxes on imports (to make them uncompetitive) or other forms of licensing arrangements. This, so the argument went, would protect infant industries while they were developing, perhaps with the assistance of government subsidies or government-directed investment. The neoliberal case against these policies relied on the view that a liberalized trade environment will lead to a more efficient allocation of resources and, ultimately, economic growth; or at least that the economic outcomes based on liberalizing trade are likely to be better than those where trade is controlled (Lal 1983: ch. 2). According to neoliberal arguments, attempts to restrict imports are likely to suffer from some of the same problems associated with price controls. The fact that imports have to be restricted means that there is a market for these goods, which in turn means that a black market for these goods is likely to develop. Licensing arrangements, the granting of rights to import certain goods, lead to competition for these licences, often resulting in the bribing of those officials who have the power to grant the licence (and of course who have an economic and/or political interest in having the ability to grant licences). In addition, the subsidizing of domestic industries is an inefficient use of scarce government resources (the goods can be imported and are likely to be sold at a price below that of the domestically produced good) and in any case is often determined more by political than by economic considerations.

The problems associated with direct control of imports were compounded, so the argument went, in a situation in which foreign exchange earnings were declining and exchange rates were fixed at an artificially high level. Exchange rate controls created a black market for the currency as foreign exchange became increasingly scarce. In the most egregious cases this led to significant forms of corrupt activities where there would be two prices for imported goods: an official price and a black market price. Access to import licences would then give an opportunity to exploit these differences (by importing at the official price, but selling at the black market prices) to those with enough money or political connections to gain access to the licences (Jeffries 1989).

Policy prescriptions

These kinds of arguments were translated directly into policy in the form of SAL. We will look in more detail at specific structural adjustment programmes in Chapter 8, but it is important to note that turning neoliberalism into development policy had two parts. The first comprised a series of policy prescriptions including the liberalization of domestic markets by reducing price controls and allowing competition; the privatization of state-owned enterprises; reducing government expenditures; ensuring macroeconomic stability, particularly reducing inflation and government deficits; and liberalizing external trade by ending exchange rate controls and import controls. Second, and crucially, structural adjustment used *conditional lending*, meaning that further tranches of support were supposed to be conditional on developing countries actually implementing the policy changes. This was thought necessary, in part, of course, to overcome the resistance to policy change that neoliberal political economy predicted. This is a clear example within the project of international development of the unravelling of the sovereign order.

Good governance

The basic idea that markets can deliver benefits and that policy reform was necessary to achieve these benefits remained central to development theory through the 1990s and beyond (Craig and Porter 2006). To this, however, was added other sets of concerns. The first can be captured under the label of 'good governance', although this rather protean term incorporates a number of different elements. The first is a concern rather narrowly with the role of institutions in development that emerged in the second half of the 1980s. The second is the more formal policy of 'good governance' that emerged first out of the World Bank in 1989 and was subsequently adopted by all development agencies. This incorporated the concern with institutions, but also included more obviously political elements such as accountability, transparency and a concern with 'civil society'. The third is a concern explicitly with democracy promotion and issues such as human rights.

The concern with the role of institutions in development emerged out of what became known as new institutional economics (NIE), associated with economists such as Douglass North and Oliver Williamson. North argued that NIE remained firmly within the neoclassical school of economics by accepting the argument that actors respond in rational ways to the incentives they face (North 1990: 5). What made NIE different was the recognition that institutions, and not just prices, created incentives. Institutions were considered in broad terms to include formal institutions and organizations, as well as unwritten rules, norms and obligations (North 1990: 304). An important concept within this work was that of 'transaction costs' (Williamson 1979). The essential insight of NIE was that economic transactions may be made more or less risky or more or less costly, depending on a host of broader institutional factors, such as how well contracts are enforced by the legal system, how easy it is to access credible information and how efficient the banking system is.

The translation of this into development thinking suggested that, in order for a market economy to work efficiently and produce the expected benefits, attention had to be paid to these institutional factors (Bates 1989). In other words, it was not enough simply to liberalize an economy; it was also necessary that the relevant institutions be constructed that would ease transactions costs for economic agents. These included the legal system, and especially contract enforcement and property rights, the banking system, the broader regulatory system and information provision systems. In turn, of course, this entailed a renewed concern with the role of the state, as it was the state which provided or created these institutions. The emergence and increasing influence of NIE within development theory coincided with a growing awareness that structural adjustment was not really producing the expected benefits. Part of this was to do with implementation, which we will discuss below. However, even when countries did implement adjustment programmes, it was becoming clear that the expected improvements in investment, productivity, output and growth were very slow in coming (World Bank 1994a). The World Bank in particular began to argue that a major reason for the poor private sector response to adjustment was the institutional environment, and given this it began to take these institutional issues more seriously.

This concern with institutions was incorporated into a much more comprehensive set of political and social concerns: good governance. The term emerged specifically out of the World Bank's analysis of the problems facing African states in *Sub-Saharan Africa: From Crisis to Sustainable Growth* (World Bank 1989b). The report argued that 'underlying the litany of Africa's development problems was a crisis of governance' (World Bank 1989b: 60). 'Ultimately, better governance requires political renewal . . . This can be done . . . by strengthening accountability, by encouraging public debate and by nurturing a free press' (World Bank 1989b: 6). In other words, significant political change was necessary for development to succeed. In some ways it is unsurprising that the term 'good governance' first emerged in the context of African development. The region had been experiencing a major development crisis since the end of the 1970s. Per capita food production in the region was lower in 1989 than it had been in 1980, export volumes had declined, external debt was rising and investment rates had fallen by 25 per cent (World Bank 1989b: 17–25). At the same time, while the World Bank had doubled its lending to the region, fewer than 50 per cent of all Bank projects undertaken in the region were rated as 'satisfactory' in terms of development outcomes (World Bank 1994a: 70). The problem was summed up by a senior World Bank staffer: 'traditional recipes are certainly not working as effectively as we expected. Whether it is structural adjustment or institutional development, somehow things are not jelling adequately' (Agarwala 1990: 51). Good governance was the Bank's answer to this problem.

It is easy to forget that when the idea was first proposed it was highly controversial, inside and outside the World Bank (Williams 2008a: 76–81). There were concerns about the Bank's knowledge and expertise in these areas and concerns about the extent to which the Bank's mandate allowed it to take political factors into consideration in its lending. Article IV(10) of the Bank's Articles of Agreement explicitly states that the 'Bank and its officers shall not interfere in the political affairs of any of its members'. In terms of the interpretation of the Bank's mandate the concern with good governance was glossed by saying that where political matters had significant direct economic effects they could be taken into consideration (Shihata 1991: 57). However, we should read into this the way in which the changing international order was redefining the boundaries of legitimate intervention.

Just as the Bank was developing the idea of good governance so the Cold War was ending, and certainly among bilateral aid donors any previous reticence they had about taking politics seriously in their relations with developing states was swept aside. Good governance became universally accepted as essential for development. Indeed, many of these bilateral donors went even further than the World Bank and started to argue that not just better governance but democracy and respect for human rights was a necessary part of development success (Carothers 1994). One of the striking things about this is how quickly other western donors embraced this language. In 1990 the British Foreign Secretary said that Britain would support those countries that 'tend towards political pluralism, respect for the rule of law, human rights and market principles' (Hurd 1990). In the same year François Mitterand said that France would link its aid to efforts designed to lead to greater liberty and democracy (Mitterand 1990). In 1991 USAID said that it would support the strengthening of democratic representation, support the participation of citizens in the political process, support the promotion of human rights and encourage 'democratic values' (USAID 1991). In a short period of time there emerged a remarkable new consensus among western development agencies about the importance of good governance and, at least among the bilateral donors, democracy and human rights. It is hard not to see the importance of the end of the Cold War and the more general triumph of liberalism here.

Main assumptions

The first main assumption behind the concern with good governance follows the same logic as that of NIE: that an 'enabling environment' for the private sector must be created which provides stability and reduces transactions costs. The logic is that private sector actors, whether they are domestic entrepreneurs or foreign investors, need to be encouraged to invest (World Bank 1991). Second, in order for the state to provide the necessary institutional and macroeconomic environment, it must be made accountable for its actions (left to their own devices politicians will not do it). This has two elements. On the one hand the state's activities must be made as transparent as possible through various information provision services and encouraging a free press and public debates. On the other hand 'civil society' groups must be 'empowered' so that they can play a key role in pressuring the state for better performance. An additional part of holding the state accountable is to decentralize administration in order to make a more direct connection between the state and its citizens. In this way pressure can be brought to bear on the state to deliver the necessary institutions and macroeconomic environment.

In terms of democracy promotion and human rights a number of arguments were at work (Carothers 1999: 56–8). The first is that liberal economics and democratic politics are mutually reinforcing: without democratic politics, market economics are threatened, and without liberal economics the promises of democracy cannot be fulfilled. Second, as the quote from Larry Diamond at the end of the last chapter indicates, democracy and the protection of human rights were thought be associated with a government's legitimacy and hence political stability. Third, there was a more general argument that democracy was associated with international peace. This was formalized within the discipline of International Relations through the so-called 'Democratic Peace Theory', which said that democracies were less likely to go to war with one another (M. Brown *et al.* 1996). Finally, we should not underestimate the more ideological reasons behind a concern with democracy promotion and human rights. Even if we are sceptical about the ability of western states to promote them effectively, and even if we know that these commitments have been hedged around by all kinds of other concerns, there seems little reason to doubt that many western policymakers believed that democracy and human rights were important regardless of whatever pragmatic reasons there may have been for promoting them.

Governance and 'globalization'

Through the second half of the 1990s and into the 2000s there was a subtle reworking of some of the arguments of good governance under the influence of the discourse surrounding 'globalization'. Dani Rodrik has argued that there 'emerged a tendency to view development – and the institutional reform needed to spark and sustain it – almost exclusively from the perspective of integration into the world economy' (Rodrik 2000: 1). He quotes Stanley Fisher, then head of the IMF, who said that 'integration to the world economy is the best way for countries to grow' (quoted in Rodrik 2000: 1). That is, the governance frameworks of developing countries were to be assessed on the basis of whether they helped or hindered the process of integrating into the globalizing economy. This kind of argument relied on the idea of 'investor confidence' on the basis that foreign investors were more likely to be attracted to states which had better governance (Rodrik 2001). It also relied on the idea that attracting foreign capital and engaging in international trade could be 'engines' of growth, to use an older phrase. Although this kind of argument was rather short-lived – collapsing in the 2008 financial crisis – it did have an impact on the ways in which development agencies pursued and justified their development programmes. It manifested itself most obviously in a concern with standards of regulation whereby developing countries would be pushed to adopt international standards for regulating banking, accounting, trade and insurance, for example, regardless of whether these were really developmentally justified, and regardless of the obvious inequalities in such an agenda – liberalizing agriculture in developing countries while protecting it in western states (Rodrik 2000, 2002). It is clear too, though, how influenced all this was by the international order of the time, in which the supposed benefits of globalization were extolled by many policymakers.

Participation, ownership and poverty reduction

As we noted above, structural adjustment had two components: a series of policy reforms and the use of conditional lending to get those reforms enacted. The broad set of issues captured under the label 'good governance' expanded the scope of the policy reforms that were deemed important for development, but it did not offer any new way of getting this expanded list of policy reforms actually enacted. Through the late 1990s and into the 2000s a new way of thinking about the relationship between development agencies and developing states emerged, utilizing the language of 'participation', 'ownership' and 'partnership' in place of conditionality. Indeed, by 2004 the DfID argued that 'it was necessary to move away from traditional approaches to conditionality', and that it was 'ineffective and inappropriate to impose policies on developing countries' (DfID 2004: 3). Even the World Bank was arguing that 'good practice' meant focusing on 'country ownership' rather than conditionality (World Bank 2005b: 11).

The stress on a new form of relationship with developing countries arose for at least three reasons. The most important was that conditionality as utilized in SAL was not a very effective mechanism for inducing policy reform. One analysis of World Bank conditionality in the 1980s found that on average only 55 per cent of policy conditions were ever implemented (Mosley *et al.* 1991: 136). DfID concluded that, 'in many cases, developing countries have not kept to the conditions they signed up to' and that, 'put simply, "conditionality" that attempts to "buy" reform from an unwilling partner has rarely worked' (DfID 2004: 4). The logic of conditional lending was that it would counter the incentives politicians and bureaucrats would have for not changing policy (owing to their own economic and political interests) by offering access to additional aid resources or threatening to end support. In reality, however, conditionality did not work like this. Borrowers became adept at working the system, delaying or fudging implementation of policy reforms, and the donors very rarely cut off additional tranches of an adjustment loan even when borrowers were making slow progress (Mosley *et al.* 1991: 166). Second, donors had few mechanisms for ensuring that policy changes were maintained once an adjustment loan had been fully dispersed. Third, and very importantly, governments that did not implement loan conditions almost always had access to further loans (Johnson and Wasty 1993). This is partly explained by the fourth factor, which was to do with the donor institutions themselves, which were unable or unwilling to police their own enforcement of supposedly conditional lending. This was especially the case with the World Bank, where promotion to senior management positions often depended in some part on how much money staff managed to lend (Portfolio Management Task Force 1992; Naim 1994). Thus staff had a strong incentive to keep lending to countries even when they did not implement the conditions of previous loans. This suggests that the common account of SAL, that it was a matter of donors imposing their conditions on developing countries, is only half-true and that in fact donors had nowhere near as much power over recipients as has sometimes been suggested.

A second reason for the emergence of a new language of donor–recipient relationship was that conditionality was becoming increasingly illegitimate (Collingwood 2003). Certainly it was very controversial and garnered a huge amount of criticism from borrower government and campaigning groups. More generally during the 1980s and 1990s donors such as the World Bank and the IMF came under attack for a host of issues such as their environmental record and their treatment of indigenous groups. In this context there were good reasons to embrace a new language of partnership and ownership. A third factor has to do with the deepening of donor–recipient relationships in the context of the end of the Cold War and the emergence of what Graham Harrison (2004) has called 'governance states'. In many developing countries donors had developed long-standing and extensive relations with recipient governments. They become enmeshed in all areas of economic life, and increasingly with good governance, politics and social life. The end of the Cold War took the heat out of the older ideological divides and the triumph of liberalism led in some states to an increasing ideological convergence between donors and recipient governments. In this context a new aid relationship was possible because donors no longer had to force states to adopt policy reforms in the way they felt they had to in the 1980s.

At the country level this new concern manifested itself most significantly in the Poverty Reduction Strategy Paper (PRSP) process initiated by the World Bank and the IMF in 1999 (Craig and Porter 2003). The idea behind this was that governments would develop a poverty reduction strategy in consultation with civil society groups. Governments needed to show that they had consulted widely not just in terms of assessing the prevalence of poverty, but also in terms of what the most appropriate policies and programmes might be for alleviating poverty. The concern with participation and ownership emerged at the project level too. Just as structural adjustment often failed, so many projects funded by donors also did not deliver their expected benefits and/or were not sustainable. The evaluation arm of the World Bank argued that there was a significant correlation between the extent of beneficiary participation and ownership and project success (World Bank 1994a, 1995b).

This new stress on participation and ownership was underpinned by several arguments. At both the country level and project level the first argument was simply that it would lead to better-designed development programmes. If the participation of governments and affected groups in the design of development projects and programmes were elicited, then such projects were more likely to be better suited to conditions on the ground. Second, it was seen as a way of generating commitment on the part of governments and project beneficiaries. 'Stakeholders', beneficiaries and local communities should be brought into the project design and implementation process and this would generate 'ownership', which would in turn lead to better and more sustainable project outcomes. This idea was not a new one within the wider development community, but it did signal a departure from the traditional 'top-down' approach to development projects that had characterized the major aid agencies. At the country level the concern with participation and ownership was also a way of disciplining governments (Abrahamsen 2000). Governments would be held to account for their performance in implementing development strategies they themselves had 'ownership' of (they could no longer say that it was all imposed from outside). Finally, for the PRSP process it was also a way of disciplining the donors themselves. Donors would sign up to support a poverty reduction strategy and agree to coordinate their assistance to countries within this strategy.

The explicit focus of the PRSP process was on poverty reduction and the end product of the process was a strategy to tackle poverty within the country. What made it innovative was the 'participatory' way this strategy was to be developed. However, the PRSP process was only one example of the ways in which an explicit concern with poverty reduction became a renewed concern of development thinking. It might seem odd to suggest that this was 'new', given that one of the most obvious justifications for the project of international development is reducing poverty, but during the 1980s explicit targeting of poverty reduction took a back seat to the necessity of economic policy reform. In another sign that structural adjustment was not really delivering, the World Bank started in the first half of the 1990s to undertake explicit Poverty Assessments. These were attempts to map and measure poverty rates within countries, to assess the particular causes of poverty, and then to provide the basis for development strategies to deal with it. By the mid-1990s these had been renamed Participatory Poverty Assessments and utilized consultation with NGOs and community groups with a view to giving the poor a 'voice' (Narayan 2000). This in turn fed into the PRSP process.

The explicit concern with poverty found its ultimate expression in the United Nations Millennium Development Goals (MDGs). These were a series of development targets established in 2000 and included such things as halving by 2014 the proportion of people living in absolute poverty (defined as living on less than one dollar a day); ensuring universal primary education; reducing by two-thirds child mortality rates; reducing maternal mortality by three-quarters; and halving the proportion of people without access to clear drinking water. In addition to these more specific targets there were more general commitments to 'integrating the principle of sustainable development' into development strategies, and developing a global partnership for development. What makes the MDGs remarkable is not so much their content as the fact there was an immediate political consensus among almost all states and development agencies about the desirability of these goals (Fukado-Parr 2004).

Conclusion: development theory and the liberal order

In some ways development theory had come a long way since the neoliberal counter-revolution of the early 1980s. The stress on conditionality had given way to a new stress on participation and ownership, the stress on economic policy reform had been joined by a concern with good governance and democracy, and poverty reduction had re-emerged as an explicit focus of international attention. Some of this is explained by the reflexivity that forms part of the project of international development, as development agencies 'learned' from previous failures and searched for new ways of pursuing development. Nonetheless, it is also clear how indebted all this is to the broader changes associated with the emergence of the liberal international order: the triumph of liberalism, the end of the Cold War, the end of political pluralism, globalization and intervention.

There is, however, a series of tensions here. There is no very good reason to think that all by itself democracy will lead to better governance (Dunn 1989).

This is one reason why the World Bank itself has been reluctant to embrace the language of democracy. Second, the new stress on ownership and partnership sits in obvious tension with the reality of the often overwhelming presence of external agencies in many developing countries. In the face of extensive reliance on foreign aid it is not clear what 'country ownership' can mean. Third, and related, the new stress on participation and ownership sits uneasily with the fact that western donors still maintain that they have privileged insight into the problems facing developing countries. It is no coincidence that most PRSPs largely reflect the particular policy concerns of the major western donors. Fourth, there are obvious tensions between 'participation', 'ownership' and democracy, and a development strategy of integrating into the globalizing economy which relies precisely on taking significant areas of political and economic life out of the process of democratic decision making so as to satisfy the demands of global capital.

Finally, there is a tension between poverty alleviation and 'development' itself. As Thandika Mkandawire has argued:

> with respect to Africa at least, 'development' is being watered down to poverty reduction and social policy's narrow concern is social protection without the transformative attributes that have been so central to successful development. And so although poverty is now discussed in the context of governance, economic growth, stabilization and security, there appears to be no coherent and consistent framework that ties these together in a developmental way.
>
> (Mkandawire 2007: 9)

In other words, the vision of social transformation to something like modernity that underpinned earlier development theory fell away, and in its place came a host of very possibly laudable objectives that do not add up to anything like 'development' in this older sense. Part of the explanation for this is the very real sense of developmental crisis in the poorest states, particularly in Africa, where anything like a social transformation to modernity seems a very long way off. As 'development' then becomes increasingly hard to imagine for these states, so in its place has come a stress on social protection and poverty alleviation. It might be argued that these are more manageable tasks but, even if they are, they do not amount to anything people used to call development. The stress on good governance, democracy and human rights, again however laudable they may be, is not buttressed by an account of the social and ideological transformations that have enabled these projects in many now developed states.

7 Development institutions in the liberal order

Introduction

Chapter 3 examined the origins and operations of development agencies during the sovereign order. This chapter traces how the institutions of the project of international development changed during the emergence and consolidation of the liberal order. In many ways the project of international development became more important during this period. This can be seen with the significant rise in aid provision over the period, particularly to the world's poorest states, and the increased importance of development within the foreign polices of many western states. The development agenda of most agencies also expanded to include new kinds of issues, such as combating HIV/Aids, and environmental protection, and the pursuit of 'development' became wrapped up with other kinds of international projects such as state building, peace building and post-conflict reconstruction. Second, this period witnessed a dramatic expansion in the role of non-governmental organizations (NGOs) in the project of international development. Third, this period saw the growth of a more integrated 'development community' in terms of policy convergence and the emergence of more coordinated relations *between* development agencies, both in general and in terms of their relations with developing countries, expressed most emblematically in the PRSP process.

For all of the agencies we examine in this chapter there are particular domestic political issues that shape what they do and how their aid programmes develop. In addition, as we have noted several times before, there is a process of 'learning' within the project of international development, and it is this that partly accounts for the rise of NGOs within development and for some of the changes in relations between development agencies. However, the changes within and between the institutions involved in the project of international development should also be understood in terms of the ways in which this project was shaped by the liberal international order. In this order 'development' becomes seen as an even more important instrument of US, and more generally western, hegemony. This was particularly the case with Britain and the United States, in both of which countries 'development' was used to pursue a host of new foreign policy objectives that were themselves made increasingly possible by the end of the Cold War. Second, the growing significance of NGOs within the project of international development was shaped by the ideological changes associated with the triumph of liberalism and the erosion of the norm of non-intervention. Third, the emergence of a more tightly integrated 'development community' was an obvious manifestation of the rise of the 'unipolar concert' more generally.

Bilateral agencies

Total bilateral aid rose steadily from the mid-1980s to the early 1990s, when it started to decline, but it rose rapidly from the early 2000s (Figure 7.1). When we look at individual donors we will see that this is a common pattern. An examination of the changing regional allocation of aid reveals a rapid rise in aid to both sub-Saharan Africa and, as a result of the invasion of Afghanistan and Iraq, the Middle East (Figure 7.2). This shows that aid and development became bound up with these larger international-political projects in a way that is not perhaps surprising, but is certainly revealing. 'Development' had come to play an important legitimizing function in the increasingly interventionist liberal order, and development had come to be seen as an important tool for dealing with the 'problems' or 'threats' that were increasingly understood to come from developing countries.

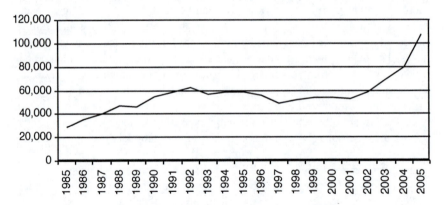

Figure 7.1 Total OECD DAC bilateral aid disbursements, 1985–2005 (US$ millions at current prices). Source: OECD.

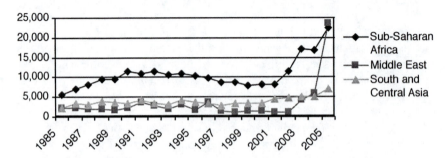

Figure 7.2 OECD DAC bilateral aid to selected regions, 1985–2005 (US$ millions at current prices). Source: OECD.

Neither of these was exactly new: since 1945 development had been wrapped up with security concerns and certainly during the Cold War the idea of 'development' was an important part of the United States' promise to help countries steer a path between colonialism and communism. However, in the liberal order these connections are amplified and 'development' became even more central to the project of western hegemony.

The United States

US bilateral aid had started to rise under the Reagan administration. Part of this was driven by more the confrontational stance the United States was taking towards communism. Aid to Central America and the Caribbean, for example, quadrupled during the 1980s in the context of Cold War-related conflicts in Nicaragua and El Salvador. However, there was also at least some humanitarian impulse at work – as witnessed by the increase in aid to states in sub-Saharan Africa partly inspired by the Ethiopian famine. Overall, US bilateral aid grew 30 per cent between 1980 and 1989 (Lancaster 2007: 82). The period from 1989 to the mid-2000s was a turbulent one for US aid with the emergence of a host of new initiatives and programmes, fluctuating aid volumes, and continued domestic political opposition. Nonetheless, by the end of the period under discussion here – the mid-2000s – US aid had nearly doubled from its level in 1989.

One new concern after 1989 was assistance to the states of Central and Eastern Europe (and then the states of the former Soviet Union) to help their political and economic 'transition' to liberal economic and political systems. We noted in Chapter 5 how the United States moved quickly to support these states, and through the first half of the 1990s aid to these states grew rapidly, particularly to support the institutionalization of democratic government. Total aid to these states rose to over US$2,500 million in 1994 and the democracy assistance programme was six times as big in 1994 as it was in 1991 (Lancaster 2007: 84; Carothers 1999: 50). Although there were specific reasons to support these particular states, including extending the United States' hegemonic reach into these new geographical areas, democracy promotion became a significant part of the US aid programme more generally during this period. Total democracy assistance aid rose from $165 million in 1991 to $435 million in 1995, and aid for democracy in sub-Saharan Africa tripled over the same period (Carothers 1999: 50–2). It covered a whole range of activities from supporting elections, political parties and civil society to legal reform. A second set of new concerns for US aid came in the area of civil wars and peace building. In 1994 USAID created a new office specifically designed to respond to conflict situations, and the United States provided aid to numerous post-conflict states, including of course in the Balkans, but also Haiti, Sierra Leone, Liberia, Colombia and Angola (Lancaster 2007: 85). Into the early 2000s this form of assistance became more high-profile in the context of conflict in Afghanistan and Iraq.

These new concerns show the ways in which the US aid programme was being used more and more as an instrument for the pursuit of all kinds of objectives related to the United States' hegemonic project. In all of these issues the same kinds of arguments were made linking aid, development, security and prosperity. At the same time, however, there were a series of domestic pressures on the US aid programme (Lancaster 2007: 85–90). The end of the Cold War had eliminated one rationale for foreign aid and emboldened some of its critics, particularly in Congress. There was also a desire on the part of the Clinton administration to cut the federal budget deficit (a legacy of Reagan) and in this context the aid budget was vulnerable. Added to this, the Republicans seized control of Congress in 1994 for the first time in 40 years. These pressures had several effects. The first was a quite significant cut in US aid provision: total aid fell from $12 billion in 1993 to $9 billion in 1996. The second was increasing Congressional direction of aid monies whereby specific allocations would be written into legislation relating to foreign aid. Third, there was an on-going attempt to get USAID merged into the State Department. The merger was successfully resisted by USAID, but there is no doubt that the mid-1990s was a time of crisis in the US aid programme, not as a result of any questioning of its utility as an instrument of US foreign policy on the part of the administration, but rather as a result of domestic political changes.

By the end of the 1990s foreign aid was again rising, but it was not until the new Bush administration that there was a really dramatic increase in US aid, so much so that the US aid budget more than doubled from 2002 to 2006 (Figure 7.3). It has sometimes been remarked that this increase in aid was a surprise coming from a Republican president (Radelet 2003a). However, in many ways it was not. Part of it is obviously explained by Afghanistan and Iraq (and Pakistan), but there are other factors at work too. First was the reorientation of the US national security strategy towards seeing developing countries as a source of 'threats' to the United States (White House 2002). Second, there was a renewed stress on the developmental aspects of US aid provision, notably through the Millennium Challenge

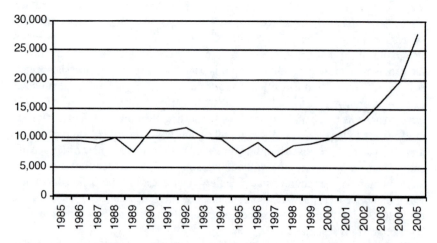

Figure 7.3 US bilateral aid disbursements, 1985–2005 (US$ millions at current prices). Source: OECD.

Account (MCA) announced in March 2001 (Radelet 2003a,b). This was to provide $5 billion a year to a select group of low-income states that were 'ruling justly, investing in their people and establishing economic freedom' (quoted in Radelet 2003b: 171). The MCA involved 16 specific indicators including controlling corruption, respect for political rights, primary education spending, inflation and trade policy. It was, according to George Bush Jr, 'a new compact for global development, defined by new accountability for both rich and poor nations alike' (quoted in Lancaster 2007: 91). It is probably the most significant innovation in US aid provision since the creation of USAID and it is important to note that it is exactly developmental in purpose and targeted at poorer states. Finally, there was a marked increase in aid specifically directed at HIV/Aids prevention and treatment. In 2004 USAID produced a policy paper that illustrates where US aid policy had got to. It announced that the goal of US aid was not simply raising living standards, but 'transformational development': 'Far-reaching, fundamental changes in institutions of governance, human capacity, and economic structure that enable a country to sustain further economic and social progress without depending on aid'. In addition, the paper identified four specific goals for US aid: strengthening fragile states, responding to humanitarian crises, supporting US strategic interests and managing global problems (USAID 2004). Given its hegemonic role this is just what we would expect and it shows that, despite the rough time that US aid had in domestic politics, it remained a fundamental component of US foreign policy.

Japan

Japan was the largest aid donor in dollar terms all through the 1990s. This position was the result of the reduction in US aid provision and a deliberate strategy to become an 'aid great power' or an 'aid superpower' (Yasutomo 1989; Lancaster 2007: ch. 4). Its aid budget doubled through the second half of the 1980s and continued to rise rapidly through the first half of the 1990s. In the second half of the 1990s and into the 2000s its aid budget declined as a result of on-going financial and economic crisis (Figure 7.4).

The growth of Japan's aid programme can be seen in part as a continuation of the developments in Japanese aid policy examined in Chapter 3. Japan's aid programme had changed from being regionally focused and commercially driven to one that was global and more 'developmental'. These trends continued, propelled by a more activist foreign policy announced in 1988 as an 'international cooperation initiative' (Yasutomo 1989: 491). This was made possible by Japan's position as the largest creditor nation in the world, and indicated a desire to move away from what had been a rather passive foreign policy ethos. This new activism manifested itself in taking a larger role in UN peacekeeping activities, for example, but it was in the area of international development that Japan most thoroughly pursued this. This was one area where Japan could act without creating anti-Japanese sentiment, and aid provision remained domestically popular (Yasutomo 1989). It was as part of this that Japan's aid budget grew so rapidly,

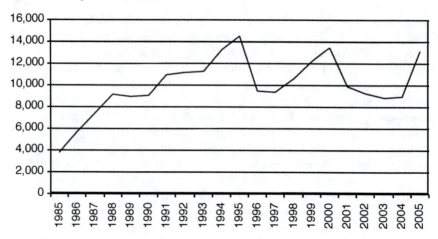

Figure 7.4 Japanese bilateral aid disbursements, 1985–2005 (US$ millions at current prices). Source: OECD.

but it also involved greater engagement with international development agencies, particularly the World Bank, and at times a more assertive (although not exactly confrontational) stance towards other western donors. This can be seen particularly with the pressure the Japanese brought to bear on the World Bank to undertake a study into the development success of East Asia, where, as the Japanese saw it, success had come by pursuing policies at odds with the neoliberalism that dominated these institutions (OECF 1991; World Bank 1993b; Wade 1996). The Japanese were also more assertive within the AsDB, where they also questioned the United States' commitment to neoliberal-style development strategies for the region (Wan 1995: 522–6).

Despite these kinds of differences, Japanese aid policy started more and more to reflect the new consensus that emerged in the first half of the 1990s about the importance of governance, human rights and democracy. The 1992 Official Development Assistance Charter spelled out the objectives of Japanese aid. It said that Japan provided aid because of a humanitarian concern for the poor, to strengthen international interdependence, and to further self-reliance. The Charter also stated that Japan would consider aid recipients' military spending in its aid allocation and that attention would be paid to promoting democracy, a market-orientated economy and the securing of basic human rights and freedoms (Lancaster 2007: 123–4). In 2003 the Charter was revised to include a stress on human security as a guiding principle of Japanese aid, as well as poverty reduction, peace building and 'addressing global issues' such as terrorism, infectious diseases, international crime and environmental protection. It also stated that 'Japan will give priority to assisting developing countries that make active efforts to pursue peace, democratization, and the protection of human rights as well as structural reform in the economic and social spheres' (MOFA 2003). Japanese aid remained institutionally fragmented through this period. In the context of the financial and economic crisis of the 1990s and beyond there was also more debate about the role and organization of Japanese aid than ever before (Sunaga 2004). Nonetheless, Japan remained one of the largest aid donors in the world through the first half of the 2000s and, as we have seen, whatever disagreements it may have had with some of the development polices being pursued by other big donors and the World Bank it also fully embraced the new development language of governance, rights and democracy.

France

It was argued in Chapter 3 that in many ways French development aid was different from that of the other major bilateral donors. It was heavily concentrated in its ex-colonies in sub-Saharan Africa, and it was based on a highly personalized set of relationships between French and African political and economic elites, often driven by political and economic interests. These features of the French aid programme were increasingly at odds with the new development agenda of good governance and democracy promotion, and with the emergence of more formalized mechanisms of cooperation between western donors. This, combined with a series of problems in French-speaking Africa, resulted a major crisis of French aid policy in the mid-1990s and an attempt to rework its institutional structure and its policy direction, although it is unclear quite how much has really changed in French aid policy as a result of this.

The first half of the 1990s was a torrid time for French aid and for France's relations with its African client states. Many of these states were experiencing the same kind of prolonged economic crisis that was afflicting other African states, but as France was the largest aid provider for most of them it clearly called into question the developmental effectiveness of French aid, as well as leading to increasing demands for French foreign aid to these states. This in turn had two important consequences. In 1993 France announced that for the first time it would refuse balance of payments support to francophone African states unless they fulfilled the terms of their agreements with the IMF and the World Bank (Cumming 1995: 390). Second, in 1994 France agreed to a 50 per cent devaluation in the CFA (Communauté Financière Africaine) franc (Chafer 2002: 4). This was a radical departure in French African policy as the CFA franc had been held at a fixed level since 1948, but the continued overvaluation of the CFA franc made exports from CFA-zone countries uncompetitive, thus putting further pressure on their balance of payments and thus putting further pressure on the French aid budget. These economic problems were compounded by the crisis in Rwanda and its aftermath, which saw the French supporting the Hutu-dominated government in the run-up to the mass killing of the Tutsi population, then intervening militarily to try (unsuccessfully) to defend the government against the Rwandan Patriotic Front. Finally, as a direct result of the crisis in Rwanda, one of France's long-time allies, President Mobutu of Zaire, was forced out (Renou 2002: 12–13).

Beyond this series of economic and political crises the ways in which French aid was managed and distributed came under increasing scrutiny. There was a growing public perception inside France that French aid was being used to prop up African dictators and enrich elements of the French political and economic elite. A series of corruption scandals involving French companies in Africa served to further heighten the sense that French aid was out of line with that of the rest of the donor community. Finally, there were budgetary pressures on French aid as it attempted to cut its government deficit to the 3 per cent of GNP required by the Maastricht agreement in preparation for European Monetary Union (Lancaster 2007: 157). This generalized crisis in French aid can be seen clearly in declining aid volumes in the second half of the 1990s (Figure 7.5).

In the late 1990s there was a concerted attempt to reform French aid. Most significant among the changes were the dismantling of the Ministry of Cooperation, which had been the central agency in managing relations with its ex-colonies, the establishment of an Interministerial Committee to oversee the management and implementation of French aid policy, and the establishment of the High Council for International Cooperation, composed of parliamentarians and representatives of NGOs, business groups and research institutions tasked with advising the government on aid policy. There are doubts about the extent to which these reforms have radically improved the coherence, transparency and effectiveness of French aid, and the OECD has remained critical of some aspects of French aid policy (OECD 2004; Lancaster 2007: 159–61). Nonetheless, and perhaps rather reluctantly, French aid policy has fallen more in line with the ideas and practices of other aid donors. Although its support for democracy has been hedged by other commitments that derive from the continuing personalized character of relations with African states, it did start to reduce its aid to some of the autocratic regimes it had previously supported, and in addition France has (again perhaps rather reluctantly) participated in the PRSP process. In this way it has taken some tentative steps towards being a more 'normal' western donor.

The United Kingdom

Britain's foreign aid programme during this period is marked by a number of important changes. The most important was the creation of a new ministry in 1997, the Department for International Development (DfID), out of the ODA. This was the first time in nearly 22 years that Britain's aid agency had been

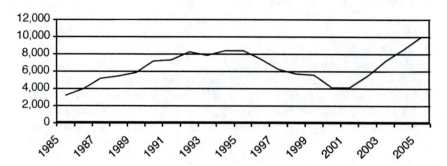

Figure 7.5 French bilateral aid disbursements, 1985–2005 (US$ millions at current prices).
    Source: OECD.

given independent ministry status and it gave the new Minister for International Development, Clare Short, a seat in cabinet. This was a sign of the increased significance that the new Labour government gave to international development. Part of this was ideological in the sense that when in government the Labour Party had always been relatively more generous with foreign aid than the Conservative Party. However, part of it was driven by the more generally internationalist stance of the new government, the more expansive development agenda that had been emerging through the 1990s, and the growing conviction that aid and 'development' were to be used as part of a host of other international projects. The heightened priority given to development is clearly seen in the rapid growth of British aid under the new government, particularly from 1999 (Figure 7.6).

Along with this expansion of aid provision, the DfID expanded its staff and its operations. It employed more people, it had more overseas offices and, more importantly, it developed a significant autonomous capacity for policy advice and engagement with other ministries – notably the Treasury and the Foreign and Commonwealth Office (Young 2001; Morrisey 2002). This sometimes led to clashes with both these ministries, but it is a sign of the increased significance of 'development' within British foreign policy (Young 2001).

At the same time, DfID wholeheartedly embraced the new policy language that emerged during the 1990s. The first White Paper produced by the DfID, *Eliminating World Poverty: A Challenge for the 21st Century*, stressed the importance of good governance, 'responsive and accountable government', human rights and the advantages of global economic integration (DfID 1997: 39). By 2000 this latter concern had become more prominent with the publication of another White Paper, *Eliminating World Poverty: Making Globalization Work for the Poor*, which argued that one of the challenges of development was to 'maximize the benefits of increased foreign investment, including that from transnational corporations, by creating strong links to the domestic economy' (DfID 2000: 49). Where Britain played a stronger role in shaping international development policy was in the area of 'partnerships'. This was a theme in the

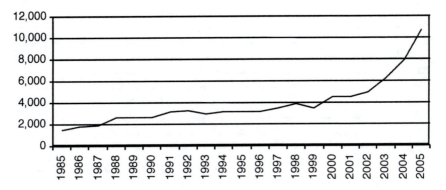

Figure 7.6 British bilateral aid disbursements, 1985–2005 (US$ millions at current prices). Source: OECD.

1997 and 2000 White Papers, and Britain was one of the first big donors to abandon (rhetorically at least) the previous stress on conditionality in favour of the
new language of partnership and country ownership. In 2002 the International
Development Act enshrined in law that the purpose of British aid was the
promotion of sustainable development and improving the welfare of people in
developing countries, and it also effectively made any attempt to 'tie' British aid
challengeable in the UK courts.

Given all of this is, it would be absurd to argue that British aid was not about
'development'. It was, and the genuine commitment of DfID and government
ministers, including the prime minister, to the cause of improving the lives of
people in developing countries is not really in doubt. Nonetheless, it is very
important to see this massive growth in aid provision, and the higher profile of
DfID more generally, in the context of the liberal international order. In particular, of course, DfID was being used as an instrument in larger international
projects in the Balkans, Kosovo, Afghanistan, Iraq and Pakistan, and in the
pursuit of the management of a variety of other international issues, from money
laundering to HIV/Aids; and in doing so British foreign aid reflected the more
interventionist stance of the 'unipolar concert' more generally.

Sweden

The Swedish aid programme too underwent a series of changes during this period.
The first was organizational and involved the creation of a new agency, Sida,
which merged the old SIDA and several other agencies into a single development
agency (Danielson and Wohlgemuth 2002). Second, Sweden joined the EU in
1995 and subsequently channelled a portion of its aid budget through the EU.
Third, Sweden expanded the number of countries it provided aid to, particularly
in Eastern Europe and the former Soviet Union (Danielson and Wohlgemuth
2002: 21). Finally, Sweden's aid programme grew substantially during the first
part of the 1990s, although in the second half of the 1990s it was affected by the
economic and financial crisis that hit several Scandinavian states (Figure 7.7).

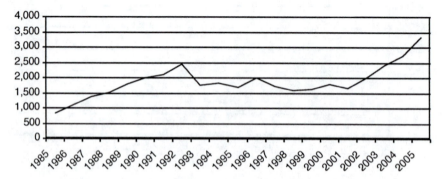

Figure 7.7 Swedish bilateral aid disbursements, 1985–2005 (US$ millions at current
prices). Source: OECD.

In terms of aid and development policy Sweden was one of the first to emphasize partnerships, particularly in the context of aid relations with Africa (G. Dahl 2001). However, although this was a genuine commitment it should also be seen in the context of the emerging consensus about good governance and democracy promotion, whereby 'partnerships' were also designed to strengthen democratic accountability and engage civil society (G. Dahl 2001: 13–14).

Multilateral agencies

The 1990s was a tricky time for multilateral development agencies. They were subjected to unprecedented levels of scrutiny from NGOs, campaigning groups and, sometimes, governments, and the rapid rise in private capital flows to many developing countries raised questions about the purpose of these agencies. These pressures led to some quite significant changes in the operations of these agencies, but despite all the criticisms and the questioning about their role, multilateral aid increased during this period (Figure 7.8).

World Bank

The World Bank's role as the leading multilateral development agency was maintained and even enhanced during this period. The Bank took the lead in developing the ideas of good governance and participation, and the end of the Cold War enabled the Bank to expand its operations into new countries in Eastern and Central Europe. It also expanded into new kinds of areas, including environmental protection and post-conflict peace building. This expansion of the World Bank's operations was crystallized in the announcement in 1999 of the Comprehensive Development Framework. This was the culmination of an attempt by James Wolfensohn, then president, and Joseph Stiglitz, then chief economist, to broaden the Bank's approach to development and to see the process of development and poverty reduction as multifaceted or 'holistic' (Pender 2001).

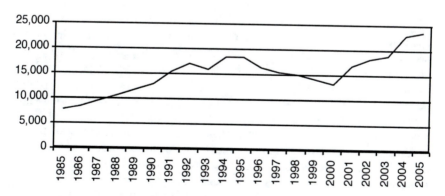

Figure 7.8 Multilateral aid disbursements, 1985–2005 (US$ millions at current prices). Source: OECD.

In this vision development involved 'good and clear government', an 'effective legal and justice system', a properly regulated financial system, strong welfare measures to assist the poorest members of society, good health and education provision, the development of water, sewerage, electricity and transport systems, the preservation of 'culture' and the physical environment, and rural development. It was also necessary, so Wolfensohn argued, to develop and include civil society in all its forms in order to engender participation and ownership (Wolfensohn 1999). As the Bank's development agenda expanded so did its lending. IDA lending, for example, grew from just under US$3,000 million in 1985 to about $7,000 million in 2005 (OECD).

In many respects then, the 1990s was a successful decade for the Bank as its lending grew and it continued to dominate the development discourse of the major western donors. At the same time, however, the Bank was subject to unprecedented external scrutiny that led to some significant changes in the way the Bank related to other actors. Part of the criticism of the Bank derived precisely from the expansion of its agenda. As the official history of the World Bank, published in 1997, pointed out, the Bank's problem by the middle of the 1990s was that its list of policy priorities had grown significantly. There were all kinds of add-ons, among them population, gender, governance, corruption and the environment (Kapur *et al.* 1997). In other words the Bank was trying to do too much. In some ways, that the Bank was able to move into new areas, such as good governance, is a sign of how powerful it had become as a result of change in international order. The expansion of the Bank's mandate, however, also came as a result of sustained criticism of it by NGOs and particularly the US Congress. In this sense the Bank found it hard to resist demands from other agencies to expand its mandate (Weaver and Leiteritz 2005).

In 1983 environmental groups persuaded the House Subcommittee on International Development Institutions and Finance to hold hearings on the environmental record of the multilateral development banks. In 1984 this committee issued a series of recommendations which included increasing the number of staff working in the World Bank on environmental issues and sharing more information with NGOs (Rich 1994: 210–12). There were also a series of high-profile campaigns about specific projects: most notably the Polonoroeste and Sardar Sarovar (Narmada) Dam projects. We saw in Chapter 4 that these kinds of projects often had adverse environmental impacts and involved the displacement of thousands of people. In these two particular projects the Bank was accused of not following its own guidelines for protecting displaced persons and especially indigenous peoples (Rich 1994: 121). NGOs and campaigning groups pressured the Bank's management and, more importantly, the executive directors of its major shareholders. The Bank was forced to stop disbursements on the Polonoroeste project pending the introduction of more effective environmental protection measures, and it was persuaded to establish a new environmental department within the Bank and to promise to undertake individual country environmental assessments as part of its lending programme (Le Pestre 1989: 199–201; Rich 1994: 136–8).

Into the 1990s the World Bank was criticized by NGOs and others using the language of 'good governance' for its own lack of accountability and transparency (Woods 2000; Nelson 2001). This pressure culminated when a Congressional committee threatened to withhold US funds for IDA until new disclosure policies were in place. In September 1993, the Bank announced new information disclosure policies and the creation of an inspection panel to hear complaints from peoples affected by Bank projects. The new disclosure polices certainly made many more Bank documents publicly available, and as the Bank's website has developed so more and more project documents, environmental assessments and reports have been made available (Nelson 2001). The inspection panel was created to hear complaints from groups affected by a Bank project on the basis that the Bank failed to follow its own internal guidelines (Udall 1997). Critics of the Bank still argued that its environmental protection measures were weak or often ignored and that the inspection panel was too narrowly conceived (Wade 2004b). Nonetheless, it is clear that the Bank was being forced to respond to external pressures.

The final set of pressures on the Bank came in the form of a good deal more introspection about how good a development institution it actually was. In 1992 the then president of the Bank, Lewis Preston, invited a retiring vice-president, Willi Wapenhams, to head a 'Portfolio Management Taskforce' to review the way the Bank managed its development projects. The taskforce report, the so-called 'Wapenhams Report', was in many ways a damming account of internal Bank practices (Portfolio Management Taskforce 1992). It found that one-third of projects were 'having major problems', that projects took on average two years longer to complete than was estimated at the time of project design, and that the gap between estimated and actual economic rates of return of projects was growing. The report argued that many of these problems stemmed from the internal culture and operation of the Bank (see also Naim 1994). It argued that there was undue emphasis on loan approval, rather than implementation and monitoring, there was too little emphasis placed on risk assessment, and there was too little internal accountability for actual developmental impact. Although the report was never officially published it was widely circulated outside the Bank and was very damaging to its reputation (Weaver and Leiteritz 2005: 373–5). Faced with this, when Wolfensohn became president in 1995 he announced a programme of renewal aimed at re-establishing the Bank as the pre-eminent development institution (Weaver and Leiteritz 2005). A review of this so-called 'strategic compact' found that the results were mixed, but that in a number of ways the Bank had improved its operations. Project success rates had improved, more staff were working in field offices, rather than in its headquarters, and it had streamlined its internal bureaucratic procedures and expanded its research capacity (Weaver and Leiteritz 2005: 377–8). It was hard to change some of the established culture of the Bank, but nonetheless the Bank had responded to these pressures, and in some ways at least had become a more open and effective development agency.

Regional development banks

The other regional development banks can be dealt with more quickly. Almost all of them saw an increase in their lending. In addition, most of them followed the World Bank in terms of the expansion of their development agendas and in terms of instituting new disclosure and accountability mechanisms – although the regional development banks tend not to have such strong policies as the World Bank (Nelson 2001). The AfDB experienced yet another funding crisis in the mid-1990s after the non-African members of the bank lost confidence in its internal procedures and its loans arrears had doubled. From 1993 to 1999 the United States made no contributions to the AfDB at all and pressure from western states led to an increase in the voting rights of non-African members.

The last important point here was the creation of a new regional development bank in 1990: the European Bank for Reconstruction and Development (EBRD), designed to assist former communist states of Central and Eastern Europe in their transition to capitalism and democracy. There was the usual political bargaining and arguments in the run-up to the establishment of the EBRD, particularly over the role of the United States and the Soviet Union in the new organization, but there was a remarkable degree of consensus on the desirability of such an institution and on its founding principles (Weber 1994). This shows how ingrained the multilateral form had become, and the EBRD shared many features with the other regional development banks in terms of governance structures and funding. There were some important and revealing differences, however. First, the EBRD had no concessional lending arm. Second, it was established with an explicit mandate to provide 60 per cent of its money to private sector organizations (in general the other multilateral development banks lend only to governments). Third, and most important, was the explicit political conditionality built into its founding charter. Article One of its Charter states that:

> the purpose of the Bank shall be to foster the transition towards open market-oriented economies and to promote private and entrepreneurial initiative in the Central and Eastern European countries committed to and applying the principles of multiparty democracy, pluralism and market economics.
>
> (EBRD 1991: 1)

The EBRD reflected the new ideological consensus that emerged with the end of the Cold War, which repeated the classic arguments about the relationship between democracy, market-led development, and peace and security. It also expressed in a very neat way the particular kind of hegemony exercised by the United States: a multilateral institution that required negotiation and compromise but at the same time advanced US interests and ideology in the region.

NGOs and development

One of the most important changes within the institutions of development during this period was the rise to prominence of NGOs. Development NGOs have

increased in number significantly in recent years and they are playing more important and varied roles within the project of international development. The standard
definition of an NGO is that it is an international organization not established
by intergovernmental agreement, that is not profit-making, does not advocate
violence, and is concerned in some way with social, political or economic affairs
(Ahmed and Potter 2006: 8). This distinguishes NGOs from a broader category
of non-state actors, which include profit-making private companies, criminal or
violent organizations, and sporting or other organizations not directly concerned
with social, political or economic issues. Emblematic NGOs thus include the Red
Cross, Amnesty International, Greenpeace and Oxfam. At one level this makes
the definition of development NGOs straightforward: a non-government, non-
profit-making formal organization dedicated to 'development' (Lewis and Kanji
2009: 10–11). There are, however, complications. The first is that many NGOs
in fact receive significant sums of money from governments and the multilateral
development banks. A second problem is that there is a huge variety of 'NGOs'
at work in the field of development, from small local community associations to
the large international development NGOs such as Care International. This has
led to a blizzard of acronyms to describe this variety from BINGOs (big international NGOs) to GROs (grassroots organizations) and VOs (village organizations)
(Lewis and Kanji 2009: 9–10). The exact definition of each need not concern us
here. The kinds of organizations captured under the label 'development NGO' are
more interesting in terms of the variety of roles that different kinds of NGOs play
in the project of international development.

Some of what international development NGOs do is of the more traditional
kind. They engage in development projects with money they raise, often for particular issues or causes. The amount of private contributions to development has
risen significantly, especially from the United States. According to some estimates
the amount of private giving for development from the United States amounts to
US$35 billion a year – substantially more than the amount of official US bilat-
eral aid – and the amount of international giving from US charitable foundations
nearly quadrupled between 1990 and 2000 (Adelman 2003). Second, NGOs
engage in advocacy work, campaigning on various issues and causes, and pressuring governments and development agencies on particular policies or projects,
as was the case with the campaign against the World Bank noted above (Lewis
and Kanji 2009: 97–107).

Beyond this, however, the significance of NGOs in the project of international
development lies in their relationship with the large bilateral and multilateral
donors (Lewis and Kanji 2009: 92–7). The amount of bilateral aid channelled
through NGOs rose rapidly from the late 1980s. The World Bank estimated that
by the mid-1990s something like US$8 billion dollars a year of official develop-
ment assistance was channelled through NGOs – roughly 15 per cent of total aid
(World Bank 1995a). For some individual donors the figure was higher. By the
mid-1990s over 30 per cent of Swedish aid was being delivered though NGOs
(Edwards and Hulme 1996: 962). By 2000 the United States was channelling over
43 per cent of its aid budget through NGOs (Ahmed and Potter 2006: 117). By the
middle of the 1990s NGOs were in involved in 50 per cent of World Bank-funded

projects – up from 20 per cent in 1989 (World Bank 1995c). The flip-side of this, of course, is that many northern NGOs themselves have become increasingly dependent on government grants. Again by the mid-1990s the largest five British development NGOs received between 18 and 52 per cent of their funds from government grants. For some US NGOs the figure was as high as 90 per cent (Edwards and Hulme 1996: 962). However, it is not just northern development NGOs that have benefited from the increasing amounts of aid being channelled to NGOs. In most developing countries there has been an explosive growth in domestic NGOs. Hundreds, sometimes thousands, of new NGOs have emerged to take advantage of the official funding being channelled to southern NGOs. Beyond the issue of funding, NGOs are also playing increasingly significant roles in the design and implementation of development projects. According to one account NGOs were involved in project design in 25 per cent of all World Bank projects (World Bank 1995c).

There are several reason why NGOs came to play a larger role in the project of international development. For the World Bank and other agencies, using NGOs was a way of improving project implementation and encouraging participation (Paul 1987a,b; L. Brown *et al.* 1991: 65). They were also a way of providing more detailed and fine-grained development interventions that targeted individual and community practices and patterns of behaviour as part of the more far-reaching development agenda that emerged in the 1990s (Williams 2008a: 68–9). In addition, as the 1990s went on, the traditional NGO opposition to the policies and practices of the big donors started to abate as structural adjustment was reformed, and as these donors started to embrace the language of good governance, human rights, participation and civil society. Second, there are reasons to do with the role of NGOs more generally in international and domestic politics that relate to the changes associated with the emergence of the liberal order. The rise of neoliberalism and the associated criticism of the state as a service provider opened the ideological space for the rise of NGOs and in this context all kinds of international agencies started to engage more with NGOs (Reimann 2006). In addition, not only did the end of the Cold War create more space for NGOs, but the supposed significant of 'civil society' in the end of communism further enhanced the legitimacy of NGOs (Lewis and Kanji 2009: ch. 6); so much so that Reimann (2006) argues that a new 'pro-NGO norm' emerged in international politics during the 1990s. In this context too, having closer ties to NGOs was seen as a way of enhancing the legitimacy of official international organizations.

NGOs are now central to the project of international development in a way they never used to be. This has significant implications for NGOs themselves, many of which have benefited from their increasing involvement in the project of international development. It obviously raises a question about the suitability of the label 'non-governmental' for these organizations as for many of them a significant portion of their budget comes from governments or multilateral development agencies. It also raises questions about the ability of these NGOs to criticize the policies and practices of those states and agencies from which they receive significant funds (Edwards and Hulme 1996; Ahmed and Potter 2006: ch.

6). It also raises issues of accountability too. One of the traditional justifications for using NGOs in project design and implementation is that they are better able to respond to the needs of local communities. However, to the extent that their funding derives from official donors the suspicion must be that they become more accountable to these donors (Edwards and Hulme 1996; Brett 1993). Despite this, many NGOs have themselves embraced this new relationship, and this is just one sign of a more general shift: the rise of a more tightly integrated development community.

A development community?

The term 'development community' or 'aid community' is used by many commentators to designate, however loosely, that collection of agencies and organizations involved in the project of international development. Despite this, relatively little effort has gone into specifying what, if anything, makes this collection of agencies and organizations something we might call a 'community'. There are problems with applying the label 'community', which has its traditional referent as a local and cohesive social group, to something as diverse as the project of international development. Nonetheless, it is argued here that the relationships between development agencies and organizations have changed significantly since the 1980s and that such organizations are now more integrated than they have ever been, that there is less diversity between them, and that they have come to share a common language and to participate in collective practices. In this sense the project of international development has paralleled the emergence of the 'unipolar concert'. This in turn, as we shall see, has significant implications for developing countries themselves. The emergence of a 'development community' can be seen in at least two ways: first, policy convergence; second, more cooperation between these agencies and participation in common practices. Although there is very little concrete research on the issue it seems there may also be a set of more amorphous changes in the professional 'culture' of international development: more staff mobility between agencies; professional qualifications; websites devoted to jobs in the industry; and so on (Morton 1996; De Waal 1997).

Policy convergence

There emerged during the 1990s a remarkable consensus among development agencies around the appropriate policies for development. As we have seen, this centred on the ideas of good governance (and possibly democracy) and 'partnership'. Although there had always been some commonly held views among development agencies, the degree of policy convergence was such as to make the policy statements of development agencies almost indistinguishable. This situation was a significant departure from that which prevailed through the 1980s in particular, when a number of states, and a great many NGOs, were very critical of both conditionality and neoliberalism. Major bilateral donors such as Japan,

Sweden and France had, for different reasons, significant reservations about the desirability of both neoliberal policy prescriptions and conditional lending.

Japan's opposition to neoliberalism during much of the 1980s was muted, and indeed Japan generally went along with the policy of structural adjustment, often making its loans linked to World Bank and IMF conditionalities (Sunaga 2004: 19). However, as we have seen, by the beginning of the 1990s Japan started to take a more activist role in the project of international development. This manifested itself most famously in a successful attempt to persuade the World Bank to undertake a study into the development success of East Asia (and to significantly fund the research) (World Bank 1993b). In 1991 the head of Japan's central bank said that:

> experience in Asia has shown that although development strategies require a healthy respect for the market mechanisms, the role of government cannot be forgotten. I would like to see the World Bank and the IMF take the lead in a wide-ranging study that would define the theoretical underpinnings of this approach and clarify the areas in which it can be successfully applied to other parts of the globe.
>
> (quoted in Wade 1996: 10)

All through the 1980s the French bilateral aid programme often ran at odds with the structural adjustment promoted by the World Bank and the IMF. The French did not make their aid conditional on the achievement of conditions laid down by the Bank and Fund (as some donors did) and socialist governments in France often publicly criticized both neoliberalism and conditionality (Cumming 1995: 387–8). Also, as we saw above, the French were reluctant for some time to devalue the CFA franc – something the Bank and Fund thought essential for structural adjustment. Sweden was less critical of the specific policy prescriptions of adjustment lending but it was often critical of conditionality as a mechanism for policy change (Karre and Svensson 1989; G. Dahl 2001). More vocal criticism came from NGOs. Criticisms of structural adjustment were varied and numerous, and included that it had a negative impact on the poorest groups; that it was implemented with a lack of understanding of the dynamics of poverty; that the measures encouraged environmental damage; that it was overly focused on growth rather than on redistribution; that it was ideological; and that it was promoted by western-dominated institutions in the interests of western states and corporations (Clark 1991: ch. 12). Oxfam went even further and argued that SAL was responsible for the 'lost decade' for development in the 1980s (Oxfam 1994).

This situation has changed significantly. All donors now embrace the new language of governance, civil society, participation, environmental protection, global economic integration and social safety nets. This policy convergence is partly explained by the triumph of liberalism and the emergence of the unipolar concert. It is also partly explained by the continued dominance of the World Bank in terms of development policy (Stern and Ferreira 1997).

In a policy world obsessed with the belief that only 'global expertise' is valuable, the Bank has no real rival. The regional development banks and the UN agencies fall over themselves to cooperate with the Bank, anxious to get a piece of the action from the large loans that follow.

(Goldman 2000)

Finally, it is also explained by the increasing participation in common institutions.

Common institutions

The problem of coordination between development agencies in their assistance to developing countries has been a long-standing one (Cassen 1986: ch. 7). Especially in the world's poorest states there may be 30 official aid agencies operating and possibly hundreds of development NGOs. In these circumstances, and especially given the relatively weak capacity of recipient governments (and a desire on the part of some donors to bypass the government), serious problems of coordination often arose. Little thought was given to how individual projects fitted into an overall development strategy; little thought was often given to how recurrent costs would be financed; and donors often funded similar projects, leading to overlap and redundancy. In addition, different donors placed different demands on recipient governments in terms of accounting, auditing and procurement. There was a growing recognition of these problems through the 1980s, leading to a more concerted attempt to coordinate donors and harmonize their policies in relations to recipient governments. Both the World Bank and UNDP took the lead in chairing donor coordination meetings, which would attempt to impose priorities on donors and impose the collective wishes of donors on recipient countries (OECD 1988). In addition, the OECD has led an attempt to harmonize policies, not just in the broad sense of development strategies, but in the narrower sense of common accounting, auditing and procurement policies (OECD 1988). This work has accelerated in recent years and culminated in 2005 with the Paris Declaration on Aid Effectiveness. This was an international agreement on the part of western donors and developing-country governments to develop country 'ownership' of development strategies, to harmonize donors' policies and to encourage mutual accountability. There are some doubts about whether this has been completely effective, but it is clear that there is a great deal more coordination and harmonization between donors than before.

More coordinated relations between donors were exemplified in the PRSP process (Craig and Porter 2003). As we saw in Chapter 6 this was an initiative developed by the IMF and the World Bank that would embody the new concern with participation and ownership in the establishment of development and poverty reduction strategies in developing countries. The novel feature of the PRSP process was the extensive participatory process that was to be used to develop the strategy. However, in terms of increasing coordination between donors the important aspect of the PRSP process was that all major development agencies signed up to this process. In principle at least it means that they have agreed to provide support for individual developing countries – in terms of both aid and debt relief – within the context of the poverty reduction strategy established by the government using a participatory approach.

It remains an open question whether the term 'development community' is really the appropriate one to describe what has emerged. Nonetheless, closer and more integrated relationships have emerged between development agencies in general and in terms of their relations with developing countries. That this has happened in the context of the dominance of the unipolar concert and the triumph of liberalism is not surprising. However, it does represent a very significant department from the sovereign order, in which there was a great deal more pluralism and a good deal less coordination and cooperation.

Conclusion

Changes within and between development institutions in the liberal order had very ambiguous consequences for developing countries. On one hand the amount of aid provided rose dramatically, and especially to the world's poorest states. In addition, the higher priority accorded to development in the foreign policies of many western states meant that the 'problem of development' was being tackled with more urgency. The increased public scrutiny of the major development agencies and the increased participation of NGOs in the project of international development led to increased transparency and accountability of development agencies, and a broader development agenda that encompasses issues such as environmental protection. On the other hand, as the limited form of political pluralism that characterized development institutions in the sovereign order has eroded, so many developing countries are faced with an increasing unified bloc of donors dominated by the World Bank and the United States, which increasingly think alike about development, and which share in the working of common institutions and practices. In this context it is not clear what developing country 'ownership' can really mean, especially given the more intrusive development agenda that emerged with 'good governance'.

8 Development practice in the liberal order

Aid in the liberal order

Introduction

We saw in the last chapter that aggregate aid provision increased considerably during the liberal order. There were also some notable changes in the sectoral composition of aid, reflecting the changes in donor priorities during this period, particularly the increased concern with good governance (Figure 8.1). There was also a more concerted attempt on the part of development agencies and academics to assess impact of development projects and programmes.

This chapter looks at the practice of development in the liberal order. It follows the same structure as Chapter 4: it looks first at aggregate aid flows during this period and the general evidence available for the success and failures of this lending; the focus then switches to the three case study countries, looking at their macroeconomic/developmental performance, aid flows and some sample projects. The same caveats apply here as in Chapter 4. Both the countries and

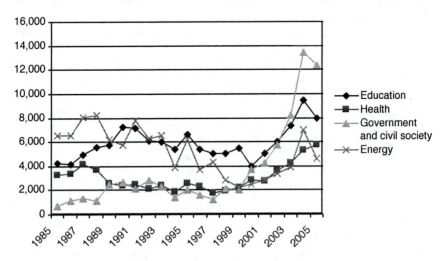

Figure 8.1 Total sectoral aid commitments, 1985–2005 (US$ millions at current prices). Source: OECD.

the specific projects are illustrative only. The book makes no claims that they are representative of the universe of developing countries or development projects, and no definitive conclusions can be drawn from them. Nonetheless, these three countries, and the specific projects examined, do illustrate some of the characteristic experiences of developing countries and some of the characteristic kinds of projects and programmes that were pursued during the liberal order.

Aggregate aid provision

There were some significant changes in the sectoral composition of aid flows. In particular there was a sharp rise in provision for government reform and civil society support (Figure 8.1).

Given that structural adjustment lending was one of the most important and controversial new features of the project of international development during this period, it is no surprise that a great deal of effort has gone into assessing its successes and failures. Assessing the outcome of adjustment operations is difficult for some of the same reasons that assessing the impact of development projects is difficult: lack of accurate data, fungibility of aid resources and the opportunity cost of aid. With adjustment lending, however, the issue of counterfactuals is even more acute. Almost by definition countries receiving adjustment loans were in a severe macroeconomic crisis, which tends to have a significant impact on the quality of services provided by the government, such as health and education, and on poverty and unemployment rates. Disentangling the effects of the adjustment programme on these issues from the effects of the initial crisis can be hard. In other words, if poverty rates rise it can be difficult to know whether they would have been better or worse in the absence of the adjustment programme. The available evidence suggests the very mixed record for structural adjustment that was discussed in Chapter 5.

In 1995 the World Bank produced a major evaluation of its structural and sectoral adjustment lending. It reviewed the experiences and outcomes of 99 adjustment programmes in 42 countries mostly from the mid-1980s onwards. Of the 88 operations given a rating, 32 were rated as 'unsatisfactory' (Jayarajah and Branson 1995: 276–9). Of the 35 operations in sub-Saharan Africa, 12 were rated as 'unsatisfactory'. Of the 42 countries undergoing Bank-supported adjustment programmes, 24 reduced their fiscal deficits (one of the central components of adjustment lending), 35 experienced devaluations and 31 increased their foreign exchange reserves (Jayarajah and Branson 1995: 2–3) – all signs that at least in some respects structural adjustment was working. In 27 of the countries, however, investment levels fell during the adjustment period – although the Bank argued that there were good reasons to think it would then rise (Jayarajah and Branson 1995: 3). The evidence on privatization is also mixed: in some countries there was substantial privatization but in others very little (Jayarajah and Branson 1995: 7). In reviewing the evidence of the social impact of adjustment the Bank concluded that it has been variable and dependent on both the initial conditions and the design of the adjustment programme. On balance urban groups seem to have suffered disproportionately more than rural groups, and within the urban groups it is the middle classes who suffered most as a result of the contraction in the formal sector and public sector job losses (Jayarajah and Branson 1995: 9). In terms of sectoral adjustment programmes, industrial sector programmes performed better than agricultural ones, of which half of the operations were rated as 'unsatisfactory' (Jayarajah and Branson 1995: 11–14).

In a specific assessment of adjustment in Africa, the World Bank argued that, of 29 countries, the six with the 'most improvement in macroeconomic policies' enjoyed higher rates of GDP per capita growth, increased growth in agriculture and higher exports (World Bank 1994b: 1). It also admitted, however, that reforms had been 'uneven across sectors and across countries' and that no African country had 'achieved a sound macroeconomic policy stance – which in broad terms means inflation under 10 per cent, a very low budget deficit and a competitive exchange rate' and that 'the politically difficult reform of the public enterprise and financial sectors lags well behind' (World Bank 1994b: 1–2). Reflecting the changing views of donors at the time, the report concluded that 'adjustment alone will not put countries in a sustained, poverty-reducing growth path. That is the challenge of long-term development, which requires better economic policies *and* more investment in human capital, infrastructure, and institution-building, along with better governance' (World Bank 1994b: 2, emphasis in original).

Beyond adjustment lending we have more data for this period on overall success rates for individual development projects and programmes. Roger Riddell has concluded that, for most donors, project success rates range from 70 to 85 per cent in this period, and that on balance success rates improved from 1965 to 1985 (Riddell 2007: 180). For the DfID, about 75 per cent of projects were deemed successful in 2000, compared with 65 per cent in the mid-1990s. In 2004 USAID rated 84 per cent of its projects as satisfactory, and the Asian Development Bank 71 per cent. The World Bank rated 78 per cent of its projects as successful in 2000–4, compared with 60 per cent in the mid-1980s (Riddell 2007: 181). These aggregate figures mask significant variations between countries and across sectors, however. The World Bank had the most success in East Asia and the Pacific (nearly 90 per cent of projects judged as successful) and the least in sub-Saharan Africa (70 per cent). In terms of sectors, the Bank rates its projects in transport, rural development and finance at 85 per cent and the environment at less than 70 per cent (World Bank 2005a). The Asian Development Bank rated transport and energy as its best performing sectors (85 per cent), but financial and agricultural sector as its worst performing (50 per cent). The African Development Bank rated 75 per cent of its agricultural development projects as successful, but only 46 per cent of its financial sector projects (Riddell 2007: 182–3). There may also be good reason to think that donors overestimate project success ratings, at least initially. Riddell has noted that some donors have downgraded their success ratings after more rigorous assessments (Riddell 2007: 186–7). These aggregate results do not tell us anything especially surprising: some projects work and other do not; adjustment lending had produced only mixed outcomes; and success has been harder to achieve in some regions than others. There does seem to have been some improvement in project success rates, which may be a sign that in some sense development agencies are getting 'better'. On the other hand, as we shall see with our case study countries, even with a somewhat improved performance, and even with more interventionist development strategies, sustained development has been hard to achieve.

Ghana

A period of political turbulence from the late 1970s ended with a coup led by Flt Lt Jerry Rawlings on December 1981. The first 18 months of the new regime was characterized by revolutionary rhetoric and political populism but, after failing to obtain financial support from other 'revolutionary' states, the government turned to the IMF and World Bank and an Economic Recovery Plan (ERP) was begun (Jeffries 1989; Nugent 1995). The initial phase of the ERP, supported by the IMF, focused on restoring macroeconomic stability and was, in some respects at least, successful. Inflation was reduced, export volumes increased and government finances were stabilized (Toye 1991). From 1987 the World Bank increasingly took the lead as the need for short-term stabilization loans receded. This marked the beginning of the longer-term process of structural adjustment. Under the leadership of the Bank the adjustment programme began to incorporate a wide-ranging set of concerns including reform and privatization of state-owned enterprises, civil service reform, improved public sector management and financial sector reform.

In 1987 the Bank approved a US$115 million *Structural Adjustment Credit*. In 1989 it approved a second *Structural Adjustment Credit* of $134 million. Both were classic structural adjustment loans. As the justification for the first credit says, the programme aimed to 'establish an incentive framework that stimulates growth, encourages savings and investment, strengthens the balance of payments, and improves resource use, particularly in the public sector' (World Bank 1987b: i). This was to be accomplished by a series of policy reforms, particularly trade liberalization, whose objective was to 'shift incentives further from trading and rent-seeking activities to production, and encourage manufacturers to shift emphasis towards exports' (World Bank 1987b: i). 'The reduced role of the state in the productive sector, the planned rehabilitation of infrastructure, and the overall improvement in incentives is intended to improve the environment for the private sector' (World Bank 1987b: ii).

The list of specific policy reforms the two credits pursued is very extensive. It amounts to more than 160 specific actions across a large range of issues (World Bank 1992). Included are such things as liberalization of trade and exchange rates (by abolishing the import licensing system, establishing foreign exchange bureaus and introducing foreign exchange auctions, among many other things); reform of the cocoa sector (by liberalizing cocoa prices, removal of input subsidies and reform of the Cocoa Marketing Board); stabilizing government finances (by tax reform and reform of the government budgeting procedures); reform of the civil service (by reducing wage rises and establishing a programme of job losses in the public sector); privatization of state-owned enterprises; and encouraging private investment (by introducing a new investment code and encouraging consultation between the government and the private sector). Some of the reforms are very detailed indeed – down to specifying specific sales tax rates, wage rises and pricing policies. These were also conditional loans. The loan was to be disbursed in two tranches with the second one being 'made available provided a review of performance . . . determines that the conditions stipulated . . . have been fulfilled' (World Bank 1987b: 38). There then follows a list of eight specific conditions that would provide the basis for deciding whether to disburse the second tranche of money, including specific targets for civil service job cuts and moves towards the privatization of state-owned enterprises.

Given that the record of structural adjustment loans in general is mixed, it is significant that the Bank judged the implementation of these programmes to have been generally a success (World Bank 1992: xii). The government did indeed enact many of the policy reforms advocated by the Bank, although the pace of privatization and civil service job cuts was slower than the Bank would have liked (World Bank 1992: xiii). According to the Bank too, the impact of the programmes on the poorest groups 'appears to have been moderately negative in the early stages and positive over the longer term', although it did admit that the extent to which households suffered as a result of the programme depended upon whether or not wage earners lost their jobs as a result of the civil service job cuts (World Bank 1992: xiii). Certainly the economic performance of Ghana was better during this period as growth rates averaged around 5 per cent. The Bank argued that the main reason behind the success of the programme was that 'the Government of Ghana was highly committed to structural adjustment and implemented a wide range of measures promptly and wholeheartedly' (World Bank 1992: xiv). This, of course, raises one of the fundamental questions about conditional lending: with a committed government it is unnecessary and with an uncommitted government it often does not work to encourage reform.

There were some problems with the programmes, however. The first was 'weakness of implementation capacity, due to deficiencies in the structure and staffing of institutions, and in management information systems in the public sector' (World Bank 1992: xvi), Second, 'the pace of implementation was slower where adjustment required changes in the structure of institutions . . . rather than just changes in rules' (World Bank 1992: xv). Third, the Bank admitted to some of its own weaknesses, particularly in terms of a lack of experience with the cocoa sector, an overly rigid approach to privatization and a too frequent turnover of Bank staff (World Bank 1992: xv–xvi). Finally, the Bank accepted that economic policy reform was not enough to generate sustained development in Ghana: 'the structural adjustment process . . . requires that in addition to providing incentives to stimulate private investment, the institutional arrangements for assisting the private investor in mobilizing resource need to be put in place' (World Bank 1992: xvi).

When it became clear that the weak link in the adjustment programme was the inadequate response of private domestic investment, emphasis shifted to the re-examination of the legal, regulatory and consultative framework in order to make it consistent with economic liberalization and the creation of a dynamic private sector.

(World Bank 1992: 6)

The relative success of these adjustment operations helped the reputation of Ghana as a success story (certainly compared with the chaos of the late 1970s) (Toye 1991; World Bank 1995d). In turn Ghana continued to receive significant amounts of development aid (Figure 8.2). A World Bank assessment of lending to Ghana concluded that in the period 1995–9, 67 per cent of its projects were 'satisfactory' (compared with 59 per cent for the Africa region as a whole) (World Bank 2000c). This masks some significant variation in performance, as only about 50 per cent of non-adjustment loans were judged 'satisfactory'.

The transition to multiparty democracy in 1992, in some part due to pressure from Ghana's donors, affected the economy as the government undertook large amounts of spending in the run-up to the election. Until the late 1990s the economy performed only modestly well, with persistently high inflation, high levels of public debt and modest levels of growth. Indeed, per capita income was by some measures lower in 2001 than it was at independence and about 40 per cent of the population was living in poverty (Table 8.1).

High levels of aid to Ghana had also created a growing situation of aid dependence. The standard definition of a highly aid-dependent country is one where aid flows are more than 10 per cent of GNP. In 1980 there were 14 such countries, but by the mid-1990s this number had risen to 34, the bulk of them in sub-Saharan Africa, reflecting the on-going crisis on the sub-continent. For a time in the mid-1990s there were a number of countries where aid constituted more than 25 per cent of GNP (Williams 2000). For many years from the late 1980s Ghana's aid amounted to 10 per cent or more of GNP, in large part because of the large inflows of aid to support the adjustment process (Whitfield and Jones 2008: 2). A 1992 World Bank paper argued that, in the most highly aid-dependent countries, 'aid can no longer be regarded as an adjunct to domestic investment resources but has

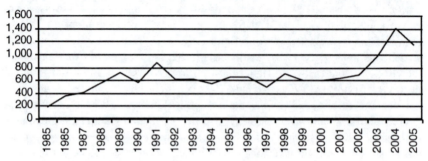

Figure 8.2 Total aid disbursements to Ghana, 1985–2005 (US$ millions at current prices). Source: OECD.

Table 8.1 Ghana: selected indicators, 1985–2004

	1985–9	1990–4	1995–9	2000–4
GDP growth rate (%)	5.1	4.1	4.4	4.6
Inflation (%)	32.6	18.8	20.7	25.6
Exports annual growth (%)	13	8	12.4	2.6
Interest payments on external debt (% of exports)	13.2	9.6	6.8	3.8
Poverty headcount at $1.25 a day (PPP) (% of population)	51 (1988)	51 (1992)	39 (1998)	n/a
Life expectancy at birth (years)	55.5	58.3	58.7	57.2
Under-5 mortality rate per 1,000	143 (1985)	120 (1990)	110 (1995)	106 (2000)

Source: World Bank.

become central to their economic management, and to the continued functioning of governments' (Lister and Stevens 1992: 8). This situation was quite different from that envisaged in any original developmental justification for aid, where it was seen as a supplement to national resources. Aid dependence can create a number of problems in addition to the problems of coordination and harmoniza- tion associated with large numbers of aid donors operating within a developing country. It leaves developing countries vulnerable to changing donor policies – as was seen in Ghana in the early 1990s when donors reduced aid provision as a result of poor economic performance immediately before and after the 1992 elections (Whitfield and Jones 2008). It also has the potential to warp government priorities as maintaining aid flows becomes a top priority. Finally, it raises questions about accountability, as government officials become more accountable to their external donors than to the people they are supposed to be governing.

It was in this context – a mixed development record and high levels of aid dependence – that the PRSP process was undertaken in Ghana. This process is not strictly a development project or programme. As was discussed in Chapters 6 and 7, it is a process for formulating a development strategy. Nonetheless, given the widespread use of PRSPs it is worth examining how the process worked in Ghana and what its results actually were. The *Ghana Poverty Reduction Strategy 2003–2005* is a remarkable document. It is an ambitious and comprehensive strat- egy that sets out the policies, programmes and projects to support growth and poverty reduction. The aim of the strategy is to 'create wealth by transforming the nature of the economy to achieve growth, accelerated poverty reduction and the protection of the vulnerable and excluded within a decentralized, democratic environment' (Government of Ghana 2003: vol. I, i). To achieve this, the *Strategy* sets out actions in six broad areas: sound macroeconomic management; 'increas- ing production and promoting sustainable livelihoods'; direct support for human development and the provision of basic services; provision of special programmes for the vulnerable and excluded; ensuring good governance and improved capacity in the public sector; and 'the active involvement of the private sector as the main engine of growth and partner in nation building' (Government of Ghana 2003: vol. I, i).

There are a number of important things to note about this. First, this list exactly replicates the development consensus among western donors and raises questions about quite how much 'ownership' there really is here. Second, in terms of encouraging the private sector by providing an 'enabling environment' including sound macroeconomic management, the *Strategy* does not deviate from the neoliberal vision that underpinned structural adjustment. The market is the way to achieve growth. Where it does differ substantially is in the focus on poverty reduction and the 'excluded and vulnerable' and in the focus on 'good governance'. As we noted in earlier chapters, the PRSP process was designed to focus explicitly on poverty reduction, and the *Strategy* begins with an assessment of poverty levels and poverty reduction trends in Ghana during the 1990s and emphasizes the need to reduce poverty not simply through economic growth, but also through expanded provision of health and education services. What the *Strategy* says about good governance is unsurprising given that it had become a key part of development policy during the 1990s, but it does include 35 specific targets for reform, including such issues as developing an anti-corruption strategy, establishing permanent mechanisms for government–civil society dialogue, strengthening the legal system and reforming land law (Government of Ghana 2003: vol. I, 125–6). There are also 23 additional targets in the area of decentralization, 18 additional targets in the area of public expenditure management and 20 additional targets in the area of transparency and accountability. In the discussion of civil society the *Strategy* says that civil society 'has a wider role as a participator in policy formulation, implementing and monitoring the outputs and evaluating the outcomes of the development process' (Government of Ghana 2003: vol. I, 133–4). Finally, one of the most striking aspects of the *Strategy* document is how detailed it is. In addition to the 96 specific targets in the areas of good governance the report contains another 54 specific targets across a large range of issues, from education and health service provision to environmental protection.

The total costs of the implementing the *Strategy* was estimated at US$5,283 million. Resource constraints and limitation of absorptive capacity, however, led to the identification of priority areas for 2003–5 that were costed at $2,515 million (Government of Ghana 2003: vol. II, 3–4) and the document includes a detailed breakdown of the funding requirements for all the specific policies and programmes included in the priority areas. It is this which provided the basis for the financial contribution of external donors. In fact, as a review conducted in 2004 showed, donor support was 'in broad conformity with the medium term priorities of the GPRS' (Government of Ghana 2005: 23). The reviews also noted, however, that, 'although the dependence on donor funds had declined, it still accounts for a greater part of the nation's investment expenditure, thus rendering development efforts extremely susceptible to the vagaries of donor resource flows' (Government of Ghana 2005: 24).

One of the distinctive features of the PRSP process was the 'participatory' process involved in its preparation. In Ghana this 'participatory' process had a number of elements (Government of Ghana 2003: vol. I, 5–10). The process started with a national forum of stakeholders involved in poverty reduction activities including the government, NGOs, civil society and advocacy groups, and donors. There then followed a more extensive consultative process involving 36 community groups, the Ghanaian media, the Trades Union Congress, student unions, professional bodies, representatives of women's groups, NGOs and religious groups involved in service delivery, the Ghana Employers Association, research institutions, political parties and members of parliament. The draft GPRS was also discussed with development agencies operating in Ghana and government ministers. A total of 35 separate participatory activities were undertaken in the preparation of the GPRS. Following the development of the *Strategy*, there was an extensive dissemination and publicity campaign (Government of Ghana 2003: vol. I, 10–12).

In many ways, then, the Ghanaian PRSP does what the PRSP process is supposed to do. There are, however, a number of questions it raises. First, who, exactly, gets to participate in this process? As the document says, 'groups for consultation were selected based on their ability to build broad legitimacy for the Ghana Poverty Reduction Strategy (GPRS). The groups were also seen as partners whose support was felt to be necessary for the implementation of the GPRS' (Government of Ghana 2003: vol. I, 5). In other words, there may be reason to think that participation in this process is limited to groups that in some way or another are thought to be important for its implementation, and that the process of consultation is as much about getting buy-in from these groups as it is about eliciting their views (Cooke and Kothari 2001). Second, there is a serious question about what difference the consultative process actually made to the content of the strategy (Stewart and Wang 2003). It is clear that the final strategy document is one that does not depart in any significant way from the views of the World Bank and other development agencies (Whitfield 2005). Third, it is wrong to think of the Ghanaian government as passive in this process, but, rather than being committed to the participatory process as a way of developing a better development strategy, it has been argued that the government saw the process as a necessary one to gain debt relief from western donors and mobilize additional donor funds (Whitfield 2010). Finally, there is the issue of conditionality. As we noted in Chapter 6, the new concern with participation, ownership and partnership was seen as a way of moving beyond the limitations of conditional lending to something often described as 'post-conditionality' (G. Harrison 2004). There are two issues here. The first is obvious and is that the PRSP process does not abandon conditionality, but shifts it to what we might call 'process conditionality'. The second is that abandoning the kind of conditionality associated with structural adjustment does not mean an end to intervention:

> rather it is that intervention is not exercised solely through conditionality and adjustment, but to a significant degree through closer involvement in state

institutions and the employment of incentive finance. This constitutes a less visible but perhaps more powerful role for donors.

(G. Harrison 2004: 77)

The Philippines

During the first half of the 1980s the Philippine economy experienced a severe economic decline. The economy contracted 7.1 per cent in 1984 and 4.5 per cent in 1985 (Mosley 1991). The Marcos regime came under severe internal pressure, and eventually external pressure too as the United States advised Marcos to resign in February 1986, and flew him and his family out of the country (the United States' continued involvement in the Philippines was also illustrated by its thwarting of at least one coup attempt against the new government of Corazon Aquino). The new government was more committed to reform of economic policy and the World Bank supported this process through a US$300 million Economic Recovery Loan. In the second half of the 1980s the economy grew modesty, although the economic recovery was hampered by the global downturn in the early 1990s.

The first of the sample projects examined here is the *Third Elementary Education Project*. In some ways this project, approved in 1996, is a more 'traditional' development project, but it also involved new elements that flow from the changing approach of donors during this period (World Bank 2007b). In particular the project stressed the inclusion of local communities and 'civil society' in educational improvement. The project was developed in the context of the Bank's assistance strategy for the Philippines, which stressed the need to help combat poverty though improved provision of basic services to the poorest groups. As was noted in Chapter 4, persistent high levels of poverty, especially rural poverty, were a major developmental problem in the Philippines. Elementary education service provision was seen as especially poor, as evidenced by low elementary education completion rates, poor student achievement and unequal provision of education funding. The 26 provinces selected to benefit from the project contained 24 per cent of the poor in the Philippines but received only 16.7 per cent of the education resources (World Bank 2007b: viii).

The project had a number of components. First, there were actions to improve the management capacity of the Department for Education, and a programme of decentralization of some of its functions. Second, the bulk of the project was directed at improving regional elementary education through the development of local education improvement plans and the funding of school improvements, teaching materials and teacher training. The project specifically aimed to involve local communities in the management of schools and the development of school improvement plans. The Bank lent US$113 million and the Japanese government slightly less, with the rest of the money coming from central and local government. The project was revised in 2001 as problems became apparent. Only 10 per cent of the loan funds had been spent, with over half of that going on consultants, and only 5 per cent of the targeted civil works had been undertaken. There was poor management and a lack of coordination between various parties (leading to logistical problems with delivering teaching materials) and a lack of consultation with schools about their local needs (World Bank 2007b: 4–5). The project was streamlined, and subsequent implementation improved although it was hindered somewhat by frequent changes in the leadership of the Department for Education (seven different Secretaries of Education during the project period) (World Bank 2007b: 7).

As a result of this, the Bank assessed the project outcomes as 'satisfactory'. Measures of educational improvement, including elementary education completion rates and student achievement rates, improved in the regions benefiting from the project, although they fell short of the targets set at the time of project approval. Completion rates rose from 55 to 61 per cent and there seems to have been an improvement in student attainment (World Bank 2007b: 14–16). Over 2,500 schools benefited in some way or another. In addition, the Bank argued that the project had a 'significant positive effect' on community involvement in education in the project regions as measured by the amount of local funds raised to support elementary education (World Bank 2007b: 20). A number of implementation problems were experienced, including problems with distribution of teaching materials, but on balance the project seems to have worked and there is some evidence that elementary education was improved as a result. It is also worth noting finally that the Bank was much more concerned with beneficiary and stakeholder participation and engagement in the project, and considered that this involvement was a crucial factor in the projects' relative success (World Bank 2007b: 20–4).

At the same time, however, the Philippines' external environment suffered a severe shock in the form of the East Asian financial crisis (Table 8.2). The Philippine currency came under severe strain during the crisis, and after an unsuccessful attempt to maintain the exchange rate the government devalued the peso. At the same time the government pursued a policy of high interest rates to support the currency.

Table 8.2 Philippines: selected indicators, 1985–2004

	1985–9	1990–4	1995–9	2000–4
GDP growth rate (%)	2.7	1.8	3.7	4.7
Inflation (%)	9.3	10.1	8	5.4
Exports annual growth (%)	6.4	7.6	5.4	7.6
Interest payments on external debt (% of exports)	18.8	10.6	5.4	6.8
Poverty headcount at $1.25 a day (PPP) (% of population)	35 (1985)	31 (1991)	22 (1997)	22 (2003)
Life expectancy at birth (years)	64	66.3	68.4	70.1
Under-5 mortality rate per 1,000	78 (1985)	59 (1990)	45 (1995)	38 (2000)

Source: World Bank.

The *Banking System Reform Loan* was a programme initiated in 1998 in the aftermath of the East Asian financial crisis. The economic problems arising from the crisis had had an adverse impact on the banking system. Non-performing loans had risen sharply and many Philippine banks were undercapitalized. In addition the regulatory system was poor, and the Philippines National Bank (PNB), one of the main state-owned banks, was in a weak financial position (World Bank 2001). The loan was designed to improve the supervision of the banking sector, develop stricter disclosure requirements and improved transparency in the banking system, develop an intervention system for troubled banks, and reform banking laws, including allowing 100 per cent foreign ownership of Philippine banks. A key part of the programme was to improve the financial position of the PNB by some form of semi-privatization whereby private capital would be brought in and a new ownership arrangement would generate the incentives to improve the performance of the bank. The World Bank loan was US$300 million and was to be disbursed in three tranches, the second and third to be disbursed when progress on reform had been demonstrated. The logic of projects of this kind is clear, especially in the context of the post-Asian crisis when banking systems in developing countries were coming under increasing scrutiny, and in the context too of the argument that a well-functioning banking system was necessary for developing countries to integrate into the global economy and benefit from the increasing flows of private capital. As the Bank put it, the reforms would help 'enhance market confidence' (World Bank 2001: 4). More generally this project shows the kinds of institutional, regulatory and legal reforms that donors were pushing during this period (Williams 2008b).

This project was not a success, however. The Bank rated its outcome as 'unsatisfactory', its sustainability as 'unlikely' and its institutional development impact as 'modest'. The Bank rated its own performance as 'satisfactory' but that of the Philippine government as 'unsatisfactory' (World Bank 2001: 2). The PNB remained a weak institution that needed additional government support to survive. There were long delays in completing the necessary audits of the bank to prepare for private investment, and the search for a strategic private investor was unsuccessful. In addition, the government sold part of its stake in the bank in order to generate cash, but as the Bank put it 'the manner in which the sale occurred was not fully transparent. And the new ownership of [the bank] was unable to generate confidence in the governance of the bank or adequately improve its financial position' (World Bank 2001:10). There were allegations of close ties between the new principal owners of the bank and the government of the Philippines at the time. On top of this, the necessary legislative changes envisaged by the reform programme were in large part not enacted by the Philippine Congress. Indeed the lack of an adequate plan on the part of the government for strengthening the PNB, and the lack of legislative changes, were deemed by the World Bank to have been sufficiently serious to prevent the disbursement of the second and third tranches of the loan and it was cancelled in May 2001 with the agreement of the new government that had come to power in January of that year

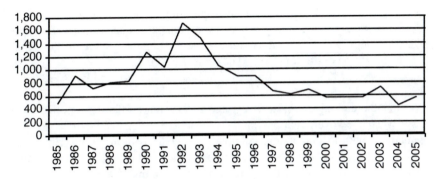

Figure 8.3 Total aid disbursements to the Philippines, 1985–2005 (US$ millions at current prices). Source: OECD.

(World Bank 2001: 6). There were some areas in which changes were made, but on balance the project was a failure.

The difficult political environment for aid agencies in the Philippines is reflected in the aid it received during this period (Figure 8.3). It is also reflected in the very mixed record of project success. The World Bank's evaluation of its lending to the Philippines concluded that from 1986 to 1989 all of its 11 loans were rated as 'satisfactory', but that this fell to 73 per cent in the period 1990–7 (World Bank 1999: 42). The Asian Development Bank's assessment of its lending to the Philippines 1986–2001 concluded that, of 36 projects fully evaluated, only 12 were rated as 'unsuccessful' (Asian Development Bank 2003: 62–4).

Argentina

Argentina too experienced a major economic and political crisis in the first half of the 1980s as a result of the debt crisis and the Falklands War. At the time the World Bank's interpretation of the problems in the Argentinian economy was derived straightforwardly from the neoliberal counter-revolution in development theory: ISI shielded domestic industry from international competition and discouraged exports, and government interventions in the economy led to slow growth and produced extensive government deficits that could be financed only by external borrowing (World Bank 1988: 1–2). This was particularly the case in the area of trade, where the Bank argued that the government had used trade policy instruments for 'non-trade objectives' (World Bank 1988: 24). In addition, ISI drove still further interventions in the economy:

> Import protection allows domestic producers to acquire some degree of monopoly power which facilitates mark-up pricing. The domestic producer has few incentives to resist wage demands, or respond with productivity enhancing adjustments, when protection allows him to pass on cost increases to consumers. The government is then tempted to control both prices and

wages. Having in effect assumed responsibility for income distribution, it becomes exposed to the pressures from organized labor and specific inter- est groups, and may try to pass the burden to unprotected groups through a combination of price and export controls.

(World Bank 1988: 34)

After the end of the military regime in 1983, there followed a period until 1989 when the government attempted to stabilize the Argentinian economy – sometimes with IMF support – culminating in 1988 with the 'Plan Primavera'. This was the start of the closer relations between the Bank and the Argentinian government and signalled the start of a more comprehensive programme of structural adjustment (World Bank 1988: 4–22). The *Trade Policy and Export Diversification Loan* and *Second Trade Policy Loan* were part of that pro- cess. These loans were sectoral adjustment loans in the sense that they were conditional loans, but the conditions targeted only one area of the economy: in this case trade liberalization. This was a mechanism used more frequently by the Bank in the later 1980s as some of the problems with full-scale structural adjustment programmes were becoming apparent (Williams 2008a: 56). It was approved in 1988 and involved a US$300 million World Bank loan to 'support the Government's program for integrating Argentina into the world economy', as the project document put it (World Bank 1988: iii).

This was to be accomplished by reforms in a number of areas: first, the removal of non-tariff barriers to imports, including quantitative restrictions and import licensing; second, the rationalizing and reduction of tariff barriers to imports; third, ending the use of anti-dumping measures that were often used to control imports; fourth, the deregulation of exports, including the removal of export controls and a reduction in export taxes; and, fifth, reform of the industrial promotion regime by reducing tax breaks and increasing the transparency of the process of selecting companies for government support (World Bank 1988: 30–4). The Bank was well aware that there were costs to this programme of reforms, particularly for workers in those firms that would not survive in a com- petitive environment (World Bank 1988: 37). However, it made two arguments in response to this: first, that demand for labour would increase in the longer term; second, that the previous system of protected production had itself caused significant hardship to the poorest groups by reducing per capita income and leading to the deterioration of public services as a result of the crisis of public finances (World Bank 1988: 36–7). The loan was disbursed in two tranches. The first tranche was to be disbursed on the basis of a number of preconditions; the second was contingent on the government's undertaking a number of highly specified actions (World Bank 1988: 38).

In the original project document the Bank admitted that success was not assured, but argued that 'it can be said safely that there is no alternative strategy that could achieve both economic stability and sustained growth' (World Bank 1988: 39). In the end Argentina made significant changes to its trade policies and by the early 1990s had eliminated almost all quantitative restriction on imports and export taxes and as a result had 'moved from one of the most closed and intransparent [sic] trade regimes to one of the most open and transparent' (World Bank 1994c: v). The Bank admitted that disentangling the effects of the changes brought about by this loan from the effects of other structural changes including privatization and more general deregulation was difficult, but argued that the impact of trade reforms was seen in the dramatic increase in trade volumes and the significant increase in consumer good imports (World Bank 1994c: v). However the process of reform was far from straightforward. The 'Plan Primavera' failed to gain domestic political support, leading to massive capital flight and hyperinflation and the Bank stopped disbursements of the loan in March 1989 because of the deteriorating economic and political situation. The economy was only restored to some kind of macroeconomic stability after President Menem came to office in mid-1989, when disbursement resumed. The Menem government was able to take more serious action, in large part because the economic crisis had eroded the power and legitimacy of some of the groups resisting reform efforts.

Despite the new government's commitment to reform there was still a significant debate about whether the second tranche of the loan should be released because the government had not liberalized exports to the extent required by the original loan agreement, particularly the ending of export taxes (World Bank 1994c: 14–15). Nonetheless the second tranche was disbursed in 1990, on the basis that the government had made good progress with liberalization in other areas, and was committed to maintaining a stable macroeconomic environment (World Bank 1994c: 15). Essentially the new government was being rewarded for good behaviour even though it had not fulfilled all the conditions, although as we noted above the Bank did stop disbursement when little progress was being made. On balance the Bank considered the programme to have been a success, and in the end Argentina complied with the loan conditions. But again, as with Ghana above, this was more the result of the commitment of the new government than the conditionality itself, as the halt to disbursement in March 1989 was ineffective as a mechanism for inducing continued policy reform.

As discussed in Chapter 5, economic crises of various kinds were a regular feature of the global economy during the 1990s and beyond, and although they were not confined to developing countries or 'emerging markets' they did occur with depressing frequency in these states. During the 1990s the Argentinian economy experienced wild fluctuations in growth and experienced a major economic crisis in the early 2000s (Table 8.3). This happened even though Argentina had engaged in a significant programme of structural adjustment after 1989, as the project above demonstrates. Indeed, the origins of the crisis in the early 2000s can be traced to the adjustment programme and attempts to combat hyperinflation.

In 1991 the Argentinian government passed the 'Convertibility Law'. This created a currency board and guaranteed convertibility of pesos to dollars at a one-to-one rate (the central bank had to keep its US dollar foreign exchange reserves at the same level as the cash in circulation in the economy). This guaranteed the currency (as it was backed by dollars and could be exchanged into dollars easily at a fixed rate) and this in turn helped restore confidence in the currency and reduce

Table 8.3 Argentina: selected indicators, 1985–2004

	1985–9	1990–4	1995–9	2000–4
GDP growth rate (%)	–1.6	6.8	2.3	0.3
Inflation (%)	854.7	444.6	–0.2	10.0
Exports annual growth (%)	5.8	6.4	10.6	4.6
Interest payments on external debt (% of exports)	38.9	16.8	25	11.6
Poverty headcount at $1.25 a day (PPP) (% of population)	2 (1986)	2 (1992)	2 (1996)	10 (2002) 8 (2004)
Life expectancy at birth (years)	71	72	73.1	74.2
Under-5 mortality rate per 1,000	34 (1985)	28 (1990)	25 (1995)	21 (2000)

Source: World Bank.

inflation rates. In the period until 1994 this system worked reasonably well, as inflation was reduced. The fixed exchange rate, however, made imports relatively cheap and there were balance of payments deficits and extensive government borrowing. In 1995 the economy contracted significantly as a result of the flight of capital from 'emerging markets' in the wake of the Mexican crisis in late 1994. The increased capital mobility encouraged during the process of structural adjustment, and the convertibility of the currency due to the 'Convertibility Law', made this capital flight much easier. Growth was restored in 1996–7 but this period also saw the appreciation of the dollar, resulting in an appreciation of the peso relative to Argentina's major trading partners, putting further pressure on the balance of payments. This situation was exacerbated by the repercussions of the East Asian financial crisis of 1997. Again there was capital flight from 'emerging markets' but a more specific problem was the devaluation of the Brazilian real, which hurt Argentinian exports to one of the country's largest trading partners (Feldstein 2002; Galiani *et al.* 2003).

Faced with rising debt the government inaugurated a programme of spending cuts, but in 2000 Argentina had to enter into an agreement with the IMF conditional on significant improvement in public finances. The economic situation deteriorated rapidly, with sharply rising unemployment, and at the beginning of 2001 a US$40 billion rescue package was assembled from the IMF, the World Bank, IADB, Spain and other private lenders. Argentina attempted to restructure its debts but the real pressure came in the form of a loss of confidence in the convertibility regime. This led in late 2001 to a huge run on the banks as people converted their pesos into dollars and sent them abroad. In response to this the government attempted to impose limits on withdrawals from bank accounts, but this only triggered widespread protests and eventually rioting. The government announced it was suspending payments on its debts (defaulting) and in early 2002 abandoned the convertibility regime.

As the Argentinian economy collapsed, so an extensive series of programmes were initiated by external agencies. The World Bank-supported *Economic and Social Transition Structural Adjustment Loan* was one of these. It was a US$500 million programme initiated in 2003 and targeted two areas: the first was provincial finances, and especially the issue of 'quasi-monies'; the second was the protection of social spending, particularly on health services (World Bank 2003). The issue of quasi-monies was a significant one. Provincial governments had been issuing their own quasi-currencies (promissory notes, drafts and bonds) to pay wages and other expenditures, in large part because of a shortage of pesos as a result of the convertibility. These quasi-monies limited the ability of the central bank to conduct monetary policy; they contributed to the growth of the informal economy and tax evasion; they affected intraprovincial trade; and they often penalized low-income individuals, who were paid in these quasi-monies, but then found that they traded at a discount to the peso (World Bank 2003: 18). By the end of 2002 some $7.7 billion worth of quasi-monies had been introduced (World Bank 2003: 18). The fact that the government no longer operated a unified currency system is a sign of how badly the economy had deteriorated. One of the objects of the loan was to help fund a Program of Monetary Unification whereby quasi-monies would be exchanged for pesos.

A second element of the loan was to help protect social spending. The economic crisis had a devastating social impact in terms of high unemployment and a great demand for health services (World Bank 2003: 25–6). The government was determined to protect and indeed increase social sector spending. As the Bank put it, this 'reverses a pattern seen in previous crises in Argentina when social spending was not protected from cuts' (World Bank 2003: 26). Also, unlike in the past, the World Bank and other international agencies were not pushing the government to cut social spending. Instead, the loan was designed to allow increased spending, particularly for health and education, to 'help mitigate the immediate social costs of the crisis, but also to minimize the potential for persistent or irreversible effects' (World Bank 2003: 26).

The loan was to be disbursed in a single tranche and was not subject to the usual forms of conditionality, beyond the agreement entered into by the government to use the money in the way described in the project, although the government had of necessity entered into an agreement with the IMF that provided some form of macroeconomic conditionality (World Bank 2003: 31). The Bank accepted that there were substantial risks associated with the loan, but concluded that these were outweighed by the risks of not assisting Argentina through its economic crisis. In the end the Bank rated that project's outcome as 'satisfactory', although it is also clear that the improvement in Argentina's economic situation was the result not simply of this particular project, but rather of the large programme of assistance offered by the international community. Monetary union was substantially restored by the end of 2003 and social spending was substantially protected (World Bank 2004: 9–10). The Bank's assessment of the loan concluded that the

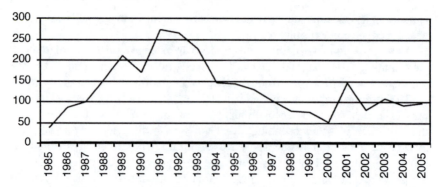

Figure 8.4 Total aid disbursements to Argentina, 1984–2005 (US$ millions at current prices). Source: OECD.

broadly successful outcomes were significantly the result of 'strong ownership' by the Argentinian government (World Bank 2004: 18).

The dramatic volatility of the Argentinian economy during this period is, of course, reflected in the aid it received (Figure 8.4). Nonetheless, overall, the World Bank's assistance to Argentina shows some improvement from the earlier period; 97 per cent of its projects from 1991 to 1999 were rated as 'satisfactory' (World Bank 2000d: 26).

Development practice in the liberal order

This review of Ghana, the Philippines and Argentina confirms how much had changed in the project of international development during the liberal order. The new issues of 'participation', good governance and regulation come to the fore. Above all we can see how much more intrusive the project of international development is: from structural adjustment to the PRSP process we can see that development agencies become concerned with a wider and wider range of issues. We can also see how the sovereignty of developing countries is at the very least downgraded, if not completely ignored, in the attempts by donors to rework not just the economies of developing countries, but also their politics and societies too (Williams 2000, 2008a). Through conditionality, the PRSP process and the fact that western development agencies are really the only source of funds for most developing countries during this period, western agencies have attempted to intervene significantly and intrusively in the internal affairs of developing countries. In this it exactly replicated the broader changes associated with the liberal international order.

However, as we also saw in Chapter 4, development agencies do not have it all their own way. Events inside and outside countries continue to play a significant role in the ability of development agencies to actually succeed. The recurrence of crises – the East Asian financial crisis and the crisis in Argentina, for example, themselves partly the product of the liberal order – pose new challenges for donors and can severely undermine the development strategies of western donors. Similarly, despite the leverage that donors do have over many developing countries, it is clear that in countries such as the Philippines political elites often do things the donors do not like. And, as structural adjustment demonstrates, there are significant limits to what donors can do. Even in countries such as Ghana, which is heavily aid dependent and which in some ways was a success story for at least some of this period, the actual developmental outcomes are and continue to be ambiguous.

Conclusion
Changing order? Changing development?

The argument presented here is that the project of international development has been crucially shaped by the international order from which it emerges and within which it operates. Far from seeing the project of international development as some kind of autonomous realm of activity, it should be understood as being structured by the prevailing international order. This is so not just in the broad sense that 'development' has been a important part of the United States' hegemonic project since the end of the Second World War, but also in the much narrower sense in that development theory, development institutions and development practice have been shaped by the international order. This connection goes right down to the individual projects funded in individual developing countries: the dam projects, the road projects, structural adjustment, the PRSP process – all these reflect the kind of international order within which they are implemented in terms of the kinds of ideas about development they embody, in terms of the kinds of interventions that are seen as possible and legitimate, and in terms of relations between development agencies. This is not to deny the internal processes of reflexivity that are also a feature of the project of international development. Development agencies have tried to learn from past experiences, and they have demonstrated a certain level of creativity in the responses to problems they have encountered. Given that these agencies have a genuine desire to do development 'better' this should not be surprising. On the other hand, that these processes of 'learning' and creativity end up replicating the broader characteristics of international order shows just how fundamentally the project of international development is shaped by this order.

Changing order?

If the basic argument of the book is correct, that the project of international development changes in line with broader changes in global politics, then the question is what changes might be happening in global politics today and how the project of international development might be changing in response to that. It is too early to say, of course. Transitions in international order take place over a period of time and predictions about the future of international politics have a habit of being proved wrong – as the prediction about American decline in the 1970s shows. Nonetheless, there is a sense in which the period from 2005 to the present has seen a number of changes that, even if they do not result in a significant change in international order, indicate that the current period is one of flux and uncertainty.

First, there is an obvious sense in which 'declinism' is back particularly in debates inside America. As one commentator has put it:

> America is in unprecedented decline. The self-inflicted wounds of the Iraq War, growing government debt, increasingly negative current-account balances and other internal economic weaknesses have cost the United States real power in today's world of rapidly spreading knowledge and technology. If present trends continue, we will look back at the Bush administration years as the death knell for American hegemony.

(Pape 2009: 1)

Francis Fukuyama has echoed these sentiments and there is barely an American news magazine that has not run articles demonstrating a considerable anxiety over the future of American power even if there is some disagreement about how serious it actually is (Beinart 2010; Fallows 2010; Kennedy 2010; Fukuyama 2011).

As with the debate about decline in the 1970s, this has both an external and internal component. Externally, the 'rise of China' and more generally other large developing countries such as Brazil and India has suggested to some that there is a fundamental shift in the distribution of power within international politics. Coupled with this is the sense that the United States has fallen victim to 'imperial overstretch': that the actions in Afghanistan and Iraq, enabled by position of dominance achieved after the end of the Cold War, have exposed the limits of US power. For some commentators there is even an inevitable logic to this process: the relatively unconstrained hegemon is tempted to do things it could not previously do, and in so doing it pushes further than it is really capable of pushing. In addition, as the hegemon becomes more active so other states increasingly see the threat to their interests and begin to balance against the hegemon. Internally, there is a sense in which the United States has lost its way with economic problems and an increasingly fractured politics.

Given that we have been here before, it is necessary to be cautious about this debate. It is particularly important to distinguish between the growing 'power' of other states and a threat to US hegemony (Magnus 2010). In other words we should be asking a more nuanced set of questions about what of US hegemony is 'threatened' by the growth of other powers and what it is about these other powers that poses a 'threat'. The US hegemonic order has several features that should shape debates about its 'decline' (Deudney and Ikenberry 1999). First, one of the great geniuses of the US hegemonic order is that it allows other states to prosper within it without threatening it. Both Japan and Germany, for example, grew economically but *within* the hegemonic order established by the United States. What would need to be shown is that China, for example, which has benefited tremendously from this hegemonic order, will in some form or another want to change, overturn or rework this order. Second, US hegemony has worked by creating forms of mutual dependence that may operate to reduce the likelihood of threats. Japan and the United States were bound together economically during the 1970s and

1980s as the largest creditor and largest debtor nations, as exporter and importer, just as China and the United States are today. What would have to be shown is that China, or any other state, would be willing to challenge or overturn the US hegemonic order despite suffering significant economic damage to itself. Third, the United States' hegemonic leadership has been accepted, however reluctantly, by many other states. In addition the United States, again sometimes reluctantly, has been willing to play the role and incur the costs of hegemonic leadership. What would have to be shown is that another state would be willing to take on this role and incur the costs of doing so, and would be accepted as a legitimate hegemonic leader by at least a decent number of states. Finally, US hegemony, as Strange was at pains to point out, is composed of a variety of structural features (military, financial, productive and ideological). Even if the United States' relative productive strength is in decline it would still need to be shown how this would affect the other features of US power in such a way as to threaten overall US hegemony.

The actual evidence at the moment that China is a 'threat' to US hegemony is pretty thin. Certainly in the economic sphere China's growth has been extraordinary and at some point it will probably become the largest economy in the world. On the other hand, financial and military power remain heavily concentrated in the United States (and its closest allies) and as yet, and despite all the talk of the BRICs (Brazil, Russia, India and China), China does not represent an attractive alternative set of ideas for many states. In addition, despite China's status as the largest creditor nation, it needs American consumers to buy its exports to maintain its impressive growth rates (this mutual dependence may reduce if China can grow its internal market). Finally, although it is clear that China is demanding more of a role in global decision making (and in some ways is being given one) there is no sign at all that China is interested in becoming anything like *the* hegemonic state. There certainly has emerged a general sentiment that the larger developing states should be given a greater role in global decision making. This can be seen in debates over reform of the IMF and the Security Council, for example, and the creation of the G20. However, this does not represent a fundamental change in the character of US hegemony; indeed it may represent another triumph of its flexibility.

The most dramatic changes have obviously come at the level of the global economy. The period from 2007 has been the most turbulent one since the Great Depression. A massive financial crisis has created an economic recession in many countries, a severe fiscal crisis for many developed states and at the time of writing a sovereign debt crisis in the euro-zone countries. The fact that many of the larger developing economies have suffered relatively less and recovered relatively quicker only reinforces the idea of a fundamental shift in the global economy from 'west' to 'east'. The question is what kinds of implications this may have. In the past, as with the Great Depression, severe economic crises have led to significant shifts in the management of the global economy – both ideologically and institutionally. Certainly the crisis is the product of the changes in the global economy during the liberal order – particularly 'globalization' and 'financialization' – and an obvious inability of global economic and financial regulatory systems to cope with these changes (Nesvetailova 2010). At the moment there is no real evidence that the general project of globalization is being called into question, although certain kinds of policies, such as capital controls, are being used more and with less criticism from organizations such as the IMF. Second, there is some sense in which the ideological triumph of neoliberalism has been called into question. It is not just that there were unforeseen (?) effects from the liberalization of global finance; it is that the legitimacy of western states telling others how to regulate their economies has been called into question. How serious this rejection of neoliberalism will be is unclear. In many western states there is no coherent alternative set of ideas that has any real political traction. Finally, there is an on-going set of domestic, regional (EU) and global attempts to draw up new forms of regulation for the financial sector – particularly in banking and derivatives regulation. What the outcome of these processes will be is unclear, but certainly at the moment there does not seem to be any very radical change in the broad ideological and institutional underpinnings of the global economy being advocated by the major states.

In terms of changes to the normative structure of international politics it is too early to say anything very much. There may be a sense in which the large-scale interventions of the Afghanistan and Iraq kind have been called into question. Clearly success has so far been elusive and the kinds of reputational and monetary costs involved have been high. At the same time, however, the 'war on terror' is throwing up a host of new potential targets for forms of intervention (Yemen, for example) and there is no obvious sign of a reassertion of the norm of non-intervention. And, as was suggested at the end of Chapter 6, the 'war on terror' makes the norm of development if anything more important, not less.

Changing development?

It is then too early to say anything definitive about the changing character of international order and probably too early to say anything concrete about changes in the project of development. There are, however, some signs of possible changes. There is some evidence, for example, of a questioning of neoliberal development theory. In a report published in 2005 the World Bank reviewed the development experience of the 1990s. Its argument was strikingly different from much of the policy literature produced by the Bank. It is worth quoting at length:

> growth entails more than the efficient use of resources. Growth entails structural transformation . . . it is . . . a process of social transformation: people will change activities and live in different places. Social relations will change, and the informal networks of rural life will be lost as other more formal networks and organizations are established . . . these changes take place over time, alongside changes in institutions that render them possible.
>
> (World Bank 2005c: 10–11)

The report says that 'what matters for growth is less the degree to which policies approximate the ideal than the extent to which a given development strategy is able to mobilize the creative forces of society and achieve ever higher levels of productivity' (World Bank 2005c: 11). In a damming criticism of development policy, the report says:

> In retrospect it is clear that in the 1990s we often mistook efficiency gains for growth. The 'one-size fits all' policy reform approach and the belief in 'best practices' exaggerated the gains from improved resource allocation and . . . proved to be both theoretically incomplete and contradicted by the evidence. Means were often mistaken for goals – that is, improvements in policies were mistaken for growth strategies as if improvements in policies were an end in themselves.
>
> (World Bank 2005c: 11)

It goes on to say that 'clearly not everything can be right at once and not everything needs to be "right" for growth to take place' (World Bank 2005c: 12).

The report makes a number of more positive arguments: first, an argument for policy flexibility; second, an argument about the 'essential' functions' that characterize successful developing countries. These functions – rapid accumulation of capital, efficient resource allocation, technological progress and sharing the benefits of growth – can be achieved by varied and various policies. Third, it argues that government discretion needs to be managed, not replaced by rules, and that there should be a pragmatic and incremental approach to public sector governance; in other words, that the state has an indispensable role in development that cannot be reduced to the observance of various rules.

These arguments have also been put forward by a number of economists, notably Dani Rodrik. As Rodrik has put it, neoliberal reforms:

> were too obsessed with deadweight-loss triangles and reaping efficiency gains from eliminating them, and did not pay enough attention to stimulating the dynamic forces that lie behind the growth process. *Seeking efficiency gains does not amount to a growth strategy.*
>
> (Rodrik 2006: 975, emphasis in original)

All this is somewhat reminiscent of the development economics of the 1950s. Indeed the World Bank report quotes from Albert Hirschman's classic text in development economics, *The Strategy of Economic Development* (Hirschman 1958).

None of this has, as yet, issued in any very substantive changes in the way development agencies actually act, and there may be good reasons for thinking at the moment that they will not change. Given the hold on development discourse and theory that various elements of liberal thought have, it seems very unlikely that development agencies and western states can be weaned off their current ways of thinking about 'development'. In addition, no development agencies are as yet questioning the importance of good governance, participation and ownership. What seems more likely is that the use of various forms of intervention, for example in financial markets, will become more acceptable and there will be more flexibility and pragmatism in the approach that development agencies take towards developing countries.

Development institutions

Aid levels have continued to rise over the last few years, suggesting the continued centrality of aid and development to international politics more generally, and to the foreign policies of western states more specifically (Table 9.1). At the moment there is little evidence of the economic crisis substantially affecting aid flows. The new Conservative-led government in the UK, for example, has pledged to protect the foreign aid budget even while engaging in substantial cuts in other areas of government spending. On the other hand, as pressure on public spending increases in western states we may yet see aid volumes falling.

The most dramatic change in the institutions of the project of international development in recent years has been the rise of China as a significant aid donor, particularly in Africa (Brautigam 2009). Total Chinese aid tripled between 2000 and 2007 to over US$3 billion, and it has been estimated that total Chinese assistance to Africa was nearly $2,500 million in 2009 (Brautigam 2009: 167, 170). Nearly half of all China's foreign assistance goes to Africa (Alden 2007 22). It is not just in terms of aid that China has become increasingly significant on the continent. Total trade between China and Africa was $10 billion in 2000 but rose to more than $50 billion in 2006 and $100 billion in 2009 (Alden 2007: 14; Brown and Chun 2009: 4). China has become the third largest trading partner with Africa (after the United States and France) and a very significant investor. In addition, China has entered into agreements on cultural exchange and cooperation with 42 African states (Brown and Chun 2009: 4–5). China is also an important supplier of military equipment and training to a number of African states (Alden 2007: 25–6). This general pattern of closer China–Africa ties was symbolized by the establishment of the Forum on China–Africa Cooperation in 2000. At the 2009 ministerial meeting a host of new initiatives were announced, including a new $10 billion loan fund and a special $1 billion loan fund for small and medium-sized African enterprises. China also announced a series of programmes to build hospitals and fund medical equipment and teacher training.

China's aid to Africa comes in a number of forms (Brautigam 2009: ch. 4). It has engaged in a programme of debt cancellation for over 30 African states, and it provides both concessional and non-concessional lending to both African governments and African corporations. As well as providing aid monies, China's development assistance programme often involves resources-for-infrastructure deals whereby China or Chinese companies get access to resources in exchange for China building a road or power station or hospital (usually using Chinese labour, materials and construction companies). In this sense it is a more diverse

Table 9.1 Aid disbursements, 2005–9 (US$ millions current prices)

	2005	*2006*	*2007*	*2008*	*2009*
OECD DAC	107,838	104,814	104,206	122,359	120,000
Multilateral	9,390	10,245	11,634	13,197	13,444

Source: OECD.

aid programme than those of many western donors. It is also institutionally fragmented. The Ministry of Finance prepares the overall aid budgets, but it is the Ministry of Commerce that manages and disburses the funds. In addition, state-owned banks, particularly the China Export–Import Bank, also play an important role. This bank supports Chinese companies engaged in construction and investment in Africa. The very diversity of Chinese aid to Africa was one of the drivers behind the creation of the Forum on China–Africa Cooperation, which has become one of the key bodies for coordinating China–Africa relations (Brown and Chun 2009).

In some ways the rationale for Chinese aid to Africa is clear. One is clearly access to natural resources. Oil is the most important African export to China and it is no coincidence that Chinese aid has been directed towards securing access to oil reserves (Alden 2007: 42–4). Beyond oil, China has an interest in securing other natural resources, including other minerals and hardwood (Butler 2007). Second, there is a clear commercial element to Chinese aid, as China has used its varied aid resources to support Chinese companies (Brautigam 2009: 87–9). Third, China has been concerned to use its aid resources to further its diplomatic objectives. This has involved, for example, displacing Taiwan's official relations with African states, garnering support for its Olympic bid and ensuring the support of African states in the UN – especially when it comes to criticisms of China's human rights record (Alden 2007: 20–3). At the most general level, China's increasing aid provision can be seen as part of its more activist foreign policy stance. Finally, China's relations with developing countries, particularly in Africa, can be seen as an embodiment of a series of principles which reflect the way that China itself would like to be treated by western states. China's Africa Policy, codified in 2006, says that its relations with Africa will be guided by four principles: sincerity, friendship and equality; mutual benefit, reciprocity and common prosperity; mutual support and close coordination; and learning from each other and seeking common development (Government of China 2006). In practice this has meant no explicit economic and political conditionality, and treating African governments as legitimate representatives of the interests of their peoples. As a Chinese diplomat at the UN said:

> Externally imposed conditions do not offer genuine solutions to African problems . . . The international community should . . . fully acquaint themselves with the real circumstances of the African countries, respect their sovereign choices and development strategies and support the continent's efforts to lift itself up by its bootstraps.
>
> (quoted in Thompson 2007: 54)

Given this it is easy to see why Chinese aid has been attractive to many African states. For some, such as Zimbabwe, it has provided a way of accessing aid resources when western states have cut off aid provision. For almost all of them the attractions of being able to access aid resources outside the demands of western states and development agencies (good governance, human rights and economic policy reform) are obvious. China's aid provision, however, has created tensions both inside and outside Africa. Western states and development agencies have often been critical of China's aid provision, precisely because it does not concern itself with issues such as good governance, corruption and human rights (Campbell 2007). '[T]here is a concern that the Chinese intend to aid and abet African dictators . . . and undo much of the progress that has been made on democracy and governance in the last 15 years in African nations' (State Department official quoted in Alden 2007: 106). In addition, China's aid has been criticized for very lax monitoring and reporting requirements, leading to suspicions that it has fuelled corruption. More generally, China's increasing involvement with Africa poses a challenge to states such as the United States, Britain and France, which have historically played an important role on the continent (Gallagher 2011). Inside Africa too there have been tensions. Many African activists have been critical of China's aid provision along much the same lines as western donors (Alden 2007: 89; Askouri 2007; Lemos and Ribeiro 2007). In addition, the presence of large numbers of Chinese workers and Chinese companies in some African states has raised tensions with local communities (Alden 2007: 85). At the most extreme, concerns have been raised that, far from providing a real alternative to western influence, Chinese aid is simply replicating the pattern of western colonialism and neocolonialism in Africa.

Some of the anxiety about the rise of China as a major aid donor, particularly in Africa, is overdone. China's aid to Africa is still quite substantially less than that provided by the United States, the World Bank, the EU or France, for example (Brautigam 2009: 172). The big question about the future is the extent to which, like those of Japan and to some extent France, China's aid programme will become socialized into existing western aid institutions and practices. In particular, there is a question about whether China will begin to provide development assistance within the framework of the PRSP process, for example, and condition its assistance on countries' fulfilling their obligations to the IMF and the World Bank. There is no doubt there will be increasing pressure for China to fall more into line with western aid practices. It is not so much that criticism of China's aid programme from NGOs and western governments will make the difference; it is that China may be forced to trade increasing compliance with western aid norms for the achievement of other foreign policy objectives. This may particularly be the case when it comes to reform of the decision-making structures of the IMF and the World Bank, in which the granting of a larger Chinese say may be accompanied by demands for greater harmonization of its aid policies and practices. On the other hand, at the moment China shows few signs of changing the way it relates to African states and any embrace of the language of good governance and human rights seems very unlikely given its own staunch defence of a more traditional view of sovereignty and non-intervention.

Development practice

It is too early to ascertain whether there is any real change in development practice. We might expect some, but at the moment there is no real change at all. In terms of our sample countries, 2005 to 2008 were modestly successful years with reasonable growth rates and relatively controlled inflation (Table 9.2). In 2008–9, however, the impact of the global financial and economic crisis began to be felt as growth rates and exports fell (Table 9.3). There is also no real sign yet of a decline in aid volumes to these countries as a result of this on-going crisis.

Table 9.2 Selected indicators for Ghana, the Philippines and Argentina, 2005–9

		2005	2006	2007	2008	2009
GDP growth rate (%)	Ghana	5.9	6.4	6.5	8.4	4.7
	Philippines	5.0	5.3	7.0	3.7	1.1
	Argentina	9.2	8.5	8.7	6.6	0.9
Inflation (%)	Ghana	15.0	80.1	16.3	20.2	16.7
	Philippines	6.5	5.2	3.0	7.4	2.6
	Argentina	8.8	13.4	14.3	19.1	10.0
Exports annual growth (%)	Ghana	9	14	1	2	n/a
	Philippines	5	13	5	–2	n/a
	Argentina	14	7	9	1	n/a
Interest payments on external debt (% of exports)	Ghana	2	2	1	2	n/a
	Philippines	6	6	5	5	n/a
	Argentina	6	7	6	5	n/a
Poverty headcount at $1.25 a day (PPP) (% of population)	Ghana	n/a	30	n/a	n/a	n/a
	Philippines	n/a	23	n/a	n/a	n/a
	Argentina	5	3	n/a	n/a	n/a
Life expectancy at birth (years)	Ghana	56.5	56.5	56.5	56.6	n/a
	Philippines	71	71.3	71.6	71.8	n/a
	Argentina	74.8	74.9	75.1	75.3	n/a
Under-5 mortality rate per 1,000	Ghana	84	80	76	72	69
	Philippines	35	35	34	34	33
	Argentina	17	16	15	15	14

Source: World Bank.

Table 9.3 Total aid disbursements to Ghana, Philippines and Argentina, 2005–9 (US $millions at current prices)

	2005	2006	2007	2008	2009
Ghana	1149	1213	1164	1305	1583
Philippines	567	565	610	48	310
Argentina	96	115	101	130	128

Source: OECD.

International development, International Relations and international order

Much of the concern of this book has been to track how the project of international development has been shaped by the changing international order. However, another aim of the book has been to use the project of international development to explore changes in international order and to see how developing countries have been affected by these changes. A number of concluding points can be made. The first is to stress a point made in the introduction that the project of international development has been a central part of International Relations since 1945, and in many respects it has been an increasingly important part as aid and 'development' have become linked to much wider foreign policy projects such as state building. Second, it follows from this that the discipline of International Relations should pay more attention to the project of international development in attempts to conceptualize the recent history of international politics. Third, it is clear that the change to a liberal international order had very important consequences for developing countries themselves. As the norm of non-intervention was eroded and the unipolar concert emerged as the dominant force in global politics, so developing states were exposed to more interventionist policies that had as their target large areas of economic, political and social life. Fourth, even if scepticism remains about the particular account given in this book, it remains the case that any adequate conceptualization of international politics ought to take as one of its reference points the place and experience of the majority of states, which, as developing countries, tend to experience this politics in very different ways from the developed world.

Finally, the concept of 'international order' upon which this book's analytical structure hinges is clearly not without its difficulties; this book has taken a fairly conventional view about what the key constituent parts of international order are, and has not substantially engaged in some of the knottier issues about the relationship between elements of international order and the process of change from one international order to another. A great deal more work could be done on these issues. Nonetheless, if we are to have some kind of account of the larger processes of change in international politics over time then something like a concept of 'international order' is likely to be useful, perhaps even indispensable, as it is only by having a picture, albeit stylized, of the main features of international politics at any given time that we can start to explore what the main differences are in international politics from one period to another.

Development, history and critique

Whatever changes do occur in the project of international development in the future, they will be fundamentally shaped by whatever broader changes take place in the character of international order. This should not be a surprise. Right from its origins as an institutionalized activity in the post-1945 sovereign order, development has been structured by the character of international order. Recognizing this does not mean that this project is wrong or misguided – although, as this book has shown, there have been plenty of things that have not worked and plenty of things that have had decidedly negative consequences. This book has not been a criticism of the project of international development. However, it has tried to be a critique. It has been animated by the thought that a more thorough historical analysis that locates the project of international development in its international context provides resources for thinking critically about development. It forces us to confront the possibility that the project of international development is not shaped primarily by what developing countries 'need' for development, nor primarily by some kind of process whereby development agencies come to 'know' the truth about development. Also, it forces us to recognize that, whatever might come in the future, there is no reason to think this will change. This is not to deny the possibility that the project of international development has 'helped' developing countries in some ways (although sometimes it clearly has not). It is, however, to say that the project of international development – its theories, its practices and its institutions – is contingent on the wider international order within which it operates.

Notes

3 Development institutions in the sovereign order

1 These include the East African Development Bank (1967), the Caribbean Development Bank (1970), the Andean Development Corporation (1970) and the Islamic Development Bank (1975). In the post-Cold War era these are joined by the European Bank for Reconstruction and Development (1991) and the North American Development Bank (1993).

6 Development theory in the liberal order

1 The term 'counter-revolution' in this context is taken from Toye (1987) and more generally from Johnson (1971).

Bibliography

Abrahamsen, R. (2000) *Disciplining Democracy: development discourse and good governance in Africa*, London: Zed Books.

Adelman, C. (2003) 'The privatization of foreign aid: reassessing national largess', *Foreign Affairs* 82, 6: 9–14.

African Development Bank (1991) 'Review of Project Performance Results 1989', Operations Evaluation Department, African Development Bank, Abidjan, 26 September.

Agarwala, R. (1990) 'Governance and institutional development in sub-Saharan Africa', in Corkery, J. and Bossuyt, J. (eds) *Governance and Institutional Development in Sub-Saharan Africa: seminar report*, Maastricht: European Centre for Development Policy Management.

Ahmed, S. and Potter, D. (2006) *NGOs in International Politics*, Bloomfield, CT: Kumarian Press.

Alden, C. (2007) *China in Africa: partner, competitor or hegemon?*, London: Zed Books.

Almond, G. (1970) *Political Development: essays in heuristic theory*, Boston: Little Brown.

Almond, G. and Powell, G. (1965) *Comparative Politics: a developmental approach*, Boston: Little Brown.

Almond, G. and Verba, S. (1965) *The Civic Culture*, Princeton: Princeton University Press.

Amuzegar, J. (1958) 'Point Four: performance and prospect', *Political Science Quarterly* 37, 4: 530–546.

Anderson, B. (1988) 'Cacique democracy and the Philippines: origins and dreams', *New Left Review* 169: 3–33.

Anderson, D. (2005) *Histories of the Hanged: Britain's dirty war in Kenya and the end of empire*, London: Weidenfeld and Nicolson.

Anderson, P. (2000) 'Renewals', *New Left Review* 1 Jan.–Feb.: 1–20.

Apter, D. (1965) *The Politics of Modernization*, Chicago: University of Chicago Press.

Asian Development Bank (2003) 'Country Assistance Program Evaluation in the Philippines', Manila, Asian Development Bank.

—— (2005) 'Sector Assistance Program Evaluation of Asian Development Bank Assistance to the Philippines Power Sector', Operations Evaluation Department, Manila, Asian Development Bank.

Askouri, A. (2007) 'China's investment in Sudan: displacing villages and destroying communities', in Manji, F. and Marks, S. (eds) *African Perspectives on China in Africa*, Nairobi: Fahamu.

Ayoob, M. and Zierler, M. (2005) 'The unipolar concert: the North–South divide trumps transatlantic differences', *World Policy Journal* 22, 1: 31–42.

Ayres, R. (1983) *Banking on the Poor: the World Bank and world poverty*, Cambridge, MA: MIT Press.

Bardhan, P. (1988) 'Alternative approaches to development economics', in Chenery, H. and Srinivasan, T. (eds) *Handbook of Development Economics*, Amsterdam: Elsevier.

—— (1993) 'Economics of development and the development of economics', *Journal of Economic Perspectives* 7, 2: 129–142.

Bates, R. (1981) *States and Markets in Tropical Africa: the political basis of agricultural policies*, Berkeley: University of California Press.

—— (1989) *Beyond the Miracle of the Market: the political economy of agrarian development*, Cambridge: Cambridge University Press.

Bauer, P. (1976) *Dissent on Development: studies and debates in development economics*, London: Weidenfeld and Nicolson.

—— (1984) *Reality and Rhetoric: studies in the economics of development*, Cambridge, MA: Harvard University Press.

Beinart, P. (2010) 'How the financial crisis has undermined US power', *Time Magazine* 175, 24: 30–31.

Bello, W., Kinley, D. and Elinson, E. (1982) *Development Debacle: the World Bank in the Philippines*, San Francisco: Institute for Food and Development Policy.

Bisley, N. (2007) *Rethinking Globalization*, Basingstoke: Palgrave.

Black, E. (1963) *The Diplomacy of Economic Development*, Clinton, MA: Colonial Press.

Brautigam, D. (2009) *The Dragon's Gift: the real story of China in Africa*, Oxford: Oxford University Press.

Brett, E. (1993) 'Voluntary agencies and development organizations: theorizing the problem of efficiency and accountability', *Development and Change* 24, 2: 269–303.

Broadberry, S. and Howlett, P. (1998) 'The United Kingdom: "victory at all costs"', in Harrison, M. (ed.) *The Economics of World War II: six Great Powers in international comparison*, Cambridge: Cambridge University Press.

Brooks, W. and Orr, R. (1985) 'Japan's economic assistance', *Asian Survey* 25, 3: 322–340.

Brown, A. (1996) *The Gorbachev Factor*, Oxford: Oxford University Press.

Brown, B. (1992) *The United States and the Politicization of the World Bank: issues of international law and policy*, London: Kegan Paul.

Brown, K. and Chun, Z. (2009) 'China in Africa: preparing for the next Forum on China–Africa Cooperation', Chatham House Briefing Note, London, June.

Brown, L., Korten, D. and Paul, S. (1991) *Nongovernmental Organizations and the World Bank: cooperation for development*, Washington, DC: World Bank.

Brown, M., Lynne-Jones, S. and Miller, S. (1996) *Debating the Democratic Peace*, Cambridge, MA: MIT Press.

Buiter, W. and Fries, S. (2002) 'What Should the Multilateral Banks Do?', EBRD Working Paper, no. 74, London: EBRD.

Butler, T. (2007) 'Growing pains and growing alliances: China, timber and Africa', in Kitissou, M. (ed.) *Africa in China's Global Strategy*, London: Adonis and Abbey.

Burley, A. (1993) 'Regulating the world: multilateralism, international law and the projection of the New Deal regulatory state', in Ruggie, J. (ed.) *Multilateralism Matters: the theory and praxis of an institutional form*, New York: Columbia University Press.

Bush, G. (1991) Speech to Congress, 6 March.

Campbell, H. (2007) 'China in Africa: challenging US hegemony', in Manji, F. and Marks, S. (eds) *African Perspectives on China in Africa*, Nairobi: Fahamu.

Carothers, T. (1991) *In the Name of Democracy: US policy towards Latin America in the Reagan years*, Berkeley: University of California Press.

—— (1994) 'The democracy nostrum', *World Policy Journal* 11, 3: 47–53.

—— (1999) *Aiding Democracy Abroad: the learning curve*, Washington, DC: Carnegie Endowment for International Peace.

Cassen, R. and Associates (1986) *Does Aid Work?* Oxford: Clarendon.

Caulfield, C. (1997) *Masters of Illusion: the World Bank and the poverty of nations*, London: Macmillan.

Cerny, P. (1993) 'Plurilateralism: structural differentiation and functional conflict in the post-Cold War world order', *Millennium* 22, 1: 27–51.

Chabbott, C. (1999) 'Development INGOs', in Boli, J. and Thomas, G. (eds) *Constructing World Culture: international nongovernmental organizations since 1875*, Stanford, CA: Stanford University Press.

Chafer, T. (2002) 'Franco-African relations: no longer so exceptional', *African Affairs* 101: 343–363.

Chandler, D. (1999) *Bosnia: faking democracy after Dayton*, London: Pluto.

—— (2000) 'International justice', *New Left Review* 6: 55–66.

Chenery, H. (1979) *Structural Change and Development Policy*, Oxford: Oxford University Press.

Chipman, J. (1989) *French Power in Africa*, Oxford: Blackwell.

CIA (1970) 'Soviet Economic Assistance to the Less Developed Countries of the Free World', Orah Cooper, 30 March, accessed at http://www.foia.cia.gov/browse_docs.asp?doc_no=0000500543

Claessens, S. and Forbes, K. (eds) (2001) *International Financial Contagion*, Dordrecht: Kluwer.

Clark, I. (2001) *The Post-Cold War Order: the spoils of peace*, Oxford: Oxford University Press.

Clark, J. (1991) *Democratizing Development: the role of voluntary organizations*, London: Earthscan.

Clausen, A. (1982) 'A concluding perspective', in Fried, E. and Owen, H. (eds) *The Future of the World Bank*, Washington, DC: Brookings Institution.

Cleveland, H. (1959) 'The convalescence of foreign aid', *American Economic Review* 49, 2: 214–231.

Cohen, E. (2004) 'History and the hyperpower', *Foreign Affairs* 83, 4: 49–63.

Collingwood, V. (2003) 'Assistance with few strings attached', *Ethics and International Affairs* 17, 1: 55–67.

Cooke, B. and Kothari, U. (eds) (2001) *Participation: the new tyranny*, London: Zed Books.

Cornia, G. (1999) 'Liberalization, Globalization and Income Distribution', UNU/WIDER Paper, Helsinki: UNU.

Cox, M. (2005) 'Beyond the West: terrors in transatlantia', *European Journal of International Relations* 11, 2: 203–233.

Cox, R. (1996) *Approaches to World Order*, Cambridge: Cambridge University Press.

Craig, D. and Porter, D. (2003) 'Poverty reduction strategy papers: a new convergence', *World Development* 31, 1: 53–69.

—— (2006) *Development beyond Neoliberalism? Governance, poverty reduction and political economy*, London: Routledge.

Critchlow, D. (1985) *The Brookings Institution 1916–1950: expertise and the public interest in a democratic society*, Dekalb, IL: North West Illinois University Press.

Culpeper, R. (1994) 'Regional development banks: exploiting their specificity', *Third World Quarterly* 15, 3: 459–482.

Cumming, G. (1995) 'French development assistance to Africa: towards a new agenda?' *African Affairs* 94: 383–398.

Dahl, G. (2001) 'Responsibility and Partnership in Swedish Aid Discourse', Nordiska Afrikainstitutet Discussion Paper 9, Uppsala.

Dahl, R. (1961) 'The behavioural approach in political science: epitaph for a monument to a successful protest', *American Political Science Review* 55, 4: 763–772

Danielson, A. and Wohlgemuth, L. (2002) 'Swedish Development Cooperation in Perspective', Lund University Department of Economics Working Paper No. 2003:8, Lund.

Desai, M. (1982) 'Homilies of a Victorian sage: a review article on Peter Bauer', *Third World Quarterly* 4, 2: 291–297.

Deudney, D. and Ikenberry, J. (1999) 'The nature and sources of liberal international order', *Review of International Studies* 25, 2: 179–196.

De Waal, A. (1997) *Famine Crimes: politics and the disaster relief industry in Africa*, Oxford: James Currey.

DfID (1997) *Eliminating World Poverty: a challenge for the 21st century*, London: DfID.

—— (2000) *Eliminating World Poverty: making globalization work for the poor*, London: DfID.

—— (2004) *Partnerships for Poverty Reduction: changing aid 'conditionality'*, London: DfID.

—— (2006) *Eliminating World Poverty: making governance work for the poor*, London: DfID.

Diamond, L. (2002) 'Winning the New Cold War on Terrorism: the democratic-governance imperative', Institute for Global Democracy Policy Paper, 1, March.

Dodge, T. (2005) 'Iraq transitions: from regime change to state collapse', *Third World Quarterly* 26, 4: 699–715.

—— (2007) 'The causes of US failure in Iraq', *Survival* 29, 1: 85–106.

Domar, E. (1957) *Essays in the Theory of Economic Growth*, Oxford: Oxford University Press.

Dunn, J. (1989) 'Conclusion', in Cruise O'Brien, D., Dunn, J. and Rathbone, R. (eds) *Contemporary West African States*, Cambridge: Cambridge University Press.

Easterly, W. (2006) *The White Man's Burden: why the West's efforts to aid the rest have done so much ill and so little good*, London: Penguin.

EBRD (1991) *Basic Documents of the European Bank for Reconstruction and Development*, London: EBRD.

Edwards, M. and Hulme, D. (1996) 'Too close for comfort? The impact of official aid on nongovernmental organizations', *World Development* 24, 6: 961–973.

Edwards, S. and Savastano, M. (1998) 'The Morning After: the Mexican Peso in the aftermath of the 1994 currency crisis', NBER Working Paper W6516, 1 April.

Eichengreen, B. (1995) 'Mainsprings of economic recovery in post-War Europe', in Eichengreen, B. (ed.) *Europe's Post-War Recovery*, Cambridge: Cambridge University Press.

Eisenstadt, S. (1966) *Modernization: protest and change*, Englewood Cliffs: Prentice-Hall.

Ellis, F. (1988) *Peasant Economics: farm households and agrarian development*, Cambridge: Cambridge University Press.

English, E. and Mule, H. (1996) *The African Development Bank*, Boulder, CO: Lynne Rienner.

Evans, P. (1997) 'The eclipse of the state? Reflections on stateness in an era of globalization', *World Politics* 50, 1: 62–87.

Fallows, J. (2010) 'How America can rise again', *Atlantic Monthly*, Jan.–Feb.: 38–52.

Feldstein, M. (2002) 'Argentina's fall: lessons from the latest financial crisis', *Foreign Affairs* 81, 2: 8–14.

Ferkiss, V. (1966) 'Theory and reality in the study of development', *Public Administration Review* 26, 2: 127–136.

Fitzgerald, F. (2000) *Way Out there in the Blue: Reagan, Star Wars and the end of the Cold War*, New York: Simon and Schuster.

Foot, R. (2000) *Rights beyond Borders: the global community and the struggle over rights in China*, Oxford: Oxford University Press.

Frank, C. and Baird, M. (1975) 'Foreign aid: its speckled past and future prospects', *International Organization* 29, 1: 133–167.

Fukado-Parr, S. (2004) 'Millennium Development Goals: why they matter', *Global Governance* 10: 395–401.

Fukuyama, F. (1989) 'The end of history', *National Interest* 16, Summer: 3–18.

—— (1992) *The End of History and the Last Man*, New York: Free Press.

—— (2004) *State-Building: governance and world order in the twenty-first century*, Ithaca, NY: Cornell University Press.

—— (2011) 'Democracy in America has less than ever to teach China', *Financial Times*, 18 January, p. 13.

Galiani, S., Heymann, D., Tommasi, M., Serven, L. and Terra, M. (2003) 'Great expectations and hard times: the Argentine Convertibility Plan', *Economia* 3, 2: 109–160.

Gallagher, J. (2011) 'Ruthless player or development partner: Britain's ambiguous reaction to China in Africa', *Review of International Studies*, forthcoming.

Giddens, A. (1990) *The Consequences of Modernity*, Stanford, CA: Stanford University Press.

Gilman, N. (2003) *Mandarins of the Future: modernization theory in Cold War America*, Baltimore: Johns Hopkins University Press.

Glynn, A., Hughes, A., Lipietz, A. and Singh, A. (1990) 'The rise and fall of the golden age', in Marglin, S. and Schor, J. (eds) *The Golden Age of Capitalism: reinterpreting the postwar experience*, Oxford: Clarendon.

Goldman, M. (1964) 'A balance sheet of Soviet foreign aid', *Foreign Affairs* 43, 349: 349–369.

Goldman, M. (2000) 'The Power of World Bank Knowledge', briefing, Bretton Woods Project, London.

Gong, G. (1984) *The Standard of 'Civilisation' in International Society*, Oxford: Clarendon.

Government of China (2006) 'China's Africa Policy', accessed at: http://www.gov.cn/misc/2006-01/12/content_156490.htm

Government of Ghana (2003) *Ghana Poverty Reduction Strategy 2003–2005: an agenda for growth and prosperity*, 2 vols, Accra: Government of Ghana.

—— (2005) 'Ghana Poverty Reduction Strategy: 2004 Annual Progress Report', Accra, Government of Ghana, March.

Government of Philippines (1972) 'Establishing Basic Policies for the Electric Power Industry', Presidential Decree no. 40.

Guan-Fu, G. (1983) 'Soviet aid to the Third World: an analysis of strategy', *Soviet Studies* 35, 1: 71–89.

Guscina, A. (2006) 'The Effects of Globalization on Labor's Share in National Income', IMF Working Paper WP/06/294, Washington, DC: IMF.

Gwin, C. (1997) 'US relations with the World Bank: 1945–1992', in Kapur, D., Lewis, J. and Webb, R. (eds) *The World Bank: its first half century, vol. 2*, Washington, DC: Brookings Institution Press.

Gyau-Boakye, P. (2001) 'The environmental impacts of the Akosombo dam and effects of climate change on the lake levels', *Environment, Development and Sustainability* 5, 1: 17–29.

Halliday, F. (1983) *The Making of the Second Cold War*, London: Verso.

—— (1994) *Rethinking International Relations*, London: Palgrave.

—— (2005) *The Middle East in International Relations: power, politics and ideology*, Cambridge: Cambridge University Press.

—— (2010) 'Third World socialism: 1989 and after', in Lawson, G., Armbruster, C. and Cox, M. (eds) *The Global 1989*, Cambridge: Cambridge University Press.

Harrison, G. (2004) *The World Bank and Africa: the construction of governance states*, London: Routledge.

Harrison, M. (1998a) 'The economics of World War II: an overview', in Harrison, M. (ed.) *The Economics of World War II: six Great Powers in international comparison*, Cambridge: Cambridge University Press.

—— (1998b) 'The Soviet Union: the defeated victor', in Harrison, M. (ed.) *The Economics of World War II: six Great Powers in international comparison*, Cambridge: Cambridge University Press.

Harrod, R. (1948) *Towards a Dynamic Economics*, London: Macmillan.

Hart, D. (1980) *The Volta River Project: a case study in politics and technology*, Edinburgh: Edinburgh University Press.

Haskell, T. (1978) 'Professionalization as cultural reform', *Humanities in Society* 1, 2: 103–114.

—— (ed.) (1984) *The Authority of Experts: studies in history and theory*, Bloomington: Indiana University Press.

Hattori, T. (2003) 'The moral politics of foreign aid', *Review of International Studies* 29, 2: 229–247.

Held, D. (1995) *Democracy and the Global Order: from the modern state to cosmopolitan governance*, Cambridge: Polity.

Held, D., Goldblatt, D. and McGrew, A. (1999) *Global Transformations: politics, economics and culture*, Cambridge: Polity.

Helleiner, E. (2006) 'Reinterpreting Bretton Woods: international development and the neglected origins of embedded liberalism', *Development and Change* 37, 5: 943–967.

Higgott, R. (1983) *Political Development Theory*, London: Routledge.

Hirschman, A. (1958) *The Strategy of Economic Development*, New Haven, CT: Yale University Press.

—— (1981) 'The rise and decline of development economics', in Hirschman, A., *Essays in Trespassing: from economics to politics and beyond*, Cambridge: Cambridge University Press.

Hirst, P. and Thompson, G. (1996) *Globalization in Question*, Oxford: Blackwell.

Honkapohja, S. (2009) 'The 1990s Financial Crisis in Nordic Countries', Bank of Finland Research Discussion Paper, 5, Helsinki.

Honkapohja, S. and Koskela, E. (1999) 'The economic crisis of the 1990s in Finland', *Economic Policy* 14, 29: 399–436.

Howe, G. (1982) 'The International Monetary Fund and the World Bank: the British approach', *International Affairs* 58, 2: 199–209.

Hull, C. (1948) *The Memoirs of Cordell Hull*, New York: Macmillan.

Huntington, S. (1968) *Political Order in Changing Societies*, New Haven, CT: Yale University Press.

—— (2002) *The Clash of Civilizations and the Remaking of World Order*, New York: Simon and Schuster.

Hurd, D. (1990) Speech given to Overseas Development Institute, London, June.

Hutchcroft, P. (1991) 'Oligarchs and cronies in the Philippine state: the politics of patrimonial plunder', *World Politics* 43, 3: 414–450.

Hyam, R. (1999) 'Bureaucracy and trusteeship in the colonial empire', in Brown, J. and Louis, W. M. (eds) *The Oxford History of the British Empire, vol. IV: the twentieth century*, Oxford: Oxford University Press.

IBRD (1951) *Sixth Annual Report*, Washington, DC: International Bank for Reconstruction and Development.

—— (1961a) 'Appraisal of the Volta River Hydroelectric Project: Ghana', report no. TO281a, 30 August.

—— (1961b) 'Appraisal of a Highway Construction and Maintenance Project: Argentina', report no. TO286, 30 June.

ICISS (2001) 'The Responsibility to Protect', Report of the International Commission on Intervention and State Sovereignty, Ottawa: International Development Research Centre.

Inkeles, A. (1969) 'Making men modern: on the causes and consequences of individual change in six developing countries', *American Journal of Sociology* 75, 2: 208–225.

—— (1975) 'Becoming modern: individual change in six developing countries', *Ethos* 3, 2: 323–342

Ikenberry, J. (1992) 'A world economy restored: expert consensus and the Anglo-American postwar settlement', *International Organization* 61, 1: 289–321.

—— (2006) *Liberal Order and Imperial Ambition: essays on American power and world politics*, Cambridge: Polity.

Inter-American Development Bank (2004) 'Final Report of the Panel of the Independent Investigation Mechanism on Yacyreta Hydroelectric Project', 27 February.

Jackson, R. (1993) *Quasi-States: sovereignty, international relations and the third world*, Cambridge: Cambridge University Press.

Jackson, S. (2007) 'Chinese Foreign Aid to Africa: a reassessment of the 1970s', paper presented to the International Studies Association Annual Meeting, Chicago, 28 February.

Jahn, B. (2005) 'Kant, Mill, and illiberal legacies in international affairs', *International Organization* 59, 4: 177–207.

Jayarajah, C. and Branson, W. (1995) *Structural and Sectoral Adjustment: World Bank experience, 1980–1992, operations evaluation study*, Washington, DC: World Bank.

Jeffries, R. (1989) 'Ghana: the political economy of personal rule', in Cruise O'Brien, D., Dunn, J. and Rathbone, R. (eds) *Contemporary West African States*, Cambridge: Cambridge University Press.

Johnson, H. (1964) *Money, Trade and Economic Growth: survey lectures in economic theory*, London: Unwin.

—— (1971) 'The Keynesian revolution and the monetarist counter-revolution', *American Economic Review* 61, 2: 1–14.

Johnson, J. and Wasty, S. (1993) 'Borrower Ownership of Adjustment Programs and the Political Economy of Reform', World Bank Discussion Paper, World Bank, Washington, DC.

Jolly, R., Emmerij, L., Ghai, D. and Lapeyre, F. (2004) *UN Contributions to Development Thinking and Practice*, Bloomington: University of Indiana Press.

Kaplan, J. (1967) *The Challenge of Foreign Aid: polices, problems and possibilities*, New York: Praeger.

Kappagoda, N. (1995) *The Asian Development Bank*, Boulder, CO: Lynne Rienner.

Kapstein, E. and Mastanduno, M. (eds) (1999) *Unipolar Politics: realism and state strategies after the Cold War*, New York: Columbia University Press.

Kapur, D., Lewis, J. and Webb, R. (eds) (1997) *The World Bank: its first half century*, Washington, DC: Brookings Institution Press.

Karre, B. and Svensson, B. (1989) 'The determinants of Swedish aid policy', in Stokke, O. (ed.) *Western Middle Powers and Global Poverty: the determinants of the aid policies of Canada, Denmark, the Netherlands, Norway and Sweden*, Uppsala: Scandinavian Institute of African Studies.

Kay, C. (1989) *Latin American Theories of Development and Underdevelopment*, London: Routledge.

Kennedy, P. (2010) 'Back to normalcy: is American really in decline?', *New Republic*, 21 December.

Kenny, C. and Williams, D. (2001) 'What do we know about economic growth? Or, why don't we know very much?', *World Development* 29, 1: 1–22.

Keohane, R. (1984) *After Hegemony: cooperation and discord in the world political economy*, Princeton, NJ: Princeton University Press.

Keren, M. and Sylvan, D. (2002) *International Intervention: sovereignty versus responsibility*, London: Routledge.

Keynes, J. (1926) *The End of Laissez Faire*, London: L. and Virginia Woolf.

—— (1936) *The General Theory of Employment, Interest and Money*, London: Macmillan.

Kiely, R. (2004) 'The World Bank and "global poverty reduction": good policies or bad data', *Journal of Contemporary Asia* 34, 1: 3–20.

—— (2007) 'Poverty reduction through liberalization: neoliberalism and the myth of global convergence', *Review of International Studies* 33, 3: 415–434.

Killick, T. (1978) *Development Economics in Action: a study of economic policies in Ghana*, London: Heinemann.

—— (2005) 'Policy autonomy and the history of British aid to Africa', *Development Policy Review* 23, 6: 665–681.

Kothari, U. (2005) 'From colonial administration to Development Studies: a post-colonial critique of the history of Development Studies', in Kothari, U. (ed.) *A Radical History of Development Studies: individuals, institutions and ideologies*, London: Zed Books.

Krasner, S. (1981) 'Power structures and regional development banks', *International Organization* 35, 2: 303–328.

—— (ed.) (1983) *International Regimes*, Ithaca, NY: Cornell University Press.

—— (1985) *Structural Conflict: the third world against global liberalism*, Berkeley: University of California Press.

Krueger, A. (1974) 'The political economy of the rent-seeking society', *American Economic Review* 64, 3: 291–303.

Kuhn, T. (1962) *The Structure of Scientific Revolutions*, Chicago: University of Chicago Press.

Lal, D. (1983) *The Poverty of 'Development Economics'*, London: IEA.

—— (1987) 'The political economy of economic liberalization', *World Bank Economic Review* 1, 2: 272–299.

Lancaster, C. (1999) *Aid to Africa: so much to do, so little done*, Chicago: University of Chicago Press.

—— (2007) *Foreign Aid: diplomacy, development and domestic politics*, Chicago: University of Chicago Press.

Larson, M. (1977) *The Rise of Professionalism: a sociological analysis*, Berkeley, University of California Press.

Lawson, G. (2010) 'Introduction: the "what", "when" and "where" of the global 1989', in Lawson, G., Armbruster, C. and Cox, M. (eds) (2010) *The Global 1989: continuity and change in world politics*, Cambridge: Cambridge University Press.

Lawson, G., Armbruster, C. and Cox, M. (eds) (2010) *The Global 1989: continuity and change in world politics*, Cambridge: Cambridge University Press.

Lawson, R. (1968) 'The Volta resettlement scheme', *African Affairs* 67, 267: 124–129.

Layne, C. (2006) *The Peace of Illusions: American grand strategy from 1940 to the present*, Ithaca, NY: Cornell University Press.

Lefebvre, J. (1991) *Arms for the Horn: US security policy in Ethiopia and Somalia, 1953–1991*, Pittsburgh: University of Pittsburgh Press.

Lemos, A. and Ribeiro, D. (2007) 'Taking ownership or just changing owners?', in Manji, F. and Marks, S. (eds) *African Perspectives on China in Africa*, Nairobi: Fahamu.

Le Pestre, P. (1989) *The World Bank and the Environmental Challenge*, London: Associated University Press.

Lewis, D. and Kanji, N. (2009) *Non-governmental Organizations and Development*, London: Routledge.

Lewis, W. (1954) 'Economic development with unlimited supplies of labour', *Manchester School* 22: 139–191.

—— (1984) 'The state of development theory', *American Economic Review* 74, 1: 1–10.

—— (2003) *The Principles of Economic Planning*, London: Routledge.

Lister, S. and Stevens, M. (1992) 'Aid Coordination and Management', internal World Bank paper, Washington, DC, 22 April.

Little, I. and Clifford, J. (1965) *International Aid: a discussion of the flow of resources from rich to poor countries*, London: Allen and Unwin.

Lumsdaine, D. (1993) *Moral Vision in International Politics: the foreign aid regime, 1949–1989*, Princeton, NJ: Princeton University Press.

McGrew, A. (2005) 'Globalization and global politics', in Baylis, J. and Smith, S. (eds) *The Globalization of World Politics: an introduction to international politics*, 3rd edn, Oxford: Oxford University Press.

McGuire, C. (1952) 'Point Four and the national power of the United States', *American Journal of Economics and Sociology* 11, 3: 343–356.

Macintyre, A. (1967) *A Short History of Ethics*, London: Routledge and Kegan Paul.

McKinlay, R. and Little, R. (1978) 'A foreign policy model of the distribution of British bilateral aid, 1960–1970', *British Journal of Political Science* 8, 3: 313–331.

McNamara, R. (1973) 'Address to the Board of Governors', Nairobi, 24 September, accessed at: http://siteresources.worldbank.org/EXTARCHIVES/Resources/Robert_McNamara_Address_Nairobi_1973.pdf

Maddison, A. (1989) *The World Economy in the 20th Century*, Paris: OECD.

Magnus, G. (2010) *Uprising: will emerging markets shake or shape the world economy?* Chichester: John Wiley.

Maier, C. (1978) 'The politics of productivity: foundations of American international economic policy after World War II', in Katzenstein, P. (ed.) *Between Power and Plenty: foreign economic policies of advanced industrial states*, Madison: University of Wisconsin Press.

Maizels, A. and Kissanke, M. (1984) 'Motivations for aid to developing countries', *World Development* 12, 9: 879–900.

Marglin, S. (1990) 'Lessons of the golden age: an overview', in Marglin, S. and Schor, J. (eds) *The Golden Age of Capitalism: reinterpreting the postwar experience*, Oxford: Clarendon.

Mason, E. and Asher, R. (1972) *The World Bank since Bretton Woods*, Washington, DC: Brookings Institution.

Mastny, V. (1998) 'The Soviet Non-Invasion of Poland in 1980–81 and the End of the Cold War', Cold War International History Working Paper no. 23, Woodrow Wilson International Center, Washington, DC, September.

Mayall, J. (1989) '1789 and the liberal theory of international society', *Review of International Studies* 15; 297–307.

Mearsheimer, J. (1990) 'Back to the future: instability in Europe after the Cold War', *International Security* 15, 1: 5–56.

Milward, A. (1984) *The Reconstruction of Western Europe, 1945–51*, London: Methuen.

Ministry of Overseas Development (1975) 'Overseas Development, the Changing Emphasis in British Aid Politics, More Help for the Poorest', Ministry of Overseas Development, London.

Mitterand, F. (1990) Interview, *Le Monde*, 20 June.

Mkandawire, T. (2007) 'Social Sciences and the Next Development Agenda', speech to the IDEAS workshop, Nairobi, 25 January.

MOFA (2003) 'Japan's Official Development Assistance Charter', Government of Japan, Ministry of Foreign Affairs, 29 August.

Morgenthau, H. (1962) 'A political theory of foreign aid', *American Political Science Review* 56, 2: 301–309.

Morrisey, O. (2002) 'British Aid Policy since 1997: Is DfID the Standard Bearer for Donors?', CREDIT Research Paper No. 02/23, Nottingham, October.

Mosley, P. (1991) 'The Philippines', in Mosley, P., Harrigan, J, and Toye, J., *Aid and Power: the World Bank and policy-based lending, vol. 2*, London: Routledge.

Mosley, P., Harrigan, J. and Toye, J. (1991) *Aid and Power: the World Bank and policy-based lending*, 2 vols, London: Routledge.

Morton, J. (1996) *The Poverty of Nations: the aid dilemma at the heart of Africa*, London: Taurus.

Moyo, D. (2008) *Dead Aid: why aid is not working and how there is another way for Africa*, London: Allen Lane.

Murphy, C. (2006) *United Nations Development Program: a better way?* Cambridge: Cambridge University Press.

Myrdal, G. (1957) *Economic Theory and Underdeveloped Areas*, London: Duckworth.

Naim, M. (1994) 'The World Bank: its role, governance and organizational culture', in *Bretton Woods: Looking to the Future*, Washington, DC: Bretton Woods Commission.

—— (2004) 'Globalization: passing fad or permanent revolution', *Harvard International Review* 26, Spring: 83–84.

Narayan, D. (2000) *Voices of the Poor: can anyone hear us?* Washington, DC: World Bank.

Nelson, P. (2001) 'Transparency mechanisms at the multilateral development banks', *World Development* 29, 11: 1835–1847.

Nesvetailova, A. (2007) *Fragile Finance: debt, speculation and crisis in the age of global credit*, London: Palgrave.

—— (2010) *Financial Alchemy in Crisis: the great liquidity illusion*, London: Pluto.

Noel, A. and Therien J. (1995) 'From domestic to international justice: the welfare state and foreign aid', *International Organization* 49, 3: 523–553.

North, D. (1990) *Institutions, Institutional Change and Economic Performance*, Cambridge: Cambridge University Press.

Nugent, P. (1995) *Big Men, Small Boys and Politics in Ghana: power, ideology and the burden of history, 1982–1994*, London: Pinter.

O'Brien, D. (1979) 'Modernization, order and the erosion of a democratic ideal: American political science, 1960–1970', in Lehmann, D. (ed.) *Development Theory: four critical studies*, London: Routledge.

OECD (1988) *Aid Coordination and Aid Effectiveness: a review of country and regional experience*, Paris: OECD.

—— (2004) 'Improving the Aid Effectiveness of Europe's Largest Donor Country', Paris, 27 May.

—— (2010) *Development Cooperation Report 2010*, Paris: OECD.

OECF (1991) 'Issues Related to the World Bank's Approach to Structural Adjustment – Proposal from a Major Partner', OECF Occasional Paper no. 1, October.

Olson, M. (1982) *The Rise and Decline of Nations: economic growth, stagflation and social rigidities*, New Haven, CT: Yale University Press.

Oxfam (1994) 'Embracing the Future: Avoiding the Challenges of World Poverty', Oxfam, Oxford.

Pape, R. (2009) 'Empire falls', *National Interest*, 22 January.

Paul, S. (1987a) 'Community Participation in Development Projects: The World Bank experience', World Bank Discussion Paper, Washington, DC: World Bank.

—— (1987b) 'Community participation in World Bank projects', *Finance and Development* 24, 4: 20–23.

Peacock, A. (1993) 'Keynes and the role of the state', in Crabtree, D. and Thirwall, A. (eds) *Keynes and the Role of the State*, New York: St. Martin's Press.

Pender, J. (2001) 'From "structural adjustment" to "Comprehensive Development Framework": conditionality transformed?', *Third World Quarterly* 22, 3: 397–411.

Pitts, J. (2005) *A Turn to Empire: the rise of imperial liberalism in Britain and France*, Princeton, NJ: Princeton University Press.

Polanyi, K. (1957) *The Great Transformation: the political and economic origins of our time*, Boston: Beacon.

Pollard, R. (1985) *Economic Security and the Origins of the Cold War, 1945–1950*, New York: Columbia University Press.

Poole, P. (1966) 'Communist China's aid diplomacy', *Asian Survey* 6, 11: 622–629.

Porter, B. (1984) *The USSR in Third World Conflicts: Soviet arms and diplomacy in local wars, 1945–1980*, Cambridge: Cambridge University Press.

Portfolio Management Taskforce (1992) 'Effective Implementation: key to development impact', September.

Prebisch, R. (1950) *The Economic Development of Latin America and its Principal Problems*, New York: United Nations.

—— (1985) 'Five stages in my thinking on development', in Meier, G. and Seers, D. (eds) *Pioneers in Development*, Oxford: Oxford University Press.

Pye, L. (1965) 'The concept of political development', *Annals of the American Academy of Political and Social Science* 358, 1: 1–15.

—— (1966) *Aspects of Political Development*, Boston: Little Brown.

Radelet, S. (2003a) 'Bush and foreign aid', *Foreign Affairs* 82, 5: 104–111.

—— (2003b) 'Will the Millennium Challenge Account be different?', *Washington Quarterly* 26, 2: 171–187.

Reichlin, L. (1995) 'The Marshall Plan reconsidered', in Eichengreen, B. (ed.) *Europe's Post-War Recovery*, Cambridge: Cambridge University Press.

Reimann, K. (2006) 'A view from the top: international politics, norms and the worldwide growth of NGOs', *International Studies Quarterly* 50, 1: 45–67.

Renou, X. (2002) 'A new French policy for Africa?', *Journal of Contemporary African Studies* 20, 1: 5–27.

Rich, B. (1994) *Mortgaging the Earth: the World Bank, environmental impoverishment and the crisis of development*, London: Earthscan.

Riddell, R. (2007) *Does Foreign Aid Really Work?*, Oxford: Clarendon.

Rodrik, D. (1995) 'Why Is There Multilateral Lending?', NBER Working Paper Series, No. w5160.

—— (2000) 'Can Integration into the Global Economy Substitute for a Development Strategy?', paper, May.

—— (2001) 'Trading in illusions', *Foreign Policy* 123, Mar.–Apr.: 54–62.

—— (2002) 'Feasible Globalizations', NBER Working Paper w9129, August.

—— (2006) 'Goodbye Washington consensus, hello Washington confusion', *Journal of Economic Literature* 44, 4: 973–987.

Rosenau, J. (1999) 'Governance in a new global order', in Held, D. and McGrew, A. (eds) *Governing Globalization: power, authority and global governance*, Cambridge: Polity.

Rosenberg, J. (2000) *Follies of Globalization Theory*, London: Verso.

Rosenstein-Rodan, P. (1943) 'Problems of industrialization in Eastern and South-Eastern Europe', *Economic Journal* 53, 2: 201–11.

Rostow, W. (1959) 'The stages of economic growth', *Economic History Review* 12, 1: 1–15.

—— (1971) *Politics and the Stages of Growth*, Cambridge: Cambridge University Press.

Ruggie, J. (1982) 'International regimes, transaction, and change: embedded liberalism in the postwar economic order', *International Organization* 36, 2: 195–231.

—— (1991) 'Embedded liberalism revisited', in Adler, E. and Crawford, B. (eds) *Progress in Postwar International Relations*, New York: Columbia University Press.

—— (1998a) 'Introduction: what makes the world hang together? Neo-utilitarianism and the social constructivist challenge', in Ruggie, J., *Constructing the World Polity: essays on international institutionalization*, London: Routledge.

——. (1998b) 'Embedded liberalism and postwar regimes', in Ruggie, J., *Constructing the World Polity: essays on international institutionalization*, London: Routledge.

Rustow, D. (1968) 'Modernization and comparative politics: prospects in research and theory', *Comparative Politics* 1, 1: 37–51.

Ruttan, W. (1975) 'Integrated Rural Development Programs: a sceptical perspective', *International Development Review* 17, 4: 9–16.

—— (1984) 'Integrated Rural Development Programs: a historical perspective', *World Development* 12, 4: 393–401.

Sachs, J. (2005) *The End of Poverty: economic possibilities for our time*, London: Penguin.

Sachs, W. (1992) 'Introduction', in Sachs, W. (ed.) *The Development Dictionary: a guide to knowledge as power*, London: Zed Books.

Scholte, J. (2000) *Globalization: a critical introduction*, Basingstoke: Macmillan.

—— (2002) 'What Is Globalization? The definitional issue – again', Centre for the Study of Globalization and Regionalization Working Paper 109, University of Warwick, December.

Schopflin, G. (1990) 'The end of communism in Eastern Europe', *International Affairs* 66, 1: 3–16.

Schraeder, P., Taylor, B. and Hook, S. (1998) 'Clarifying the foreign aid puzzle: a comparison of American, Japanese, French and Swedish aid flows', *World Politics* 50, 2: 294–323.

Schultz, T. (1964) *Transforming Traditional Agriculture*, New Haven, CT: Yale University Press.

Scott, J. (1996) *Deciding to Intervene: The Reagan Doctrine and American foreign policy*, Chapel Hill, NC: Duke University Press.

Seers, D. (1963) 'The limitations of the special case', *Bulletin of the Oxford University Institute of Economics and Statistics* 25, 2: 77–98.

Shihata, I. (1991) 'The World Bank and "governance" issues in its borrowing countries', in Shihata, I., *The World Bank in a Changing World: selected essays*, Dordrecht: Martinus Nijhoff.

Shipway, M. (2008) *Decolonization and Its Impact: a comparative approach to the end of the colonial empires*, London: Blackwell.

Singer, H. (1950) 'US foreign investment in underdeveloped areas', *American Economic Review* 40, 2: 473–485.

—— (1996) 'Is Development Economics Still Relevant?', Development Thinking and Practice Conference, Washington, DC, 3–5 September.

Slaughter, A. (2004) *A New World Order*, Princeton, NJ: Princeton University Press.

Sluglett, P. (2005) 'The Cold War in the Middle East', in Fawcett, L. (ed.) *International Relations of the Middle East*, Oxford: Oxford University Press.

Snow, P. (1994) 'China and Africa: consensus and camouflage', in Robinson, T. and Shambaugh, D. (eds) *Chinese Foreign Policy: theory and practice*, Oxford: Clarendon.

Springhall, J. (2001) *Decolonization since 1945*, Basingstoke: Palgrave.

Stern, N. and Ferreira, F. (1997) 'The World Bank as "intellectual actor"', in Kapur, D., Lewis, J. and Webb, R. (eds) *The World Bank: its first half century, vol. 2*, Washington, DC: Brookings Institution Press.

Stewart, F. and Wang, M. (2003) 'Do PRSPs Empower Poor Countries and Disempower the World Bank, or Is It the Other Way Round?', Queen Elizabeth House Working Paper 108, Oxford, October.

Stiglitz, J. (2002) *Globalization and Its Discontents*, London: Penguin.

Stokke, O. (ed.) (1989) *Western Middle Powers and Global Poverty: the determinants of the aid policies of Canada, Denmark, the Netherlands, Norway and Sweden*, Uppsala: Scandinavian Institute of African Studies.

—— (2009) *The UN and Development: from aid to cooperation*, Bloomington: University of Indiana Press.

Strange, S. (1987) 'The persistent myth of lost hegemony', *International Organization* 41, 4: 551–574.

—— (1988) 'The future of the American empire', *Journal of International Affairs* 42, 1: 1–18.

Strayer, R. (1998) *Why Did the Soviet Union Collapse?: understanding historical change*, New York: M. E. Sharpe.

Sunaga, K. (2004) 'The Reshaping of Japan's Official Development Assistance (ODA) Charter', FASID Discussion Paper on Development Assistance No. 3, Tokyo, November.

Thomas, G. and Lauderdale, P. (1988) 'State authority and national welfare programs in the world system context', *Sociological Forum* 3, 3: 383–399.

Thompson, D. (2007) 'US Responses in China's Rise in Africa: policy and policy options', in Kitissou, M. (ed.) *Africa in China's Global Strategy*, London: Adonis and Abbey.

Toye, J. (1987) *Dilemmas of Development*, Oxford: Blackwell.

—— (1991) 'Ghana', in Mosley, P., Harrigan, J. and Toye, J. (eds), *Aid and Power: the World Bank and policy-based lending, vol. 2*, London: Routledge.

—— (1992) 'Interest group politics and the implementation of adjustment policies in sub-Saharan Africa', *Journal of International Development* 4, 2: 183–197.

Tully, J. (ed.) (1988) *Meaning and Context: Quentin Skinner and his critics*, Princeton, NJ: Princeton University Press.

Tussie, D. (1995) *The Inter-American Development Bank*, Boulder, CO: Lynne Rienner.

Udall, L. (1997) *The World Bank Inspection Panel: a three year review*, Washington, DC: World Bank Information Center.

UN (1960) 'Declaration on the Granting of Independence to Colonial Countries and Peoples', UN General Assembly Resolution 1514, 12 December.

—— (1969) 'Declaration on Social Progress and Development', 11 December.

—— (1986) 'Declaration on the Right to Development', 4 December.

United States (1951) Mutual Security Act, Public Law 165, 82nd Congress, 10 October.

USAID (1991) 'Democracy and Governance Paper', Washington, DC, November.

—— (2003) *Foreign Aid in the National Interest: promoting freedom, security and opportunity*, Washington DC: USAID.

—— (2004) *US Foreign Aid: meeting the challenges of the twenty-first century*, Washington, DC: USAID.

Wade, R. (1996) 'Japan, the World Bank, and the art of paradigm maintenance: the East Asian Miracle in political perspective', *New Left Review* 217: 3–36.

—— (2004a) 'Is globalization reducing poverty and inequality?', *World Development* 32, 4: 567–589.

—— (2004b) 'The World Bank and the environment', in Boas, M. and McNeil, D (eds) *Global Institutions and Development: framing the world?*, London: Routledge.

Walton, M. (2004) 'Neoliberalism in Latin America: good, bad or incomplete', *Latin American Research Review* 39, 3: 165–183.

Waltz, K. (2000) 'Structural realism after the Cold War', *International Security* 25, 1: 5–41.

Wan, M. (1995) 'Japan and the Asian Development Bank', *Pacific Affairs* 68, 4: 509–528.

Weaver, C. and Leiteritz, R. (2005) ' "Our poverty is a world full of dreams": reforming the World Bank', *Global Governance* 11: 369–88.

Weber, S. (1994) 'Origins of the European Bank for Reconstruction and Development', *International Organization* 48, 1: 1–38.

Weigle, M. and Butterfield, J. (1992) 'Civil society in reforming communist regimes: the logic of emergence', *Comparative Politics* 25, 1: 1–23.

Weiss, L. (1998) *The Myth of the Powerless State*, Ithaca, NY: Cornell University Press.

Westad, O. (2007) *The Global Cold War*, Cambridge: Cambridge University Press.

Wexler, I (1983) *The Marshall Plan Revisited: the economic recovery program in economic perspective*, Westport, CT: Greenwood Press.

Weyland, K. (2004) 'Neoliberalism in Latin America: introduction to a debate', *Latin American Research Review* 39, 3: 143–149.

Wheeler, N. (2000) *Saving Strangers: humanitarian intervention in international society*, Oxford: Oxford University Press.

White House (1985) 'Statement on Signing the International Security and Development Cooperation Act', 8 August.

—— (1992) 'Freedom Support Act of 1992 Fact Sheet', Office of the Press Secretary, 1 April.

—— (2002) *National Security Strategy of the United States of America*, Washington, DC: White House.

Whitfield, L. (2005) 'Trustees of development from conditionality to governance: Poverty Reduction Strategy Papers in Ghana', *Journal of Modern African Studies* 43, 4: 641–64.

—— (2010) 'The state elites, PRSPs and policy implementation in aid dependent Ghana', *Third World Quarterly* 31, 5: 721–737.

Whitfield, L. and Jones, E. (2008) 'Ghana: the political dimensions of aid dependence', Global Economic Governance Working Paper 2007/32, Oxford, February.

Williams, D. (2000) 'Aid and sovereignty: quasi-states and the international financial institutions', *Review of International Studies* 26, 4: 557–573.

—— (2008a) *The World Bank and Social Transformation in International Politics: liberalism, governance and sovereignty*, London: Routledge.

—— (2008b) ' "Development" and global governance: the World Bank, financial sector reform and the "will to govern" ', *International Politics* 45, 2: 212–227.

Williams, D. and Young, T. (2009) 'The international politics of social transformation: trusteeship and intervention in historical perspective', in Duffield, M. and Hewitt, V. (eds) *Empire, Development and Colonialism: the past in the present*, London: James Currey.

Williamson, O. (1979) 'Transaction cost economics: the governance of contractual relations', *Journal of Law and Economics* 22, 2: 233–261.

Willner, A. (1964) 'The underdeveloped study of political development', *World Politics* 16, 3: 468–482.

Wittkopf, E. (1973) 'Foreign aid and United Nations votes: a comparative study', *American Political Science Review* 67, 3: 868–888.

Wittrock, B., Wagner, P. and Wollman, H. (1991) 'Social science and the modern state: policy knowledge and political institutions in Western Europe and the United States', in Wagner, P., Weiss, C., Wittrock, B. and Wollman, H. (eds) *Social Sciences and Modern States: national experiences and theoretical crossroads*, Cambridge: Cambridge University Press.

Wohlforth, W. (1994) 'Realism and the end of the Cold War', *International Security* 19, 3: 91–129.

Wolfensohn, J. (1999) 'A Proposal for a Comprehensive Development Framework', paper, 21 January.

Woods, N. (2000) 'The challenge of good governance for the World Bank and IMF themselves', *World Development* 28, 5: 828–841.

World Bank (1969) 'Appraisal of a Second Highway Project: Argentina', report no. PTR-13a, 10 June.

—— (1974) 'Philippines: appraisal of the Sixth Power Project', Report No. 421a-PH, 30 June.

—— (1976) 'Appraisal of the Upper Regional Agricultural Development Project', Report No. 1061aGH, 3 June.

—— (1979a) 'Fisheries Training Project: Philippines', Staff Appraisal Report, Report No. 1786-PH, 30 November.

—— (1979b) 'Argentina Paraguay Yacyreta Hydroelectric Project', Staff Appraisal Report, Report No. 2342AR, 21 September.

—— (1983a) 'Philippines: Sixth Power Project', Project Completion Report, Report No. 4847, 22 December.

—— (1983b) 'Argentina: Third Highway Project', Report No. 4341, 3 March.

—— (1987a) 'Project Completion Report Ghana: Upper Regional Agricultural Development Project', Report No. 6755, 5 May.

—— (1987b) 'Report and Recommendation of the President, Ghana: Structural; Adjustment Credit', Report No. P-4403-GH, 23 March.

—— (1988) 'President's Report and Recommendation, Argentina: Second Trade Policy Loan', Report No. P-4856-AR, 3 October.

—— (1989a) 'Argentina: Fourth Highway Loan Project', Project Completion Report, Report No. 8211, 11 December.

—— (1989b) *Sub-Saharan Africa: from crisis to sustainable growth*, Washington, DC: World Bank.

—— (1990) 'Fisheries Training Project', Project Performance Assessment Report, Report No. 8788, 25 June.

—— (1991) *World Development Report 1991*, Washington, DC: World Bank.

—— (1992) 'Program Performance Audit Report, Ghana: First and Second Structural Adjustment Credits', Report No. 10686, 29 May.

—— (1993a) 'Argentina: Highway Sector project', Project Completion Report, Report No. 12453, 4 November.

—— (1993b) *East Asian Miracle: economic growth and public policy*, Oxford: Oxford University Press.

—— (1994a) *Evaluation Results 1992*, Washington, DC: World Bank.

—— (1994b) *Adjustment in Africa: reform, results and the road ahead*, Washington, DC: World Bank.

—— (1994c) 'Program Completion Report, Argentina: Trade Policy and Export Diversification Loan and Second Trade Policy Loan', Report No. 12747, 9 February.

—— (1995a) 'Argentina: Yacyreta Hydroelectric Project', Project Completion Report, Report No. 14056, 14 March.

—— (1995b) *Evaluation Results 1993*, Washington, DC: World Bank.

—— (1995c) 'Cooperation between the World Bank and NGOs: FY 1994 progress report', World Bank paper.

—— (1995d) 'Ghana: Country Assistance Review', Operations Evaluation Department.

—— (1999) 'Philippines: from crisis to opportunity', Country Assistance Review, World Bank, Washington, DC.

—— (2000a) 'Argentina: Country Assistance Evaluation', Operations Evaluation Department, 10 July.

—— (2000b) *World Development Report 2000*, Oxford: Oxford University Press.

—— (2000c) 'Ghana: Country Assistance Evaluation', Operations Evaluation Department, Report No. 20328.

—— (2000d) 'Argentina: Country Assistance Evaluation', Operations Evaluation Department, 10 July.

—— (2001) 'Implementation Completion Report, Philippines: Banking System Reform Loan', Report No. 22824, 14 December.

—— (2003) 'Argentina: Economic and Social Transition Structural Adjustment Loan', Report No. 25860-AR, 2 May.

—— (2004) 'Implementation Completion Report, Argentina: Economic and Social Transition Structural Adjustment Loan', Report No. 29637-AR, 30 June.

—— (2005a) *Evaluation Results 2004*, Washington, DC: World Bank.

—— (2005b) 'Review of World Bank Conditionality', Operations Policy and Country Services, 9 September.

—— (2005c) *Economic Growth in the 1990s: learning from a decade of growth*, Washington, DC: World Bank.

—— (2007a) *World Development Indicators*, Washington DC: World Bank.
—— (2007b) 'Implementation and Completion Results Report, Philippines: Third Elementary Education Project', Report No. ICR0000204, 31 January.
—— (n.d.) 'Towards a Financially Sound and Efficient Power Sector', accessed at http://siteresources.worldbank.org/INTPHILIPPINES/Resources/DB14-Power-June23.pdf.
World Bank Inspection Panel (2004) 'Executive Summary of World Bank Inspection Panel Yacyreta Hydroelectric Project', Washington, DC.
Yasutomo, D. (1989) 'Why aid? Japan as an "aid great power"', *Pacific Affairs* 62,4: 490–503.
Young, R. (2001) 'New Labour and international development: a research report', *Progress in Development Studies* 1, 3: 247–253.

Index